William Howard Taft
A BIBLIOGRAPHY

Meckler's Bibliographies of the Presidents of the United States

Series Editor: Carol Bondhus Fitzgerald

1. George Washington
2. John Adams
3. Thomas Jefferson
4. James Madison
5. James Monroe
6. John Quincy Adams
7. Andrew Jackson
8. Martin Van Buren
9. William Henry Harrison
10. John Tyler
11. James Knox Polk
12. Zachary Taylor
13. Millard Fillmore
14. Franklin Pierce
15. James Buchanan
16. Abraham Lincoln
17. Andrew Johnson
18. Ulysses S. Grant
19. Rutherford B. Hayes
20. James A. Garfield
21. Chester A. Arthur
22. Grover Cleveland
23. Benjamin Harrison
24. William McKinley
25. Theodore Roosevelt
26. William Howard Taft
27. Woodrow Wilson
28. Warren G. Harding
29. Calvin Coolidge
30. Herbert C. Hoover
31. Franklin D. Roosevelt
32. Harry S. Truman
33. Dwight D. Eisenhower
34. John F. Kennedy
35. Lyndon B. Johnson
36. Richard M. Nixon
37. Gerald R. Ford
38. Jimmy Carter
39. Ronald Reagan
40. George Bush

William Howard Taft
A BIBLIOGRAPHY

Paolo E. Coletta

Bibliographies of the
Presidents of
the United States
No. 26

Meckler
Westport • London

Library of Congress Cataloging-in-Publication Data

Coletta, Paolo Enrico, 1916-
  William Howard Taft : a bibliography.

  (Meckler's bibliographies of the presidents of the
United States ; 26)
  Includes index.
  1. Taft, William H. (William Howard), 1857-1930--
Bibliography. 2. United States--Politics and government--
1909-1913--Bibliography. I. Title. II. Series.
Z8857.88.C64 1989 016.97391'2'092   89-3388
[E762]
ISBN 0-88736-140-4 (alk. paper)

British Library Cataloguing in Publication Data

Coletta, Paolo E. (Paolo Enrico), *1916 -*
  William Howard Taft : a bibliography. - (Bibliographies
  of the Presidents of the United States : no. 26).
  1. United States. Taft, William Howard, 1857-1930 -
  Bibliographies
  I. Title. II. Series
  016. 97391 ' 20924

  ISBN 0-88736-140-4

Copyright © 1989 Meckler Corporation. All rights reserved.
No part of this publication may be reproduced in any form by
any means without prior written permission from the publisher,
except by a reviewer who may quote brief passages in review.

Meckler Corporation, 11 Ferry Lane West, Westport, CT 06880.
Meckler Ltd., Grosvenor Gardens House, Grosvenor Gardens,
   London SW1W 0BS, U.K.

Printed on acid free paper.
Printed in the United States of America.

Contents

Foreword ix
Editor's Preface xiii
Acknowledgments xv
Introduction xvii
Abbreviations xix
Chronology xxi

1. Manuscript and Archival Sources
    A. Manuscript and Archival Sources for William H. Taft 1
    B. Published William Howard Taft Papers 3
    C. Unpublished Personal and Administrative
        Papers of Presidential Associates 5
    D. Published Personal and Administrative
        Papers of Presidential Associates 10
    E. Contemporary Newspapers 10
2. Published Writings of William Howard Taft
    A. Published Writings of William Howard Taft 13
    B. Unpublished Writings of William Howard Taft 25
3. Autobiographical and Biographical Publications 27
4. Childhood and Early Development, 1857-1878
    A. The Ohio Environment 31
    B. Ancestry 32
    C. Childhood 32
5. Early Career, 1878-1888 35
6. Mature Years, 1888-1908
    A. Introduction 37
    B. Solicitor General and Circuit Court Judge, 1890-1900 38
    C. In the Philippines, 1900-1904 38
    D. Secretary of War, 1904-1908 41
7. The Election of 1908 47
8. The Presidency
    A. Bibliographic Guides 55
    B. Presidential Studies 56
    C. Presidential Elections 66
    D. Presidential Power 70
    E. The Inauguration, March 4, 1909 75
    F. The Cabinet 78
    G. Taft as Administrator 79
    H. Taft as Commander in Chief 82
    I. Progressivism: General 87

1. The Antitrust Crusade 91
2. Banking and Currency Reform 96
3. Children's Bureau 97
4. Civil Service 98
5. Conservation 98
6. The Direct Election of Senators 104
7. A Federal Budget 105
8. A Federal Corporation Tax 106
9. A Federal Income Tax 106
10. Governmental Reorganization 108
11. Immigration 109
12. The Judicial System 110
13. Labor 111
14. Black Americans 113
15. Parcel Post 118
16. Postal Savings Banks 119
17. Public Health 119
18. Railroad Regulation 120
19. Shipping 121
20. Tariff Reform 122
21. Tariff Reciprocity with Canada 127
22. Women's Suffrage 130
J. Foreign Affairs 131
1. General 132
2. Taft and Foreign Affairs 133
3. The Monroe Doctrine 133
4. Dollar Diplomacy, General 134
5. Argentina 134
6. Brazil 134
7. Canada 135
8. China 135
9. Colombia 136
10. Cuba 136
11. Ecuador 137
12. Germany 137
13. Great Britain 137
14. Honduras 137
15. Japan 137
16. Mexico 138
17. Near (Middle) East 138
18. Montenegro 138
19. Morocco 139

20. Nicaragua	139
21. Open Door	139
22. Panama	140
23. The Panama Tolls Question	140
24. Pan Americanism	141
25. The Philippines	141
26. Puerto Rico	141
27. Russia	141
28. San Domingo	142
29. Treaties	142
30. World Peace	142

9. Administration Personnel
    A. Cabinet Members 145
    B. Vice Presidents and Cabinet Members 149
    C. Congressmen 149
    D. Military Leaders 160
    E. Naval Officers 161
    F. State Department and Foreign Service 164
    G. Supreme Court Justices 168
10. Elections of 1910 173
11. Elections of 1912 179
12. Post-Presidential Career, 1913-1930 187
    A. Professor of Law 190
    B. On World War I 193
    C. Member of the National War Labor Board 193
    D. On World Peace 194
    E. On Women 198
    F. On Prohibition 198
13. Chief Justice of the Supreme Court, 1921-1930
    A. The Supreme Court: General 201
    B. The Personnel of Taft's Court 209
    C. The Most Important Decisions of Taft's Court 213
14. Taft's Personal Life
    A. Personal Characteristics 221
    B. Health 222
    C. Religion 223
    D. Marriage 224
    E. Children 226
    F. Mrs. William Howard Taft 229
15. Historiographical Materials
    A. Biographers and Others 231
    B. On Taft's Contributions to History 232

    C. Bibliographies 237
    D. Oral Histories 237
    E. In Memoriam 238
16. Iconography 243
Index to Authors 247
Index to Subjects 265
Appendix: Serials Consulted 269

Foreword

Nothing in the American constitutional order continues to excite so much scholarly interest, debate, and controversy as the role of the presidency. This remains the case in spite of the complaint, so common in the historical profession a generation ago, about the tyranny of "the presidential synthesis" in the writing of American history.

This complaint had its point. It is true enough that the deep currents in social, economic, and intellectual history, in demography, family structure, collective mentalities, flow on without regard to presidential administrations. To deal with these underlying trends, the "new history" began in the 1950s and 1960s to reach out beyond traditional history to anthropology, sociology, psychology, and statistics. For a season social-science history pushed politics and personalities off the historical stage.

But in time social-science history displayed its limitations. It did not turn out to be, as its apostles had promised, a philosopher's—or historian's—stone. "Most of the great problems of history," wrote Lawrence Stone, himself a distinguished practitioner of the new history, "remain as insoluble as ever, if not more so." In particular, the new history had no interest in public policy—the decisions a nation makes through the political process—and proved impotent to explain it. Yet one can reasonably argue that, at least in a democracy, public policy reveals the true meaning of the past, the moods, preoccupations, values, and dreams of a nation, more clearly and trenchantly than almost anything else.

The tide of historical interest is now turning again—from deep currents to events, from underlying trends to decisions. While the history of public policy requires an accounting of the total culture from which national decisions emerge, such history must center in the end on the decisions themselves and on the people who make (and resist) them. Historians today are returning to the insights of classical history—to the recognition that the state, political authority, military power, elections, statutes, wars, the ideas, ambitions, delusions and wills of individuals, make a difference to history.

This is far from a reversion to "great man" theories. But it is a valuable corrective to the assumption, nourished by social-science history, that public policy is merely a passive reflection of underlying historical forces. For the ultimate fascination of history lies precisely in the interplay between the individual and his environment. "It is true," wrote Tocqueville, "that around every man a fatal circle is traced beyond which he cannot pass; but within the wide verge of that circle he is powerful and free; as it is with man, so with communities."

The *Bibliographies of the Presidents* series therefore needs no apology. Public policy is a powerful key to an understanding of the past; and in the United States the presidency is the battleground where issues of public policy are fought out and resolved. The history of American presidents is far from the total history of America. But American history without the presidents would leave the essential part of the story untold.

Recent years have seen a great expansion in the resources available for students of the presidency. The National Historical Publications Commission has done superb work in stimulating and sponsoring editions, both letterpress and microform, of hitherto inaccessible materials. "Documents," as President Kennedy said in 1963, "are the primary sources of history; they are the means by which later generations draw close to historical events and enter into the thoughts, fears and hopes of the past." He saluted the NHPC program as "this great effort to enable the American people to repossess its historical heritage."

At the same time, there has been a rich outpouring of scholarly monographs on presidents, their associates, their problems, and their times. And the social-science challenge to narrative history has had its impact on presidential scholarship. The interdisciplinary approach has raised new questions, developed new methods and uncovered new sources. It has notably extended the historian's methodological arsenal.

This profuse presidential literature has heretofore lacked a guide. The *Bibliographies of the Presidents* series thus fills a great lacuna in American scholarship. It provides comprehensive annotated bibliographies, president by president, covering manuscripts and archives, biographies and monographs, articles and dissertations, government documents and oral histories, libraries, museums, and iconographic resources. The editors are all scholars who have mastered their presidents. The series places the study of American presidents on a solid bibliographical foundation.

In so doing, it will demonstrate the wide sweep of approaches to our presidents, from analysis to anecdotage, from hagiography to vilification. It will illustrate the rise and fall of presidential reputations—fluctuations that often throw as much light on historians as on presidents. It will provide evidence for and against Bryce's famous proposition "Why Great Men Are Not Chosen Presidents." It will remind us that superior men have somehow made it to the White House but also that, as the Supreme Court said in *ex parte Milligan*, the republic has "no right to expect that it will always have wise and humane rulers, sincerely attached to the principles of the Constitution. Wicked men, ambitious of power, with hatred of liberty and contempt of law, may fill the place once occupied by Washington and Lincoln."

Above all, it will show how, and to what degree, the American presidency has been the focus of the concerns, apprehensions and aspirations of the people and the times. The history of the presidency is a history of nobility and of pettiness, of courage and of cunning, of forthrightness and of trickery, of quarrel and of consensus. The turmoil perennially swirling around the White House illuminates the heart of American democracy. The literature reflects the turmoil, and the *Bibliographies of the Presidents* supply at last the light that will enable scholars and citizens to find their way through the literature.

Arthur Schlesinger, Jr.

Editor's Preface

As a central force in government, the presidents of the United States have been both the authors and the subjects of an enormous quantity of literature. However, accessing presidential materials has been a haphazard exercise. Few of the presidents have been the subject of comprehensive monographic bibliographies, and scholars have had to piece together their own bibliographies from catalogs, indexes, and elsewhere.

This bibliographic series seeks to serve contemporary research by organizing the widest possible range of materials. Each president is the subject of a comprehensive, booklength bibliography, compiled by an eminent scholar. The bibliographies itemize and annotate primary resources such as government documents and manuscript collections, monographs, articles, chapters and essays, dissertations and theses, and oral history if available. Each volume follows a uniform format, including a detailed subject index. The study of the individual presidents will be facilitated, and it will also be possible to systematically search topics across presidential administrations. Closer scrutiny of the life and times of each president, whether he is rated a greater or a lesser one, will benefit all presidential scholarship.

Carol Bondhus Fitzgerald

Acknowledgments

Data offered herein attempts to place William Howard Taft in historical perspective. Although he served only one term as President of the United States, 1909-1913, he began his public service at the age of twenty-four years. With the exception of his years as a Professor of Law at Yale University, 1913-1921, he did not leave it until he resigned after having served for nine years as Chief Justice of the Supreme Court. This was only a month before his death in 1930.

Following the chronology, the chapters begin with what bibliographical matter is available on the subject covered, then list data in monographs, documents, and articles in periodicals or essays in books. Dissertations and theses are not mentioned if they have been included in book form. Multiple works by the same author are listed chronologically. A list of abbreviations is provided.

Arabic numbers in the author and subject indices match the consecutive numbers that precede each title in the text. If a title has been reissued, both the original year of publication and later year and publisher will be noted.

Annotations are provided only if the point of view or the content of an item cited is not obvious from the title or the subject category in which it appears.

Several individuals have assisted with the preparation of this work. Carol Bondhus Fitzgerald, Series Editor, Bibliographies of the Presidents of the United States, 1789-1989, Meckler Corporation, provided excellent direction on content and format. Titles were expertly ferreted out in the Nimitz Library, U.S. Naval Academy, by the staff of Prof. Richard A. Evans, Librarian; at the Mansucript Division of the Library of Congress by Dr. David Wigdor; and in the General Reading Rooms Division of the Library of Congress by Virigina Steel Wood. Steve Margeton, Librarian of the Supreme Court, helped with the records of that court, and Ms. Gail Galloway with the construction of the Supreme Court building. In Ohio, requests for information were cheerfully answered by Ella Rayburn, Historian, William Howard Taft National Historic Site, Cincinnati, Ohio; J. Richard Abell, Head, History Department, the Public Library of Cincinnati and Hamilton County; the director of the Library of the University of Cincinnati; Mr. Jeff Thomas, Archives and Library Division, Ohio Historical Society; and Rosemary Burke of the Cincinnati Public Library. Information on its holdings on Taft in the Yale University Library was kindly furnished by Judith Ann Schiff, Chief Research Archivist, Manuscripts and Archives.

Paolo E. Coletta
Annapolis, Maryland

William Howard Taft (Photograph from the Collections of the Library of Congress)

Introduction

There is such an abundance of documentation for both the private and public life of William Howard Taft that his bibliographer has had to be selective, and he apologizes for any errors or notable omissions from the titles offered. There are ample family records and about a million documents spawned while Taft filled many appointive offices and served as President of the United States. His public speeches while president alone fill several volumes, as do his decisions while serving as a federal judge, 1892-1900, President of the Philippine Commission, Civil Governor of the Philippines, 1900-1904, and Secretary of War, 1904-1908. He is also a major subject in works dealing with the elections of 1908 and 1912.

Among secondary works are several biographies, a study of his years as president, and works on his career as Chief Justice of the Supreme Court. He has also been mentioned frequently in studies of the Office of the President, the reference being mainly to his limited conception of its powers. Unlike Theodore Roosevelt, who acted and then sought justification for doing so, Taft would act only after finding authority to do so in the Constitution or in law.

For each important period in Taft's life titles are offered from primary sources, books, dissertations, and periodical articles. These reveal that Taft came from a moderately wealthy family. His father served in high Republican circles; his brothers and half brothers had considerable political influence in Ohio, in the Republican Party, and in Washington. The main criticism of him as a federal circuit judge was his bias against organized labor and willingness to grant free rein to personal and property rights. As Civil Governor of the Philippines he put into effect the recommendations of the Philippine Commission he had chaired for President William McKinley and started Filipinos on their road to self-government. The construction of the Panama Canal is a monument to his work while secretary of war and president. Various trips to the Far East should have prepared him to deal with at least Pacific foreign affairs while president.

Though his life's ambition was to serve on the Supreme Court, Taft declined several offers of an appointment to it by Roosevelt because he wanted to help the latter with projects already under way. He sought the presidency largely because of pressure from his ambitious wife, Helen "Nellie" Herron Taft, and his brothers—and with Roosevelt's blessing. However, his crediting the financial support given him by his brother Charles for winning the election of 1908 angered his mentor, Roosevelt. During the year it took Nellie to recover from a stroke suffered in May 1909, he was deprived of the sage advice she could have given him while he served his first year in the White House.

As president, Taft was determined to give legal effect to various Rooseveltian reforms, especially in the field of conservation; he would consolidate progress already made. While enjoying jokes of which he himself was the butt, particularly about his obesity, he lacked skill in handling journalists and in achieving political compromises with his Congresses. Unfortunately, he procrastinated in reaching decisions and in preparing speeches. In one speech he badly errred by highly praising the controversial Payne-Aldrich Tariff of 1909. For this reason, and others, he was opposed in Congress by the Insurgents, largely Midwestern Republicans of the progressive stamp. Yet he was able in four years to achieve more reforms than Roosevelt had in seven. Using methods Roosevelt taught him, he rigged the Republican national convention of 1912 against Roosevelt, who had broken with him in 1910 and entered the presidential race.

In foreign affairs Taft was a noninterventionist. His attempt through Dollar Diplomacy to gain favor—and profits—for the United States by substituting dollars for bullets led to the charge that he had a "shopkeeper" mentality. While president, he sought to obtain world peace through arbitration treaties. He later sought the same goal as president of the League to Enforce Peace.

Historians have rated Taft as president as "average," as neither "near great" nor near the bottom of the list.

Included for Taft's presidency are titles dealing with the major personalities of his administration and, while Chief Justice, those dealing with his associate justices.

Except for a leave of absence in 1917-1918 to serve as a member of the National Labor War Board, Taft taught constitutional law at Yale University from 1913 to 1921, and was beloved by its students and staff and also by New Haven's citizenry. Then, finally, he achieved his lifelong ambition when President Warren G. Harding appointed him Chief Justice of the Supreme Court. He was so happy with the appointment that he said that it made him forget that he had been president. Alice Longworth Roosevelt thereupon quipped, "So has the country." As Chief Justice, Taft is best remembered for an increasing compassion for the cause of labor, his reforming of court procedures, and his crusade that eventuated in the construction of the current Supreme Court building. He has been rated as one of the best of the Chief Justices.

Abbreviations

Acad.	Academy	NA	National Archives
Adm.	Admiral	NARG	National Archives Record Group
BGen	Brigadier General	NARS	National Archives Record Service
Bos.	Boston		
Bull.	Bulletin	NIP	Naval Institute Press
		NWCR	Naval War College Review
Capt.	Captain		
Chap.	Chapter	Pub.	Publisher/Publishers
Coau.	Coauthor	PUP	Princeton University Press
Col.	Colonel	RAdm.	Rear Admiral
Comdr.	Commander	rept.	reprint
		rev.	revised
Ed./ed.	Editor		
enl.	enlarged	Soc.	Society
GCNY	Garden City, N.Y.	U.	University
		UP.	University Press
Hist.	History/Historical	USA	United States Army
		USMC	U.S. Marine Corps
LC	Library of Congress	USN	U.S. Navy
LCdr.	Lieutenant Commander	USNI	U.S. Naval Institute
LGen	Lieutenant General	USNIP	U.S. Naval Institute *Proceedings*
Lib.	Library		
LT	Lieutenant		
		v./vol.	volume
MA	Master's thesis	VAdm.	Vice Admiral
		Wash.	Washington

Chronology

1857

Sept. 15. Born to Louisa Torrey, second wife of Alphonso Taft, Cincinnati, Ohio. There were two sons from a previous marriage, to Fannie Phelps (d. 1852): Charles Phelps and Peter Rawson.

1859

May 27. Brother, Henry Waters, born.

1861

Dec. 28. Brother, Horace Dutton, born.

1865

Fall. Enrolled in Sixteenth District School, Mt. Auburn section of Cincinnati.

Sister, Frances Louise, born. Father filled an interim appointment as judge of the Cincinnati Supreme Court, a post to which he was nominated in 1869.

1866

Suffered a bad cut on the head and a slight fracture when he fell from a runaway horse-drawn carriage.

1869

Dec. 24. Was first in his class, with an average of 95.

1874

Graduated as salutatorian from Woodward High School, Cincinnati.

1876

Father served as Secretary of War and Attorney General under President U.S. Grant.

1878

Awarded a B.A. from Yale University. Graduated second in a class of 132.

Summer. Started reading law in his father's office.

Fall. Entered Cincinnati Law School and worked as the court reporter for the *Cincinnati Commercial*.

1880

Graduated from Cincinnati Law School and admitted to the Ohio Bar, but continued working as a court reporter rather than beginning a law practice.

Oct. 25. Appointed assistant prosecuting attorney of Hamilton County, Ohio, to begin work on Jan. 3, 1881.

Campaigned throughout Ohio for the Republican state and national tickets.

1882

Appointed by President Chester A. Arthur the Collector of Internal Revenue for the first district of Ohio.

1883

Assumed private law practice. During the summer visited his parents at the American embassy in Vienna. Also visited Ireland, Scotland, England, and Switzerland.

1884

Campaigned for the Republican national ticket.
Father appointed U.S. minister to Russia.

1885

Mar. Engaged to Helen ("Nellie") Herron (1860-1943).

1886

June 19. Married, took wedding trip through France, England, and Scotland. In the fall occupied a new house in the Walnut Hills section of Cincinnati.

1887

Mar. Appointed to Superior Court of Ohio by Governor Joseph B. Foraker.

1888

Elected to a full term as Superior Court judge.

1889

Sept. 8. Son, Robert Alphonso Taft, born.

1890

Wrote the opinion of the court against a bricklayer's union, ruling that the secondary boycott was illegal—a decision that was held against him when he campaigned for President.

Feb. 4. Appointed U.S. Solicitor General by President Benjamin Harrison. Was sworn in on Feb. 14. Lived in a small rented house on Dupont Circle, Washington, D.C.

1891

Argued successfully for the government in a controversy with Great Britain over the protection of the Bering Sea seals. A Canadian sealer had been condemned after capture by a revenue cutter. When Great Britain appealed the case to the Supreme Court, Taft asserted that Britain could not transfer the case from the executive branch of the government to the courts.

Aug. 1. Daughter, Helen Herron Taft, born.

1892

Mar. 7. Resigned as U.S. Solicitor General and appointed Judge of the Sixth Federal Circuit Court by President Harrison. His territory included Ohio, Kentucky, Michigan, and Tennessee. He traveled much but the family returned to Cincinnati and lived in a rented house.

1896

Dean and Professor of Property at the Cincinnati Law School. Gave two hour-long lectures per week.

1897

Sept. 20. Son, Charles Phelps Taft, born.

1900

Mar. 15. Although he preferred an appointment offered to the Supreme Court, Taft accepted an appointment as President of the Philippine Commission by President William McKinley.

Apr. 17. Sailed from San Francisco for the Philippines with the other members of the Philippine Commission.

Sept. 1. Taft and Secretary of War Elihu Root had a large hand in establishing policy to be followed by the Philippine Commission. A civilian would have full legislative powers, but a military man would be the executive—a point to which Taft objected.

1901

Mar. 10. The members of the Philippine Commission, their familes, and various others began a tour of the southern provinces.

Mar. 22. With the capture of insurgent leader Emilio Aguinaldo, the Filipino insurrection was all but over.

July 4. Taft was appointed as the first Governor of the Philippines by President McKinley and took his oath of office.

Dec. 24. Taft returned home to recuperate from an operation and also to testify before Senate committee hearings on the Philippines.

1902

On President Roosevelt's order, Taft asked the Pope to replace the Spanish friars in the Philippines by another order and that church land be sold to the Philippine government at a fair price. At his urging, in 1903 the land was purchased for $7.5 million and sold in small lots to natives. American and native priests gradually replaced Spanish priests.

Aug. 22. Upon his return to Manila, Taft pledged that steps to allow popular government would soon begin.

1903

Although again offered appointment to the Supreme Court, Taft declined it because he felt it his duty to remain the Philippines.

Dec. 23. Left Manila to succeed Elihu Root as Secretary of War. Two reasons that prompted him to do so were his having contracted amoebic dysentery and the improved economic situation in the Philippines.

1904

Feb. 1. Appointed Secretary of War by President Theodore Roosevelt. While in this office he made trips to the Far East in 1905 and 1907.

Mar. 22. Roosevelt directed that Taft would be in general command of the Isthmian Canal Commission, of which RAdm. John G. Walker was the first chairman.

Spring and summer. Campaigned for Roosevelt's election, which occurred on November 8.

Nov. 26. Arrived in the Panama Canal Zone on a goodwill tour and to confer with the engineers building the canal.

1905

While Roosevelt vacationed, Taft "sat on the lid" of the difficult Dominican situation.

Apr. 26. In the absence of Secretary of State John Hay, Taft's talks with the British ambassador helped set the stage for the Algeciras Conference respecting Morocco in 1906.

June 28. John F. Stevens replaced John F. Wallace as chief engineer in the Panama Canal Zone.

Summer. Took a trip to the Far East. In talks with Count Taro Katsura, agreed that Japan could acquire suzerainty over Korea. He also led a congressional party to the Philippines in order to gain favorable legislation for the islands.

Under a physician's direction, dieted and by summer of 1906 had gone from 320 to 250 pounds.

Oct. 21. In supporting the reelection in Ohio of Governor Myron T. Herrick, Taft disavowed Boss George B. Cox.

1906

Rushed Army supplies and tents for the survivors of the great San Francisco earthquake.

Aug. 14. The members of three Negro companies of soldiers were blamed for the death of a man in a fracas at Brownsville, Texas. Although reluctantly, at Roosevelt's direction Taft signed the dismissal orders for all three companies.

Sept. 16. With a rebellion in Cuba threatening American military and business interests, Taft visited the island on a fact-finding mission.

Sept. 29. Roosevelt appointed Taft provisional governor of Cuba when Cubans could not elect a new president. Taft let Cubans know that he would serve only until stability had been restored.

Oct. 13. Taft was succeeded by Charles E. Magoon as provisional governor of Cuba, which elected a new president on Jan. 28, 1909, and had its government restored.

Dec. 12. Because Mrs. Taft and others advised him that he could win a presidential nomination, Taft sat by while Roosevelt appointed William H. Moody to the Supreme Court.

1907

On Taft's recommendation, Roosevelt had Maj. George W. Goethals succeed John F. Stevens as chief engineer of the Panama Canal.

Apr. 30. In a speech in New York City, Democratic presidential hopeful William Jennings Bryan lost much ground with conservatives by advocating, as a last resort to control their rates, the government ownership of railroads.

July 29. Although Gov. Joseph B. Foraker opposed Taft's nomination for president, the Ohio Republican State Central Committee voted for him. Thus ended Foraker's political power.

Sept. 28. On his way to the Philippines, Taft stopped in Tokyo, where he was assured that Japan had only friendly intentions with respect to the United States.

Oct. After opening the Filipino Assembly in Manila, on his return home Taft made a brief call upon the Czar of Russia.

Dec. 7. Taft's mother, one of the few who advised him not to seek the presidency, died. He did not arrive from Europe in time for her funeral.

1908

Spring and summer. Campaigned for the Republican presidential nomination.

May 17. Returned to Washington after settling labor problems in the Panama Canal Zone.

June 18. Nominated for president by the Republican national convention held in Chicago. His running mate was James S. "Sunny Jim" Sherman. His compromise wording on the platform plank on injunctions pleased neither business nor labor.

June 30. Resigned as Secretary of War in order to devote full time to the campaign.

July 8. At the Democratic national convention, William Jennings Bryan won a third presidential nomination.

Sept. 17. Taft refused to answer questions about his stand on prohibition voiced by Carry Nation. He favored local option because he believed that federal legislation could not be enforced. Major criticisms during his campaign were about his Unitarian religion (he did not believe in Jesus Christ), and his playing golf, considered an effete sport.

Sept. 19. Directed the Treasurer of the Republican National Committee not to accept contributions from Standard Oil, a directive later amended to include all corporations. Exempt was the contribution from Andrew Carnegie, who had retired from business. While Bryan demanded the publication of contributions prior to election time, Taft would publicize them only after the election.

Nov. 3. Elected President of the United States with 321 electoral votes to Bryan's 162, but his popular vote was less than half that of Roosevelt in 1904.

Dec. By declining Roosevelt's advice and that of others to unhorse "Uncle Joe" Cannon, Speaker of the House of Representatives, Taft lost the confidence of the Insurgents, defined as progressive Republican reformers.

1909

Mar. 4. Because of a blizzard, the inaugural ceremonies were held in the Senate Chamber rather than outdoors. Seeking men who knew both the law and business, for his cabinet Taft chose mostly corporation lawyers. By not living up to what Roosevelt believed was a promise to keep his own cabinet, Taft began an estrangement from Roosevelt. The makeup of the cabinet was: Philander C. Knox, Secretary of State; George W. Wickersham, Attorney General; Jacob McG. Dickinson, Secretary of War; Frank Hitchcock, Postmaster General; Charles Nagel, Secretary of Commerce and Labor; Richard A. Ballinger, Secretary of the Interior—lawyers. Franklin MacVeagh served as Secretary of the Treasury; James Wilson as the perennial Secretary of Agriculture; and the experienced diplomat and administrator George von Lengerke Meyer as Secretary of the Navy.

Mar. The Insurgents failed to unseat Speaker Cannon.

Mar. 18. Taft received a tumultuous greeting when he visited Yale University.

May 17. Mrs. Taft suffered a stroke which left her speech impaired. During the approximate year of her recovery, she was unable to give her husband political advice which he much needed.

June 16. To make up for revenue lost by tariff reductions, Taft proposed a 2 percent tax on the net income of all corporations except banks. He also proposed the adoption of a constitutional amendment permitting the collection of personal federal income taxes.

Aug. 5. Signed the Payne-Aldrich Tariff Act, which displeased tariff reformers. The Act also established a Tariff Board that would recommend tariff rates changes based upon differences in the costs of production at home and abroad.

Sept. 17. While on a fence-mending swing about the country, at Winona, Minnesota, Taft lost much credibility by saying that the Payne-Aldrich Tariff bill was "the best" tariff bill ever passed by the Republican Party.

Oct. 16. Exchanged visits at El Paso, Texas, and Juarez, Mexico, with the dictator of Mexico since 1876, Porfirio Díaz, who verged upon losing power.

Nov. 10. Returned from his swing about the country, including a steamboat trip down the Mississippi and demands for scrapping the pork barrel in favor of conservation of both land and water resources. Unfortunately, he permitted himself to be photographed with Cannon.

Nov. 13. Louis R. Glavis, chief of the Field Division of the Department of the Interior, charged Ballinger with conspiracy to defraud the public domain in the Alaskan coal lands. Taft upheld Ballinger and fired Glavis.

Nov. 20. Special government prosecutor Frank G. Kellogg succeeded in finding Standard Oil a monopoly and in violation of the Sherman Antitrust Act.

Dec. 7. By ascribing a large post office deficit to the low rates charged for mailing newspapers and magazines, Taft won the disapprobation of the fourth estate and of the public, which turned against him in the elections of 1910.

Dec. 20. Two important Taft appointments made Gen. Leonard Wood the Chief of Staff of the Army and elevated Circuit Judge Horace H. Lurton, aged 69 years, to the Supreme Court. Lurton displeased many because of his age and organized labor because of his conservatism.

1910

Jan. 7. Long opposed to his conservation policies, Taft finally fired Gifford Pinchot, a Roosevelt favorite, as the Chief Forester. The estrangement of Taft and Roosevelt was thereby broadened.

Feb. Secretary of State Knox set out on a good-will tour of Central and South America in which he garnered little good will.

Mar. 17. With legislative legerdemain, Rep. George W. Norris won approval for having the members of the House Rules Committee elected rather than named by Cannon. Cannon remained the Speaker, but with much reduced power.

May 20. Attorney Louis D. Brandeis, representing Glavis at a congressional investigation into reputed land fraud by Ballinger, revealed that Taft had ordered the predating of an investigative report prepared by Attorney General Wickersham, thereby reducing the credibility of the Taft administration.

May 21. Treaty between the United States and Great Britain fixing the boundary line in Passamaquoddy Bay.

May 31. Taft obtained an injunction to prevent western railroads from raising freight rates in violation of the Sherman Act. A week later the railroads stated that they would not raise rates until a new law was passed that authorized the Interstate Commerce Commission to examine them.

June. Taft obtained $100,000 from Congress with which to study the fiscal operations of the government. This was the first step in his creation of a federal budget system.

June 18. Taft still further distanced himself from Roosevelt by not personally welcoming the latter upon his return from a year in Africa and Europe.

June 20. Roosevelt declined Taft's invitation to visit him in the White House.

June 25. Taft signed the Postal Savings Bank Act. One bank in each state, under strict federal supervision, could give 2 percent interest on accounts limited to $500.

June 30. Accompanied by his Harvard classmate, Sen. Henry Cabot Lodge, Roosevelt made a perfunctory call upon Taft at the latter's summer home in Beverly, Massachusetts.

July 17. The call upon him of two of Taft's Beverly neighbors, nabobs Henry C. Frick and J.P. Morgan, displeased insurgents.

Aug. 18. Special agreement between the United States and Great Britain for the submission of outstanding pecuniary claims to arbitration.

Sept. 5. Taft rejected a proposal to have a dinner given to both him and Roosevelt at the National Conservation Congress at St. Paul, Minnesota. The two former friends addressed the convention on different days.

Sept. 10. Following Roosevelt's call for a New Nationalism in a speech at Osawatomie, Kansas, Taft said that the program could not be implemented without revising the Constitution.

Sept. 19. When Taft and Roosevelt met in New Haven, Connecticut, they discussed merely the forthcoming New York State Republican Convention, to be held in Saratoga.

Sept 27. At Saratoga, Taft supported Roosevelt against Vice President Sherman and others of the Old Guard and in nominating Roosevelt's choice for governor, Henry L. Stimson.

Oct. Appointed Gov. Charles Evans Hughes to be Associate Justice of the Supreme Court to replace David J. Brewer, deceased. Melvin W. Fuller was 76 years old, and John M. Harlan did no work, yet following the death of Rufus W. Peckham on Oct. 24, 1909, Taft had appointed as his successor the 69-year-old Horace Lurton.

Nov. 4. In the elections of that date, Stimson was defeated. Also defeated was Warren Harding, to whose campaign Taft had contributed $5,000, as governor of Ohio. The new governor of New Jersey was the reform-minded Woodrow Wilson.

After William H. Moody resigned from the Supreme Court because of poor health, Taft made a bad move in appointing Willis Van Devanter.

Dec. By declining to seek a successor to "Uncle Joe" Cannon, Taft displeased Roosevelt and the Insurgents.

Pronounced himself pleased with what he saw on a visit to the Panama Canal Zone.

1911

Jan. Appointed Joseph R. Lamar to be an Associate Justice of the Supreme Court.

Jan. 12. Minutes of Conference held at Washington the 9th, 10th, 11th, and 12th of January, 1911, as to the application of the award delivered on the 7th September 1910, in the North Atlantic Coast Fisheries Arbitration to Existing Relations of Canada and Newfoundland.

Jan. 14. Minutes of Conferences held at Washington the 13th and 14th of January, 1911, as to the Objections of the United States to existing laws and fishery regulations of Canada as recorded in Protocol XXX of the Proceedings upon the North Atlantic Coast Fisheries Arbitration.

Feb. 7. Treaty between the United States and Great Britain providing for the preservation and protection of fur seals.

Feb. 15. An amendment to the Interstate Commerce law provided a U.S. Commerce court and also increased the powers of the Interstate Commerce Commission.

Mar. 2. Taft appointed a commission to investigate postal rates for newspapers and magazines. Its report helped convince Congress that a rate increase was justified.

Mar. 6. When the American Ambassador to Mexico, Henry Lane Wilson, reported his concern for the safety of American residents in Mexico, on the pretext of their holding maneuvers Taft ordered the mobilization of 20,000 soldiers along the Mexican border.

Mar. 7. Appointed Walter L. Fisher, who followed Gifford Pinchot's policies on conservation, as Secretary of the Interior to replace Ballinger, who resigned.

Mar. 16. Appointed Henry L. Stimson as Secretary of War to replace Dickinson.

May 24. After President Díaz of Mexico resigned, the idealistic reformer Francisco Madero was elected to succeed him, but popular unrest continued.

June 6. A treaty with Nicaragua containing protectorate terms similar to those for San Domingo was signed. The Senate rejected it.

June 17. Sen. Robert M. La Follette, of Wisconsin, announced his candidacy for the Republican presidential nomination.

July 26. Taft signed the Canadian Tariff Reciprocity Agreement, which sat badly with Midwestern farmers. In elections held in Canada on September 21, the Agreement and Sir Wilfrid Laurier and his Liberal government were defeated.

Aug. 3. Taft signed general arbitration treaties with France and England. Roosevelt and H. C. Lodge had led the charge against them.

Aug. 18. Taft vetoed rate reductions in the tariff on wool and woolen goods, saying that the Tariff Board had not completed its investigation.

Autumn. Taft took the issue of the arbitration treaties to the people on a Western tour. In March 1912, although the Senate confirmed watered-down treaties, they proved to be unacceptable to Britain and France.

Oct. 24. In a suit Taft filed against U.S. Steel for violating the Sherman Act, it was alleged that Roosevelt had been deceived during the Panic of 1907 into allowing the corporation to purchase the Tennessee Coal & Iron Company. The allegation provided a final blow to the Taft-Roosevelt friendship. In March 1920, the Supreme Court ruled in favor of U.S. Steel.

Nov. 15. Attorney General Wickersham notified Taft that the National City Bank of New York was in violation of the National Banking Act. On the advice of Knox and McVeagh, Taft decided not to prosecute.

Dec. 12. Taft submitted the Tariff Board's report on the wool and woolen rates. Because the cost of raising wool—Taft's criterion—varied greatly from place to place, great doubt existed that cost could be used to fix tariff rates.

The most important issue in foreign affairs in 1911 was the settlement of differences between the United States and Canada with respect to fishing rights on the North Atlantic Coast Fisheries in conferences held in Washington. These were finally settled in a treaty between the United States and Great Britain signed on July 20, 1912. Meanwhile, on Feb. 7, 1911, a treaty between the United States and Great Britain was signed providing for the preservation and protection of pelagic fur seals in Bering Sea waters.

1912

Jan. 6. New Mexico admitted as the forty-seventh state.

Jan. 17. Taft urged the adoption of an annual federal budget. When Congress drastically lowered the funds he sought for the Commission on Efficiency and Government and placed a very low limit on the salaries its members could be paid, many members resigned.

Feb. 14. Arizona admitted as the forty-eighth state.

Feb. 22. In a speech in Ohio, Roosevelt said that his hat was in the ring but alienated big business by advocating the recall of judicial decisions.

Mar. Because of differences with Secretary of Agriculture Wilson, Dr. Harvey W. Wiley, his head chemist, resigned. The resignation became an issue in the 1912 elections particularly for consumer groups and women's clubs.

Mar. 13. Mahlon Pitney took the oath as Associate Justice of the Supreme Court. Having appointed six new men to it, Taft hoped to have a majority that would defend the Constitution against Theodore Roosevelt.

Mar. 27. Mrs. Taft planted along the Tidal Basin in the Capital the first of the Japanese cherry trees given to the United States.

Apr. 15. In appointing Julia Lathrop the chief of the newly-created Children's Bureau, Taft placed a woman in a responsible position for the first time.

June 22. Taft's name was placed in nomination for the presidency by Warren Harding at the Republican national convention held in Chicago. Chairman Elihu Root caused Roosevelt to fail in his challenge to regular party delegations. Taft received 561 votes, Roosevelt 107. Sherman was renominated for vice president.

July 2. At Baltimore, Woodrow Wilson was named as the Democratic presidential candidate.

Aug. 5. Roosevelt was nominated as president by the Progressive (Bull Moose) Party.

Aug. 9. Taft vetoed a compromise tariff bill because its writers had not followed the recommendations of the Tariff Board.

Aug. 24. Alaska was granted a territorial form of government.

Aug. 24. Taft signed a bill exempting American coastwise shipping from paying tolls to transit the Panama Canal. Many Americans as well as Britons considered the bill to contravene the terms of the Hay-Pauncefote Treaty of 1901. At President Wilson's request, Congress repealed the exemptions in March 1914.

Sept. 24. Marines were sent to restore order in Santo Domingo and a request was made that the latter honor its treaty with the United States.

Oct. 29. Following the death of Vice President Sherman, the President of Columbia University, Nicholas Murray Butler, was chosen to succeed him as the nominee.

Nov. 5. The electoral returns gave Wilson 435 votes; Roosevelt, 88; and Taft 8. The popular vote was: Wilson, 6,286,214; Roosevelt, 4,126,020; Taft, 3,483,922. Taft was glad that at least Roosevelt had been defeated.

Dec. Taft made an inspection trip to Panama.

1913

Jan. 1. Parcel post service began.

Feb. 14. Although it was favored by labor, Taft vetoed a bill calling for a literary test for immigrants.

Feb. 18. Gen. Victoriano Huerta engineered the overthrow of Madero and his murder. Taft obstinately refused popular clamor to intervene in Mexico.

Feb. 25. The Sixteenth Amendment was ratified. Congress now had the power to collect taxes on incomes.

Mar. 4. Woodrow Wilson inaugurated as President. The Tafts then left for a vacation in Augusta, Georgia, after which Taft assumed his duties as president of the American Bar Association.

Apr. 1. Taft was greeted by some 3,000 students and faculty upon his return to Yale to accept duty as Kent Professor of Constitutional Law. While serving he also earned from $150 to $1,000 for speaking engagements and also fees for magazine articles.

Summer. Justice Lurton died. Wilson's appointment of Louis Brandeis to the Supreme Court shocked Taft, who had signed a petition of the American Bar Association to the Senate Judiciary Committee saying that Brandeis was unfit.

1915

Jan. In a lecture on "The Presidency" at the University of Virginia, Taft criticized Roosevelt's broadening the use of executive power. As he saw it, a president "has no initiative in respect to legislation given him by law, except that of mere recommendation, and no legal or formal method of entering into the argument and discussion of the proposed legislation while pending in Congress."

Apr. Taft and Roosevelt were stiffly cordial while serving as pallbearers at the burial of a mutual friend.

June 17. Taft was named President of the League to Enforce Peace, which included an international police force.

1916

Mar. Although Elihu Root, President of the American Bar Association, Taft, and four other past presidents wrote to the Senate protesting Wilson's appointment of Brandeis to the Supreme Court, the Senate confirmed him.

May 15. Following the sinking of the *Lusitania* on May 7, 1915, Taft suggested to President Wilson that he break diplomatic relations with Germany. Wilson declined to do so. Angered when Democrats used his support for Wilson in the war crisis as political ammunition against the Republican Party, Taft questioned the Wilson administration's preparedness program and policies. With the sinking of the unarmed French Channel steamer *Sussex*, however, Taft supported Wilson's new preparedness demands and successfully invited him to address a meeting of the League to Enforce Peace.

June. Taft applauded the Republicans' choice of Charles Evans Hughes as their presidential candidate. Roosevelt declined to be named by the Progressive Party. Both Taft and Roosevelt campaigned for Hughes.

Nov. Woodrow Wilson was re-elected.

1917

Taft was named as joint chairman with Frank P. Walsh of the National War Labor Board, charged with reducing labor problems in vital war industries "for the duration." He thereupon moved to Washington. Although he opposed yellow-dog contracts (workers hired by a firm would agree not to join a union), these had been declared legal and enforceable by the Supreme Court. As he learned more about the working conditions and wage levels of the working classes, he softened his formerly hard line on labor rights.

Dec. 12. Although Ambassador Walter Hines Page had suggested that Taft go to England to explain Wilson's policies and purposes in the war, Wilson vetoed the suggestion. Again, after his alter ego, Col. E. M. House, recommended to Wilson that Taft be appointed as a member of the Versailles Peace Conference, Wilson declined to do so.

1918

Mar. 28. Taft and A. Lawrence Lowell, President of Harvard University, suggested to Wilson the holding of a convention of the League to Enforce Peace with the British League of Nations Society. Wilson approved as long as details of a peace program were not discussed.

May. Meeting by chance in Chicago, Taft and Roosevelt reunited politically and worked successfully to help elect a Republican Congress in November.

1919

Jan. 5. Taft attended Roosevelt's funeral, staying until the last and crying.

Feb. Taft toured through fifteen states in an attempt to gain popular support for the League of Nations.

Nov. Warren Harding was elected President. Because he did not support the League of Nations, Taft was criticized for supporting him.

Dec. 24. Taft breakfasted with Harding, who said that he would name him the Chief Justice of the Supreme Court when a vacancy therein occurred.

1921

May 19. Chief Justice Edward White died.

June 30. Harding appointed Taft the Chief Justice of the Supreme Court. The latter took the oath of office on Oct. 3, 1921.

1923

Feb. Judge Edward T. Sanford, of the Circuit Court of Appeals, was chosen to succeed Mahlon Pitney.

Feb. and Apr. Taft had heart attacks. He gave up golf and horseback riding.

Aug. President Harding died and Vice President Calvin Coolidge became President.

1925

Feb. 13. The Judiciary Act, for which Taft had worked hard, passed. It gave the Supreme Court greater power to decide which cases it would hear.

1929

Mar. Taft administered the oath at the inauguration of President Herbert Hoover.

Dec. Taft's half brother, Charles P. Taft, died in Cincinnati. Although not feeling well, Taft insisted upon attending the funeral. His efforts weakened his resistance to cardiovascular collapse.

1930

Feb. 3. Taft sent his resignation as Chief Justice to President Hoover.

Mar. 8. Taft died at his home in Washington at the age of seventy-two years. He was the first president to be buried in Arlington National Cemetery.

Dec. 13. The bar and officers of the Supreme Court held a memorial service for Taft.

1
Manuscript and Archival Sources

A. Manuscript and Archival Sources for William H. Taft

The William Howard Taft Papers in the Manuscript Division of the Library of Congress remain the best single source for information on Taft's life and career. Among the 750,000 items are data on his writings, materials while he was the Secretary of War, President, Professor of Law at Yale University, and Chief Justice of the U.S. Supreme Court. In addition there are his correspondence with family members, diaries, scrapbooks, legal papers, law lectures, and many items from his presidential administration. A microfilm of these papers has been available since 1972 and can be purchased from the Chief, Photoduplication Service, Library of Congress, Washington, D.C. 20540.

A breakdown of the Series follows:

1. Series 1. Family correspondence and related items, 1805-1909.

2. Series 2. W.H. Taft-Helen Herron Taft correspondence, 1881-1929.

3. Series 3. General correspondence and related material, 1877-1930. This series is especially good for Taft's service as Secretary of War, Yale Law Professor, and Chief Justice of the Supreme Court.

4. Series 4. W.H. Taft-Theodore Roosevelt Correspondence, 1897-1918.

5. Series 5. Executive Office Correspondence (Presidential Series No. 1), 1909-1910.

6. Series 6. Executive Office Correspondence (Presidential Series No. 2), 1910-1913.

7. Series 7. The Presidential Personnel File (Presidential Series No. 3), 1909-1913.

8. Series 8. Letterbooks, 1872-1921. Herein are especially valuable outgoing letters for Taft's period as Solicitor General, 1890-1891, Philippine Commission, 1900-1903, and Secretary of War period, 1904-1909. In addition there are Semi-official Letters, 1904-1905; Orders, 1905-1908; Presidential Letterbooks, 1909-1913; and Yale Letterbooks, 1913-1921.

9. Series 9. Speeches, articles, and messages, 1850-1929, arranged in rough chronological order.

10. Series 10. Professional Diaries, 1902-1918. These are chronologically arranged within the following groups:

> Official, 1902-1913. Chiefly diaries kept by Taft's military aides.
>
> Social, 1908-1913. Chiefly social activities, personal appointments, and speaking engagements.
>
> Personal Diaries, 1904-1908. Chiefly reports of Taft's personal appointments and speaking engagements.
>
> Secretarial, 1906-1908. Diaries kept by Taft's personal secretaries.

11. Series 11. Family Diaries and Miscellaneous Personal volumes, 1835-1930.

12. Series 12. Legal Papers of Alphonso Taft [father], 1784-1889.

13. Series 13. Legal Papers of William Howard Taft, 1880-1929.

14. Series 14. Legal Notebooks, 1887-1900. Notebooks Taft kept while he served as Judge of the Superior Court, Cincinnati, Ohio, and while Judge of the Sixth U.S. Circuit Court.

15. Series 15. Miscellaneous Legal Manuscripts, 1881-1930.

16. Series 16. Law Lectures and Related Material, 1897-1930.

17. Series 17. Scrapbooks, 1879-1922.

18. Series 18. Taft Family Financial Papers, 1880-1930.

19. Series 19. Taft Family Financial Account Books and Related Material, 1831-1926.

20. Series. 20. Miscellaneous Correspondence and Related Material, ca. 1797-1941.

21. Series 21. Special Correspondence, 1890-1909.

22. Series 22. Miscellaneous Addresses, Articles, and Related Material, ca. 1807-1909.

23. Series 23. Miscellaneous Reports and Minutes, 1905-1929.

24. Series 24. Miscellaneous Messages, 1903-1913.

25. Series 25. Miscellany.

26. In the Taft Correspondence, Miscellaneous, dated December 1929, is a biographical sketch by Charles D. Hilles, "The Unique Career of William Howard Taft." Hilles was one of Taft's secretaries.

27. There is a Subject File of Titles and also an alphabetical Index of names.

28. Mischler, Wendell W., Papers, Manuscript Division, Library of Congress. Mischler began serving as Taft's secretary when Taft was Secretary of War, 1904-1908, and stayed with Taft while the latter was President, at Yale, and at the Supreme Court. Among the papers are Taft's speeches on law (he was president of the American Bar Association in 1913), to churches, charitable and teacher organizations, at dedication ceremonies, Red Cross and Liberty Loan drives, on peace and the League of Nations, and while he campaigned for Hughes for president in 1916.

B. Published William Howard Taft Papers

Helpful are:

29. Fitzgerald, Carol Bondhus. "The Presidential Papers, George Washington to Calvin Coolidge: An Introduction to the Presidential Papers Microfilm Series," *History Teacher* 17 (Aug. 1984):545-65 (Taft on p. 563).

30. Rowland, Buford. "The Papers of the Presidents," *American Archivist* 13 (July 1950):195-211.

31. Shelley, Fred. "The Presidential Papers Program of the Library of Congress," *American Archivist* 25 (1962):429-34.

32. Stewart, Kate. "The William Howard Taft Papers," *Quarterly Journal of the Library of Congress*, November 1957.

33. Willard, Martha. Swarthmore College, "Notes for a Biographer, Based on the Taft Private Papers, 1810-1891." Unpublished Ms., Library of Congress, 1935.

34. Taft, William Howard. Collected Addresses, Messages, Opinions, etc., 1887-1917. Manuscript Division, Library of Congress.

35. ———. *Addresses: Five Lectures on the Edward Page Foundation, before Seniors at the Sheffield Scientific School at Yale University.* 1914; rept. Port Washington, N.Y.: Kennikat Press, 1969.

36. ———. Addresses, Pamphlets, etc., Relating to the Philippines, 1902-1905. Assembled by the Library of Congress.

37. ———. *Decisions Rendered by Hon. William H. Taft in Cases Coming Before Him as Judge in which Were Involved Questions Affecting Boycotts.* Washington: Sudworth Co., 1908.

38. ———. *Popular Government: Its Essence, Its Permanence, and Its Perils.* New Haven: Yale University Press, 1913. Biweekly lectures at Yale University on "Questions of Modern Government," 1913. Taft lectured at the University of Virginia in October 1914, University of Chicago in November 1914, University of Toronto in February 1915, and at Columbia University in October 1915.

39. The lectures at the University of Virginia, on Barbour-Page Foundation, were published as *The Presidency: Its Duties, Its Powers, Its Opportunities and Its Limitations.* New York: Charles Scribner's Sons, 1915.

40. The Columbia University lectures were published under the title of *The President and His Powers* by New York: Columbia University Press, 1915. They were reprinted by that press in 1925 and also by New York: Charles Scribner's Sons, 1916, and by New York: Johnson Reprint Corp., 1972.

41. ———. *Liberty Under Law: An Interpretation of the Principles of Our Constitutional Government.* New Haven: Yale University Press, 1922. Includes two lectures given at Town Hall, New York City; the law schools of Boston University, University of Minnesota, and Albany; and at Amherst, Bryn Mawr, Smith, Vassar, Harvard, and Wesleyan Universities.

42. ———. *Taft Papers on the League of Nations*. Marburg, Theodore, and Horace C. Flack, eds. New York: Macmillan, 1920.

43. "William Howard Taft and Myron T. Herrick: Selected Letters, 1912-1916." Phillip R. Shriver, ed. *Historical and Philosophical Society of Ohio Bulletin* 14 (Oct. 1956):22131. Taft helped Herrick win reelection as governor of Ohio in 1905; Herrick helped Taft win the presidential nomination in 1912 and was named by Taft as his Ambassador to France.

44. U.S. President. *The State of the Union Messages of the Presidents, 1790-1966*, 3 vols. Ed. by Fred L. Israel. New York: Chelsea House, 1966, 3:2338-2543.

Other important collections are of Taft's cabinet officers in various record groups in the National Archives.

45. Agriculture
Attorney General
Commerce and Labor
Interior
Navy
Post Office
State
Treasury
War

These collections contain various subsidiary groupings that facilitate their use. The Department of State uses a decimal file system that indicates the relations of the United States with every other nation. Under Navy, there are, for example, the General Correspondence of the Secretary of the Navy, RG 80; the Records of the General Board of the Navy, 400 Series; Naval Aviation, RG 72; Court Martial Records, RG 125; and Marine Corps, RG 127.

C. Unpublished Personal and Administrative Papers of Presidential Associates

46. Aldrich, Nelson. Papers. Manuscript Division, Library of Congress. Reveal the career of a conservative; a member of the Old Guard in Congress upon whom Taft as president depended.

47. Anderson, Chandler P. Papers. Manuscript Division, Library of Congress. Important for foreign affairs during Taft's presidency.

48. Ballinger, Richard A. Papers. Microfilm, University of Washington Libraries. Of four subgroups, the most pertinent is II: Secretary of the Interior Period, 1909-1911. Included are correspondence, newspaper clippings, scrapbooks, memoranda on the Forest Service, records of hearings at which Ballinger was a principal witness, and speeches and writings. Citations must give credit to the University of Washington Libraries.

49. Borah, William E. Papers. Manuscript Division, Library of Congress, reveal the career of a Republican progressive who was not a Progressive and of one who sought world peace through disarmament.

50. Brandeis, Louis D. Papers. Law School Library, University of Louisville. Taft thoroughly disliked his brand of sociological jurisprudence.

51. Bristow, Joseph L. Papers. Kansas Historical Society. Reveal the thought and actions of an Insurgent.

52. Butler, Nicholas Murray. Papers. Columbia University Library. Butler was a conservative Republican who nevertheless demanded low tariff rates.

53. Cannon, Joseph G. Papers. Illinois State Historical Society, reveal the record of a conservative.

54. Carnegie, Andrew. Papers. Manuscript Division, Library of Congress. Important for the world peace crusade.

55. Clapp, Moses. Papers. Minnesota Historical Society. The papers of an anti-Taft Insurgent.

56. Cummins, Albert B. Papers. Historical and Art Department of Iowa, at Des Moines. The papers of an anti-Taft Insurgent.

57. Dickinson, Jacob McGavock. Papers. Tennessee Archives and Library. Show the difficulties experienced by a Democrat and Southerner in Taft's cabinet.

58. Dolliver, Jonathan. Papers. Iowa State Historical Society, Iowa City. The papers of an anti-Taft Insurgent.

59. Fisher, Walter. Papers. Manuscript Division, Library of Congress. The papers of Taft's second Secretary of the Interior.

60. Foraker, Joseph Benson. Papers. Some 11,000 items in the Historical and Philosophical Society of Ohio, Cincinnati. Governor of Ohio and a U.S. Senator, Foraker originally befriended but in the end opposed Taft as president.

61. Harrison, Benjamin. Papers. Manuscript Division, Library of Congress. The papers of the president who gave Taft his earliest federal offices.

62. Hughes, Charles Evans. Papers. Manuscript Division, Library of Congress. The papers of New York State governor, Secretary of State, and Supreme Court Justice.

63. Johnson, Hiram. Papers. Brancroft Library, University of California, Berkeley. The papers of an anti-Taft Insurgent.

64. Kent, William. Papers. Yale University. The papers of a West Coast anti-Taft Insurgent.

65. Knox, Philander Chase. Papers. Manuscript Division, Library of Congress. About 8,450 items that deal especially with Knox as Attorney General of the United States, 1901-1904; U.S. Senator from Pennsylvania, 1904-1909 and 1917-1921; Secretary of State, 1909-1913; and his goodwill tour of Central America while Secretary.

66. La Follette, Robert M. Papers. Manuscript Division, Library of Congress. Contain data on a state reform governor, U.S. Senator, and one who as a Republican Progressive lost the presidential nomination to Roosevelt in 1912.

67. Lodge, Henry Cabot. Papers. Massachusetts Historical Society. A Theodore Roosevelt Harvard classmate who opposed Taft's general arbitration treaties and angered Taft with his corollary to the Monroe Doctrine.

68. Marburg, Theodore. Papers. Manuscript Division, Library of Congress. Great supporter of Taft in the world peace movement.

69. MacVeagh, Franklin. Papers. Manuscript Division, Library of Congress. Illustrate Treasury matters during Taft's presidential tenure.

70. Mann, James R. Papers. Manuscript Division, Library of Congress. Much on railroad regulation during Taft's presidential tenure.

71. Meyer, George von Lengerke. Papers. Manuscript Division, Library of Congress. Nine volumes and diaries January 4, 1901, to October 1, 1909, and one portfolio of photographs and other memorabilia. Other papers are in the Massachusetts Historical Society. His papers as Secretary of the Navy, however, are in National Archives, Washington, D.C.

72. Moody, William Henry. Papers. Manuscript Division, Library of Congress. Important because he was Taft's colleague in Theodore Roosevelt's cabinet and then a Supreme Court Justice.

73. Nagel, Charles. Papers. Yale University Library. The papers of Taft's Secretary of Commerce and Labor.

74. Newlands, Francis J. Papers. Yale University Library. A Western U.S. Senator much interested in the conservation of natural resources.

75. Norris, George W. Papers. Manuscript Division, Library of Congress, reveal the crusade of an Insurgent in Taft's day.

76. Perkins, George. Papers. Historical, Memorial, and Art Department of Iowa. Exemplar of a former trust magnate who supported reform via Theodore Roosevelt after the latter left the White House.

77. Pinchot, Amos. Papers. Manuscript Division, Library of Congress. A Roosevelt supporter via the Progressive Republican Party, 1912-1916.

78. Poindexter, Miles P. Papers. Microfilm copy in the Manuscript Division of the Library of Congress of the Papers in the University of Washington Libraries. A Western Republican anti-Taft Insurgent.

79. Roosevelt, Theodore. Papers. Manuscript Division, Library of Congress.

80. Sherman, James Schoolcraft. Papers. New York Public Library.

81. Simmons, Furnifold M. Papers. Duke University. A leading anti-Taft Democratic tariff reformer.

82. Sims, William S. Papers. Manuscript Division, Library of Congress. Naval operations and reforms during Taft's tenure as president.

83. Smith, Herbert Knox. Papers. Manuscript Division, Library of Congress. Smith was the Commissioner of Corporations.

84. Spooner, John C. Papers. Manuscript Division, Library of Congress. Republican U.S. Senator and anti-Taft Insurgent.

85. Straight, Willard. Papers. Cornell University Library. Illuminate Dollar Diplomacy in China during Taft's Presidential tenure.

86. Stimson, Henry L. Papers. Yale University. Much on Republican politics during Taft's tenure as president.

87. Taft, Charles Phelps (son), 1897-1983. Papers. Some 160,000 items that reveal the life of a lawyer, public official, Protestant lay leader, and mayor of Cincinnati.

88. Taft, Robert Alphonso "Mr. Republican," (the other son). Papers. Manuscript Division, Library of Congress.

89. Washington, Booker T. Papers. Manuscript Division, Library of Congress. Illuminate the Negro leader's failure to win Taft over to providing greater freedoms for Negroes.

90. Webb, Edwin Y. Papers. University of North Carolina Library. Important for the prohibition crusade.

91. Wickersham, George. Papers. These papers, which must shed light on the work of Taft's Attorney General, are held by the family and are not available to students.

92. Wilson, Francis Maris Huntington. Papers. Ursinus College, Collegeville, Pa. (Microfilm). Important for Taft's relations with Mexico and Central America.

93. Wood, Leonard. Papers. Manuscript Division, Library of Congress. Reveal attempts at reforms in the Army during Taft's tenure as president.

94. Helpful also is John J. McDonough and Marilyn K. Parr. *Members of Congress: A Checklist of Their Papers in the Manuscript Division, Library of Congress*. Washington: Library of Congress, 1980.

D. Published Personal and Administrative Papers of Presidential Associates

95. Butt, Archibald. *The Letters of Archie Butt: Personal Aide to President Roosevelt.* Lawrence Abbott, ed. 1924; rept. R. West, 1978.

96. Knox, Philander C. *Speeches Incident to the Visit of Philander Chase Knox, Secretary of State of the United States of America, to the Countries of the Caribbean, February 23, to April 17, 1912.* Washington: GPO, 1912. Knox gathered little good will on his good-will tour.

97. *The Letters of Franklin K. Lane, Personal and Political.* Lane, Anne W., and Louise H. Walls, eds. Boston: Houghton Mifflin, 1922. Lane was a West Coast progressive and member of the Interstate Commerce Commission.

98. *Selections from the Correspondence of Henry Cabot Lodge and Theodore Roosevelt*, 2 vols. Henry Cabot Lodge, ed. New York: Charles Scribner's Sons, 1925. Contains revealing insights into the Roosevelt-Taft relationships and Lodge's opposition to many of Taft's foreign policies.

99. Newlands, Francis G. *The Public Papers of Francis G. Newlands.* Arthur H. Darling, ed., 2 vols. Boston: Houghton Mifflin, 1932. Important for the conservation movement.

100. Roosevelt, Theodore. *The Letters of Theodore Roosevelt.* Elting E. Morison and others, eds., 8 vols. Boston: Houghton Mifflin, 1951-1954. A most judicious and beautifully edited selection.

101. See also the annual Departmental reports of each of Taft's cabinet members, the *Yearbooks* published by the Department of Agriculture, and the Department of State's *Papers Relating to the Foreign Relations of the United States.*

E. Contemporary Newspapers

102. Ohio Historical Society. *Guide to Ohio Newspapers.* Stephen C. Gugesell, ed. Columbus, Ohio: 1973.

103. Curl, Donald W. *Murat Halstead and the Cincinnati Commercial.* Boca Raton, Fla.: University Presses of Florida, 1980. This work is important because Taft served Halstead as a court reporter.

104. Among the more consistent pro-Roosevelt, hence anti Taft, newspapers, were the *Chicago Tribune, Des Moines Register*, and *Kansas City Star*. The *New York Sun* was the voice of extreme conservatism on the East coast, the *Los Angeles Times* on the West Coast, but the *San Francisco Argonaut* was not far behind.

Two independent newspapers were the *New York Post* and the *Springfield (Massachusetts) Republican*.

Of all the pro-administration papers between 1901 and 1923, the *New York Tribune* was the best; it was inclined to be more favorable to Taft than to Roosevelt. Also supporting Taft was the *Washington Post*.

Thoroughly opposed to Taft was the *American Federationist*, the voice of trade unions.

Cautious supporters of Taft's banking and currency reforms and Dollar Diplomacy were New York's *Commercial and Financial Chronicle, Journal of Commerce*, and *Wall Street Journal*.

Strongly Democratic were the *New York World*—which Taft refused to read—the *Baltimore Sun, New York Times, Louisville Courier-Journal, St. Louis Post-Dispatch*, and *Raleigh (North Carolina) News and Observer*.

Particularly useful for information on the activities of the federal government was the *Washington (D.C.) Bee*.

The *New Haven (Conn.) Journal Courier* and the student publication, *Yale Daily News*, spoke highly of Taft while president, Professor of Law at Yale, and Chief Justice of the Supreme Court.

105. See also Daniel C. Walter. *Black Journals of the United States*. Westport, Conn.: Greenwood Press, 1982. Most of these journals, such as *The Crisis*, edited by W.E.B. Du Bois, opposed Taft.

2
Published Writings of William Howard Taft

The major published writings of William Howard Taft consist of the many addresses he delivered between 1909 and 1913 and of his annual and special messages to Congress. For the latter see the entry under Fred L. Israel and the synthesis of them in the following section.

A. Published Writings of William Howard Taft

Major compilations of Taft's addresses and speeches are:

106. *Presidential Addresses and State Papers of William Howard Taft, from March 4, 1909, to March 4, 1910.* New York: Doubleday and Co, 1910.

107. *Four Aspects of Civic Duty.* New York: Charles Scribner's Sons, 1906, and New Haven: Yale University Press, 1911.

108. *Present Day Problems: A Collection of Addresses Delivered on Various Occasions.* 1908; rept. Freeport, N.Y.: Books for Libraries Press, 1967.

109. *Political Issues and Outlooks: Speeches Delivered between August 1908 and February 1909.* New York: Doubleday, Page, 1909. This title contains Taft's 1908 campaign speeches and those delivered between his election and inauguration.

110. Many of Taft's presidential addresses can also be found in *CIS. U.S. Serial Set Index.* Washington: CIS Congressional Information Service, 1975. Part VII: 61st 63rd Congresses, 1909-1915. These will be indicated by the notation *CIS*, the number of the Congress, whether a House or Senate document, and a number that refers to the actual material on file.

In chronological order, a number of addresses by Taft follow:

111. "The Security of Private Property." Address before the Alumni and Students of the Law Department, Wednesday, June 27, 1894. Ann Arbor, Michigan: The University, 1894.

112. The address above also appeared as "The Right of Private Property," *Michigan Law Journal* 3 (1894):215-33. Charges had been made that federal

judges had usurped their powers in protecting corporations and injured organized labor. Taft welcomed criticism of the judicial system because it forced judges to act as scrupulously as possible. Provides insight into Taft's views on property and its social contributions.

113. Address. "Recent Criticism of the Federal Judiciary." Delivered before the American Bar Association, Detroit, Michigan, August 28, 1895. In *Present Day Problems*, pp. 290-332.

114. "Inaugural Address as Civil Governor of the Philippines." Manila, Philippine Islands, July 4, 1900. In *Present Day Problems*, pp. 1-10. Taft was happy with the transition from military to civil government, in which Filipino members would be asked to take part. How to improve education and solve the tariff question would be important problems to resolve.

115. "Administration of Criminal Law." To the Graduating Classes of the Law School of Yale University on June 26, 1905. In *Present Day Problems*, pp. 333-55. The problems faced by practitioners of civil law in criminal cases and how to extend the writ of *habeas corpus* and trial by jury to the dependencies of the United States.

116. "Philippines," *National Geographic Magazine* 16 (Aug. 1905):361-75.

117. "Philippines Revisited," *National Geographic Magazine* 19 (Nov. 1905):1015-20.

118. "Panama Canal," *The Outlook* 81 (Dec. 9, 1905):869-73.

119. "The Panama Canal." At the Meeting of the Ohio State Bar Association, Put-in-Bay, July 11, 1906. In *Present Day Problems*, pp. 95-112. On the choice of the Panama over the Nicaraguan route, engineering and medical problems encountered during construction, and the remote possibility of building a sea-level canal.

120. "A Republican Congress and Administration, and Their Work from 1904 to 1906." Boise City, Idaho, November 3, 1906. In *Present Day Problems*, pp. 123-54. Under a Republican president, Senate, and House, the country has prospered materially and the administration has tackled the trust, railroad rate, and tariff problems, passed pure food and drug legislation, started construction on the Panama Canal, helped end the Russo-Japanese War, provided self-government for the Filipinos, and promoted labor unionization.

121. U.S. National Coast Defense Board. *Coast Defenses of the United States and the Insular Possessions. Message from the President. Transmitting a Letter from the Secretary of War with a Report of the National Coast Defense Board.* Washington: GPO, 1906.

122. Taft, William Howard. "Panama Canal," *The Century Magazine* 72 (Dec. 1906):300-13.

123. ———. "Some Recent Instances of National Altruism: The Efforts of the United States to Aid the Peoples of Cuba, Puerto Rico, and the Philippines," *National Geographic Magazine* 18 (July 1907):429-38.

124. ———. "The Legislative Policies of the Present Administration." Columbus, Ohio, August 19,1907. In *Present Day Problems*, pp. 155-205. Practically a repetition of the speech delivered in the title above.

125. ———. Address. "Southern Democracy and Republican Principles." Lexington, Ky., Aug. 22, 1907. In Taft, *Present Day Problems*, pp. 221-40. "The reason why the South exerts so little political influence in the guidance of the nation is because one single issue has made it the perpetual tail of the Democratic party, so that however small the Northern head, it wags that tail." Taft saw an "era of good feelings" in which the race issue would soon be worked out as Negroes learned better skills particularly in the agricultural sector.

126. ———. "The Inauguration of the Philippine Assembly." Manila, Philippine Islands, October 16, 1907. In *Present Day Problems*, pp. 11-42. The avowed policy of the administration was to govern the islands with regard to the interest and welfare of the Filipino people and to prepare them for self-government.

127. ———. "The People Rule: Mr. Taft's Reply to Mr. Bryan at Hot Springs, Virginia, August 21, 1908." In *Addresses* of William Howard Taft. Excesses of big business require a limitation upon the use of property and capital, but social legislation must be examined with "care and caution."

128. ———. "Abraham Lincoln," *Cosmopolitan Magazine* 46 (Mar. 1909):361.

129. ———. "My Predecessor," *Collier's Magazine* 42 (Mar. 6, 1909): 25.

130. ———. "Answer to Panama Canal Critics," *McClure's Magazine* 33 (May 1909):3-14.

131. "Panama Canal Tolls." *CIS*, 63-1, S. Doc. 11, 6335; 63-2. Sen. Report 469, 6552.

132. ———. "Judicial Decisions as an Issue in Politics," *McClure's Magazine* 33 (June 1909):201-9.

133. "Establishment of Children's Bureau in the Department of Commerce and Labor," *CIS*, 61-2, S. Report 417, 5583.

134. "Establishment of Children's Bureau in the Department of Commerce and Labor," *CIS*, 6102, H. Report 1675, 5593.

135. "Tariff Speech of President Taft at Winona, Minn., September 17, 1909." *CIS*, 61-2. S. Doc. 164, 5657.

136. ———. *Address of President Taft at the Banquet Given in His Honor by the Americans Club, Pittsburgh, Pa., May 2, 1910.* N.p., 1910?

137. ———. *Address of President Taft before the National Conservation Congress at St. Paul, Minnesota, Sept. 5, 1910.* Washington: GPO. 1910. Taft's conception of conservation as opposed to Roosevelt's.

138. "Address by President Taft at Cleveland, Ohio, January 19, 1911, discussing Republican Party Platform, Tariff, and Foreign Policy." *CIS*, 62-2. S.Doc. 292. 6175.

139. ———. *Address of President Taft at the Banquet of the American Society for the Judicial Settlement of National Disputes, at the New Willard, Dec. 17, 1910.* Washington: GPO, 1911. Taft greatly favored such settlement.

140. ———. "Address to the Pocatello, Idaho, Chamber of Commerce in 1911," *New York Evening Post*, Oct. 6, 1911, p.3. On his love for the judicial system.

141. "Message of the President Recommending an Amendment to Tariff Bill for Tax on Net Income of Corporations." *CIS*, 61-1. S. Doc. 98, 5569.

142. "Address of President Taft at Lincoln Birthday Banquet in New York City on Republican Party Platform and Revision of Tariff." *CIS*, 61-2. S. Doc. 361. 5657.

143. "Address by President Taft on Public Health." *CIS*, 62-1. S.Doc. 84. 6107.

144. "Message of President Submitting Budget," *CIS*, 62-3, S. Doc. 1113, 6353.

145. ———. "Reciprocity with Canada," *Journal of Political Economy* 19 (1911):513-17.

146. "Address on Reciprocity With Canada by William Howard Taft, Indianapolis, Indiana, July 4, 1911." *CIS* 62-1, S. Doc. 63, 6107

147. ———. "World Peace and the General Arbitration Treaties," *The World's Work* 23 (Dec. 1911):143-48. Taft favored general arbitration treaties.

148. "Address by President Taft At Marion, Indiana, on Foreign Policy and Treaties of Arbitration." *CIS* 62-1. S. Doc. 79. 6107.

149. ———. *Canadian Reciprocity*." Chicago, June 3, 1911. Washington: GPO, 1911. Speech in favor. This also appears as "Address by President Taft of United States on Canadian Reciprocity." *CIS*, 61-2. S. Doc. 43. 6100.

150. ———. *Dawn of Peace*. New York City: American Association for National Conciliation, 1911. Hope that world peace could come through general arbitration treaties.

151. ———. *Address by President Taft on Arbitration*. Washington: 1911. Same as above.

152. "Address of President Taft at Boston, Mass., March 18, 1912, on Government and the Judiciary." *CIS*, 62-2. S. Doc. 451. 6175.

153. "Address by President Taft on Judiciary and Progress." *CIS*, 62-2. S. Doc. 408. 6175.

154. "Address by President Taft on Howard University." *CIS*, 62-2. S. DOC. 568. 6176.

155. "Presidential Message Relating to Termination of Treaty of Commerce and Navigation of 1832 between United States and Russia." *CIS* 62-2. S. Doc. 161. 6174.

156. ———. *Address of William Howard Taft, President of the United States, Delivered in Boston, Massachusetts, Apr. 25, 1912*. Washington:

GPO, 1912. The same appears under title of "Address of President Taft, Boston, Massachusetts, April 25, 1912, on Theodore Roosevelt and the Judiciary, Election of Senator Lorimer of Illinois, Payne Tariff, Anti-Trust Law, and Presidential Election." In *CIS*, 62-2. S. Doc. 615. 6177.

157. ———. "What I Am Trying to Do," *The World's Work* 24 (June 1912):173-75. To bring about tariff revision, business prosperity, arbitration, and the indpendence of the judiciary.

158. "Speech of President Taft Accepting Renomination." *CIS* 62-2. S. Doc. 902. 6179.

159. "Economy and Efficiency in Government Service: Message of President with Recommendations," *CIS*, 62-2, H.Doc. 459, 6296.

160. "Message of President Relating to Fur Seals Convention," *CIS*, 62-2, S. Doc. 997, 6364.

161. "Address of President Taft At Concord, New Hampshire, on Tariff, Arbitration Treaties, and the Judiciary." *CIS*, 62-2. S. Doc. 552. 6176.

162. "Message of President Relating to Fur Seals of Alaska," *CIS*, 62-3, S.Doc. 921, 6179.

163. "Address of President Taft for United Daughters of the Confederacy on Erection of Monument to Heroic War Dead of the South in Arlington National Cemetery." *CIS*, 62-3. S. Doc. 971. 6364.

164. "Recent Anti-Trust and Labor Injunction Legislation. Address by William A. Taft before the American Bar Association." *CIS*, 63-2. S. Doc. 614. 6596.

165. ———. "The Social Importance of Proper Standards for Admission to the Bar," *American Bar Association Reports* 38 (1913):924-36. Knowledge of social needs will help judges to temper the demands of reformers and thus avoid "radical and impractical changes in the law and government."

166. ———. *Opinion of the Hon. William H. Taft on the Complaint of Joint Committee of Cincinnati Business Organizations on Cincinnati Freight Rate Discriminations.* Cincinnati? 1913.

167. "Message of President Vetoing Immigration Bill." *CIS*, 63-3, H. Doc. 1527, 6889.

168. ———. *Popular Government*. New Haven: Yale University Press, 1913, 1914.

169. "Message of President, Mar. 5, 1914, Relating to Panama Canal Tolls," *CIS* 63-2, H. Doc. 813, 6755.

170. ———. "Address of the President," *American Bar Association Reports* 39 (1914):368. "We are in danger of excessive regulation which will really interfere with that freedom of trade and unrestricted initiative which has helped so much the material progress of the country heretofore."

171. ———. "Address." *American Bar Association Reports* 41 (Aug. 30, 1914):741. On court reforms.

172. ———. *The Anti-Trust Act and the Supreme Court*. New York: Harper, 1914. Taft's view on the Sherman Act and monopolies. While aware of the "slot machine" theory of judging, he conceded that "the courts are affected by the times in which they live."

173. ———. *The United States and Peace*. 1914; rept. Kraus Reprint Co., 1971. A collection of four Taft lectures before the New York Peace Society. A valuable source for Taft's views on the Monroe Doctrine, immigration, model aribitration treaties, world organization, and an international court of justice.

174. ———. "Is a National Standard of Education Practical?" National Education Association, 1915. Pamphlet.

175. ———. "Yale's Contribution to the Spanish American War." In *Book of the Yale Pageant*. G.H. Nettleton ed. New Haven: Yale University Press, 1916.

176. ———. *Our Chief Magistrate and His Powers*. New York: Columbia University Press, 1916.

177. ———. *World Peace: A Written Debate between William Howard Taft and William J. Bryan*. 1917; rept. New York: Kraus Reprint Co., 1970. Taft would have an international military force enforce peace; Bryan would not.

178. ———. "America Can't Quit . . . An Address on the League of Nations, La Crosse, Wisconsin, July 2, 1919." New York: League to Enforce Peace, 1919.

179. ———. *The Paris Covenant for a League of Nations.* New York: League to Enforce Peace, 1919.

180. ———. "Adequate Machinery for Judicial Business." Address Delivered at the Forty-fourth Meeting of the American Bar Association, at Cincinnati, Ohio, Aug. 30, 1921. *American Bar Association Journal* 7 (Sept. 1921):453. Congress has failed to provide adequate judicial machinery. More judges should be added and an executive director should be provided to assign them their work and to schedule judicial conferences.

181. ———. "Three Needed Steps of Progress," *American Bar Association Journal* 8 (1922):24. Same as 180.

182. ———. "Possible and Needed Reforms in the Administration of Justice," *American Bar Association Journal* 8 (1922):601. Same as 180.

183. ———. "Statement before the Committee of the Judiciary, U.S. Senate," 67th Cong., 1st Sess., p. 16, Oct. 5, 1921. On court reform.

184. ———. *The Presidency: Its Duties, Its Powers, Its Opportunities and Its Liberty Under Law: An Interpretation of the Principles of Our Constitution and Government.* New Haven: Yale University Press, 1922.

185. ———. "The Supreme Court and the Public Welfare," *The Outlook* 130 (June 20, 1923):67-68. At the unveiling of a monument to Chief Justice Salmon Portland Chase, Taft responded to criticism of the Supreme Court Judges as "actually Supreme Rulers."

186. ———. "Statement of Chief Justice William Howard Taft." *Hearings before the Committee on the Judiciary.* House of Representatives, 68th Cong., 2d Sess., on HR 8206, Dec. 18, 1924. On court reform.

187. ———. "The Attack on the Courts and Legal Procedure," *Kentucky Law Journal* 5 (1924):18. Taft's recommendation that by reducing the Supreme Court's obligatory jurisdiction and extending discretionary review he hoped to reroute many cases on appeal to the Circuit Courts.

188. ———. "The Jurisdiction of the Supreme Court under the Act of February 13, 1925," *Yale Law Journal* 35 (Nov. 1925):2. Explains how the court could be more selective in the cases it chose to hear under the law he had fought for.

189. ———. "W.H. Taft to C.E. Hughes, April 27, 1926," *American Bar Association Journal* 12 (May 1926):326. Taft blasted local bar associations for being social groups rather than agencies attempting to secure self-discipline and "real reform measures of legal procedure."

Summaries follow of Taft's annual and special messages to Congress.

190. June 16, 1909. Special message to Congress recommending a constitutional amendment that would give the federal government the power to levy taxes on income. The amendment was proposed to the state legislatures by Congress on July 2, 1909, and ratified on February 25, 1913.

191. December 7, 1909. First Annual Message on the State of the Union. After dealing with foreign relations, Taft asked for a reorganization of the Department of State that would further American trade and interests abroad. On domestic affairs he noted that "Perhaps the most important question presented to this Administration is that of economy in expenditures and sufficiency of revenue." He asked that Congress appoint a committee to report on how a better system could be devised. Meanwhile, to reduce expenditures, he severely cut funds for the military services. To obtain information on tariff rates he asked for the establishment of a Tariff Commission. He also asked for changes in judicial procedures that would avoid the "deplorable delays in the administration of civil and criminal law" and that clearer language be provided with respect to the issue of the writ of injunction. By recommending higher postal rates for newspapers and magazines he incurred the hostility of the fourth estate, and by asking for postal savings banks he incurred the hostility of established banks. Lastly, he asked for improved methods of conserving the nation's natural resources and for a law requiring that candidates for membership in the House of Representatives publicize their expenditures.

192. December 6, 1910. Second Annual Message. Taft applauded progress made on arbitrating the fisheries dispute with Great Britain, the settlement of the Passamaquoddy Bay boundary with Canada, and steps taken to forward world peace through disarmament and an International Prize Court. He was pleased that the Portuguese monarchy had been overthrown in favor of a republic and that China was looking kindly upon American loans to stabilize her currency and for railroad building. He noted that great improvement had

been made because of the new tariff law and that new business had been obtained by Americans in consequence of his Dollar Diplomacy. He again voiced his demand for what amounted to a federal budget system, for the simplification of judicial procedures and for those respecting the issue of writs of injunction, and for a rural parcel post system. He was pleased that a beginning had been made with postal savings banks, that higher rates had enabled the Post Office Department to wipe out a deficit, and with the reorganization of the Navy Department and with the economy with which it operated. What was still needed was legislation on conservation, on a new Department of Health, and on a federal budget.

193. December 5, 1911. Third Annual Message. Part I. Because of the number of subjects to be covered, Taft promised a number of special messages in addition to the regular annual one. He started with the antitrust law. He was pleased with the Supreme Court's upholding of the Sherman Antitrust Law in decisions against the Standard Oil and American Tobacco Co. trusts but wanted its wording changed so that its meaning to businessmen would be amply clear and that Congress would provide for the federal incorporation of corporations.

194. December 7, 1911. Part II. On Foreign Relations. Taft was pleased with the "general movement on the part of the Powers for broader arbitration." He had taken the precaution of sending troops to maneuver along the Mexican border and warships off its coasts because of civil disturbances in Mexico that threatened American lives and property. He was neutral with respect to the contending Mexican factions and was determined not to intervene if possible. Dollar Diplomacy was working well in Central America and in China, to which two loans had been made, and a new treaty of commerce and navigation between the United States and Japan in 1911 extended the one signed in 1894. Because of Russia's mistreatment of foreigners, he hesitated to renew the treaty of 1832. Outstanding was the Fur Seal treaty of 1911 that ended pelagic sealing by the United States, Japan, Great Britain, and Russia. In light of profitable foreign trade, American merchant shipping should be subsidized.

195. December 20, 1911. Part III. Having received some reports from his Tariff Commission, Taft asked Congress to reconsider amending Schedule K, on wool, and to reduce the rates.

196. December 21, 1911. Part IV. On the financial condition of the treasury, needed banking and currency reform, and departmental questions. Taft was pleased with the condition of the Treasury. For the first time in twenty-seven

years the Post Office Department had a surplus. The interest bearing debt of the nation was below $1 billion, and improved efficiency in the Treasury Department made it possible to eliminate 134 positions in 1912.

The Congressional Monetary Commission established in consequence of the Panic of 1907 had not reported fully, yet Taft believed that the current banking organization need not be changed radically, certainly not in favor of a central bank. He awaited additional reports and hoped that the issue would not become a political one.

Taft sought reforms in the War Department that would increase its efficiency yet reduce its expenditures and asked that the Memorial Amphitheater at Arlington National Cemetary be built with funds already appropriated. Construction of the Panama Canal should be completed as of July 1, 1913, eighteen months early, and he wished that Congress would authorize him to set the rate of tolls to be charged and that American shipping be exempted from payment. In addition to asking that justice be provided more speedily and cheaply, he wanted an adequate workmen's compensation law, the building of two battleships per year until forty such ships were provided, and ranks higher than rear admiral for naval officers. He again urged upon Congress the creation of a Council of National Defense, one that could recommend to the President and to Congress whatever measures it deemed necessary.

197. January 17, 1912. Special Message On Economy and Efficiency in the Government Service. On June 25, 1910, Congress had provided $100,000 with which the President could inquire, for the first time in history, into government procedures and recommend improvements therein. The Commission he had appointed had reported on five fields: organization, personnel, business methods, accounting and reporting, and the budget. The nation had no budget. One should be provided that not only offered a definite annual program of business to be financed but how all business would be paid for as well. He desired that Congress appropriate more funds to continue the work of the Commission and defray the costs of printing its reports.

198. December 3, 1912. Fourth Annual Message. Part I. Foreign trade prospers and "the relations of the United States with all foreign powers remain upon a sound basis of peace, harmony, and friendship." The new "geographical desk" reorganization of 1909 of the Department of State was working well, but he was sorry that the Senate disagreed with his suggestion of using arbitration treaties as a method of avoiding war. Dollar Diplomacy was working well in China and should be expanded in Central America. He praised the sailors and Marines who had quelled a Nicaraguan revolution in 1912 and trusted that Secretary of State Knox had gained some goodwill on his goodwill tour of Central America. As for the two-year-old internal strife in

Mexico, he prayed that it would soon end. The United States was in no way involved in the war between Italy and Turkey and was highly pleased that China was now a republic.

199. Part II. On fiscal, judicial, military, and insular affairs. "The business condition of the country with reference to business could hardly be better," yet improvement must be made in its banking and currency system. As of yore, Taft asked that tariff rates be fixed on the basis of the difference of costs of production abroad and at home. He would soon ask Congress to provide for a federal budget. Puerto Rico and the Philippines were making progress, with independence for the latter to be granted in eight years. Congress should pass vitally needed legislation to control waterpower projects so that they might help make waterways navigable. He would study Great Britain's complaint against his exempting American shipping from paying the Panama Canal tolls. He highly praised Meyer's reorganization of the Navy Department via an Aide system and asked that a Naval Reserve be created. Finally, he continued his demands for swifter and cheaper justice and for a workmen's compensation act.

200. December 19, 1912. Part III. Concerning the work of several departments and the District of Columbia. Taft wanted Congress to authorize Cabinet members to have seats in Congress and to speak therein and to answer questions. The postal savings banks and parcel post system were working well. The Interior Department had more problems than any other, and Congress should legislate on the subject of the conservation of natural resources. Moreover, appeals should be permitted under the Pure Food and Drug law. "The trust question in the enforcement of the Sherman antitrust law is gradually solving itself...."

The District of Columbia was growing rapidly and could stand some improvement in the direction of its public utilities and school system. However, he was strongly opposed to granting the district an elective government.

201. See also *The American Yearbook: A Record of Events and Progress.* New York and London: Appleton, 1911(none for 1920-1924) under title of "Government and Administration."

B. Unpublished Writings of William Howard Taft

202. The unpublished writings of William Howard Taft consist of the approximately 750,000 items in his papers at the Manuscript Division, Library of Congress, small collections in repositories in Cincinnati and in Columbus, Ohio, and letters that he wrote to individuals who maintain them in their private collections.

3
Autobiographical and Biographical Publications

Bibliographic Guides

203. Barclay, Barbara. *Lamps to the Light the Way of Our Presidents: Presidential Portraits by Celeste Swayne-Courtney.* Glendale, Calif.: Bowman, 1970.

204. Bassett, Margaret Byrd. *Profiles and Portraits of American Presidents and Their Wives.* Freeport, Me.: B. Wheelright Co., 1969. Taft, pp. 71-73, 119.

205. Cooke, Donald E. *Atlas of the Presidency*, rev. ed. Maplewood, N.J.: Hammond, 1977. Short biographies of the president to date of publication. For juveniles.

206. Dargin, Marion. *Guide to American Biography. Part II: 1815-1933.* Albuquerque: The University of New Mexico Press, 1952. Taft, pp. 440-41.

207. Kane, Joseph Nathan. *Facts About the Presidents: A Compilation of Biography and Historical Information*, 4th ed. New York: H.W. Wilson Co., 1981. Taft, pp. 177-82.

208. Magill, Frank Northen, ed. *The American Presidents*, 3 vols. Pasadena, Calif.: Salem Press, 1986. Taft, 2:482-99.

209. Morgan, James. *Brief Biographies of Our Chief Magistrates from Washington to Eisenhower*, 2d enl. ed. New York: Macmillan, 1958. Presidents are born, not made! Taft, pp. 163-67.

210. Taylor, Tim. *Book of the Presidents.* New York: Arno Press, 1972. Statistics about each president and a chronology of major events occurring during each term in office. Taft, pp. 310-22.

211. *Selected List of Biographies of the Presidents of the United States.* Washington: Library of Congress, Bibliography Division, 1926. Contains chronologies and a listing of only 75 books. Taft, pp. 310-22.

212. World Book Encyclopedia. *Presidents of the United States.* Chicago: Field Enterprises Educational Corp., 1973. Various paging. Presidential biographies excerpted from the encyclopedia. "William Howard Taft," s.v.

Monographs

213. *Academic American Encyclopedia*, 21 vols. Princeton, N.J.: Areta Pub. Co., 1980. Taft, 5:218; 16:174; 18:357; 19:452.

214. Beard, Charles A. *The Presidents in American History.* New York: Julian Messner, 1935. Taft, pp. 121-24.

215. Brown, William B. *The People's Choice: The Presidential Image in Campaign Biography.* Baton Rouge: Lousiana State University Press, 1960. Campaign biographers tend to idealize their subjects. Taft, pp. 26, 29, 41, 42, 52, 55, 95.

216. Cunliffe, Marcus, and the editors of *American Heritage. A History of the Presidency.* New York: American Heritage Pub. Co., 1965. Taft, s. v.

217. DeGregorio, William A. *The Complete Book of United States Presidents.* New York: Dember Books, 1984. Taft, pp. 393-408.

218. *Dictionary of American Biography.* John A. Garraty, ed., 1974. "William Howard Taft," s.v.

219. Editors of *American Heritage. The American Heritage History of the Confident Years.* New York: American Heritage Pub. Co., n.d. Taft, pp. 333, 341, 364, 367-77.

220. Editors of *American Heritage.* Editor-in Chief, Kenneth W. Leish. *American Heritage Pictorial History of the Presidents*, 2 vols. New York: American Heritage Pub. Co., 1968. Taft, s.v.

221. *Encyclopedia Americana.* "William Howard Taft," s.v.

222. *Encyclopedia Britannica*, 11th ed. 1931. Wickersham, George W. "William Howard Taft."

223. *Encyclopedia Britannica: Macropedia*, 1977. "William Howard Taft," IX:764.

A. Autobiographical and Biographical Publications

224. Anderson, Donald. *William Howard Taft: A Conservative Conception of the Presidency*. Ithaca: Cornell University Press, 1968. Theodore Roosevelt would act and then seek justification in the Constitution, whereas Taft would do nothing unless he found specific authorization to do so in the Constitution.

225. ———. "A Mountain of Misery: An Intimate History of William Howard Taft." Ph.D. diss., University of California, Los Angeles, 1973.

226. Anderson, Judith Icke. *William Howard Taft: An Intimate History*. New York: W.W. Norton, 1981. An outgrowth of a doctoral dissertation that seeks to ascribe Taft's laziness and other physiological and psychological characteristics to his obesity. His problem in reaching decisions began in his childhood and was complicated by his marriage to a woman who had a powerful influence over him. He was also a product and a victim of his ties to those he loved, especially Theodore Roosevelt.

227. Barker, Charles E. *With President Taft in the White House*. Chicago: A. Kroch and Son, 1947. By his physician while Taft was in the White House. Has especially good details on Taft's fighting the "battle of the bulge."

228. Burt, Nathaniel. *First Families: The Making of an American Aristocracy*. Boston: Little Brown, 1970. Taft, pp. 305, 319, 325.

229. Burton, David H. *William Howard Taft: In the Public Service*. Malabar, Fla.: R.E. Krieger Pub. Co., 1985. The author claims that Taft desired to become President and to make himself independent of Roosevelt. He also praises Taft as a far-sighted Court administrator and reformer and a learned jurist.

230. Butt, Archibald Willingham. *Taft and Roosevelt: Intimate Letter of Archie Butt*, 2 vols. Garden City, N.Y.: Doubleday, Doran, 1930. Perceptive comments on both principals by their military aide until he went down with the *Titanic* in 1912.

231. Coletta, Paolo E. *The Presidency of William Howard Taft*. Lawrence: University of Kansas Press, 1973. The only study to date that centers on the presidency itself. After relating the status of the country when Taft assumed the presidency, it deals with his actions on tariff reform and conservation, his losing fight against the Insurgents and his defeat in the elections of 1910, his great success in achieving a number of economic reforms except with respect to the trusts, his work for world peace, his foreign policies, his break

with Theodore Roosevelt, and the split in the Republican party that enabled the Democrats to win the elections of 1912. When viewed in the era of transition from Rooseveltian to Wilsonian progressivism, Taft appeared to be a constitutional conservator.

232. ———. "William Howard Taft." In Henry F. Graff, ed., *The Presidents: A Reference History*. New York: Charles Scribner's Sons, 1984, pp. 413-34. A concise survey of Taft's presidential domestic and diplomatic affairs.

233. Cotton, Edward. *William Howard Taft: A Character Study*. Boston: Beacon Press, 1932. The story of a consistent, honest, and at times even courageous conservative.

234. Davis, Oscar King. *William Howard Taft: The Man of the Hour*. Philadelphia: P.W. Ziegler, 1908. A capable campaign biography by an excellent journalist.

235. Hall, Harry Orville. *William Howard Taft*. Washington: 1909. From the *Washington Herald* of Mar. 4, 1909.

236. Hargrove, Erwin C. "William Howard Taft: The Judge." In Erwin C. Hargrove, *Presidential Leadership: Personality and Political Style*. New York: Macmillan, 1966, pp. 77-96. Above all, Taft desired order and stability with legality. He dominated the Supreme Court while its Chief Justice and worked hard to obtain unanimous decisions. Rated poorly as president.

237. Hess, Stephen. *America's Political Dynasties from Adams to Kennedy*. Garden City, N.Y.: Doubleday, 1966. The Taft dynasty, including sons Charles and Robert. The latter, "Mr. Republican," is covered on pp. 299-338.

238. ———. "Big Bill Taft," *American Heritage* 17 (Oct. 1976):32-37. A brief life sketch, well illustrated, that says essentially what he said in the work above.

239. Hicks, Frederick C. *William Howard Taft: Yale Professor of Law and New Haven*. New Haven: Yale University Press, 1945. A perceptive and favorable picture of man beloved by the Yale faculty and student body and the citizens of New Haven.

240. Hoover, Irwin Hood. *Forty-two Years in the White House*. Boston: Houghton Mifflin, 1934. "Ike" Hoover, the Chief Usher at the White House, was quite critical of changes Mrs. Taft made in the management of the White House.

241. Josephson, Matthew. *The President Makers: The Culture of Politics and Leadership in an Age of Enlightenment, 1896-1919.* New York: Harcourt, Brace, 1940. See Chapter 9, "An Attempted Restoration," and Chapter 10, "The Ballinger Case."

242. McHale, Francis. *President and Chief Justice: The Life and Services of William Howard Taft.* Philadelphia: Dorrance & Co., 1931. A quick overview.

243. Manners, Will. *TR and Will: A Friendship that Split the Republican Party.* New York: Harcourt, Brace & World, 1969. A popularly written account.

244. Martin, Asa E. *After the White House.* State College, Pa.: Penns Valley Publishers, 1951. See Chapter 21: "His Honor, the Chief Justice," pp. 384-407.

245. Mason, Alpheus Thomas. *William Howard Taft: Chief Justice.* New York: Simon and Schuster, 1965. Well researched and well written by one familiar with the law.

246. Myers, Elisabeth P. *William Howard Taft.* Chicago: Reilly and Lee, 1970.

247. Patterson, Raymond Albert. *Taft's Training for the Presidency.* Boston: Chapple Press, 1908. A campaign biography.

248. Pringle, Henry F. *The Life and Times of William Howard Taft.* New York: Farrar & Rinehart, 1939, 2 vols. The fullest and best biography to date.

249. ———. *Theodore Roosevelt: A Biography.* New York: Harcourt Brace & World, 1931, 1956. Contains much on Taft's relations with Roosevelt.

250. Ragan, Allan. *Chief Justice Taft.* Columbus: Ohio State Archaeological and Historical Society, 1938. Covers the same ground as Mason, q.v., but not quite as well.

251. Roosevelt, Theodore. *An Autobiography.* 1913; rept. Da Capo Press, 1985. Care must be exercised in knowing when Roovevelt took more credit for certain events than he deserved.

252. Severn, Bill. *William Howard Taft: The President Who became Chief Justice.* New York: McKay, 1970.

253. Stoddard, Henry Luther. *As I Knew Them: Presidents and Politics from Grant to Coolidge.* 1927; rept. Port Washington, N.Y.: Kennikat Press, 1971. Includes the journalist's memories of Taft, pp. 341-88. 417.

254. Taft, Charles P. "William Howard Taft: My Father the Chief Justice," Supreme Court Historical Society. *Yearbook* 2 (1977):5-10.

255. Taft, Horace Dutton. *Memories and Opinions.* New York: Macmillan, 1942. Chapter X on his brother William Howard; Chapter XI on T. Roosevelt.

256. Taft, Helen Herron (Mrs. W. H. Taft). *Recollections of Full Years.* New York: Dodd, Mead, 1914. A disappointing story because it tells little about Taft's presidential policies or politics.

257. Thompson, Charles Willis. *Presidents I've Known and Two Near Presidents.* Indianapolis: Bobbs-Merrill, 1929. Includes the memoirs of Taft by a newspaper reporter who specialized in political affairs. Taft, *passim.*

258. White, William Allen. *Masks in a Pageant.* 1928; rept. Westport, Conn.: Greenwood Press, 1971. Taft was born politically out of his time. As Theodore Roosevelt put it, Taft was a good lieutenant but a poor captain.

4
Childhood and Early Development, 1857-1878

A. The Ohio Environment

259. Federal Writers' Program. Ohio. *Cincinnati: A Guide to the Queen City and Its Neighbors*. Compiled by the Workers of the Writers' Program of the Works Projects Administration of the State of Ohio. Cincinnati: Wilson-Hart Press, 1943.

260. Federal Writers' Program. *The Ohio Guide*. New York: 1940; rept. Somerset Pub., n.d.

261. Goss, Charles Frederick. *Cincinnati: The Queen City, 1788-1912*. Chicago: S.J. Clarke Co., 1912.

262. Izant, Grace (Goulder). *This Is Ohio's 88 Counties in Words and Pictures*. Cleveland: World, 1953.

263. Kayser, Pat. *Cincinnati without Fears or Tears*. Cincinnati: Tourcrafters, 1978.

264. Perry, Enos J. *Boyhood Days of Our Presidents*. Chicago: Adams, 1971. Taft, pp. 212-18.

265. Pringle, *William Howard Taft*, 1:25-44. No. 248.

266. Smith, Bessie White. *The Boyhoods of the Presidents*. Boston: Lothrop, Lee and Shepart, Taft, s.v.

267. Taft, William Howard, and George B. Edwards, "Letters of Roommates: William H. Taft and George B. Edwards." Ed. by Walter P. Armstrong. *American Bar Association Journal* 34 (May 1948):383-85.

268. Tucker, Louis Leonard, "Cincinnati: Athens of the West," *Ohio History* 75 (Winter 1966):10-25.

B. Ancestry

269. Faber, Doris. *The Mothers of American Presidents*. New York: New American Library, 1968.

270. Hampton, William Judson. *Our Presidents and their Mothers*. Boston: Cornhill, 1922.

271. Henry, Reginald B. *Genealogies of the Families of the Presidents*. Rutland, Ver.: Tuttle, 1935.

272. Hess, Stephen. *America's Political Dynasties From Adams to Kennedy*. New York: Doubleday, 1966. American families in which more than one individual has been nationally politically influential. Taft, pp. 194-331, 489, 590, 640.

273. Leonard, Lewis Alexander. *Life of Alphonso Taft* [father]. New York: Hawke Publishing Co., 1920.

274. Montgomery-Massingberg, Hugh, ed. *Burke's Presidential Families of the United States of America*. London: Burke's Peerage, 1975. Provides a chapter on each president including a short biographical study, chronology of important events, and the president's writings. The emphasis is upon the president's antecedents and family.

275. Ross, Ishbel. *An American Family: The Tafts, 1678-1964*. Cleveland: World, 1964. A history of the antecedents, birth, marriage, political, teaching, and judicial career of William Howard Taft and of Mrs. W. H. Taft and their children as well. For Taft's childhood, Chapter 3.

276. Taft, Alphonso, 1810-1891. Portrait, *World's Work* 14 (July 1907):9135, and *Harper's Weekly* 53 (Jan. 16, 1909):24.

277. Washburn, Mabel T.R. *Ancestry of William Howard Taft*. New York: Frank Allaben Genealogical Co., 1908.

278. Zorn, Walter Lewis. *The Descendants of the Presidents of the United States of America*. Monroe, Mich.: The Author, 1955. Taft, p. 117.

C. Childhood

279. Harris, Irving D. "The Psychologies of Presidents," *History of Childhood Quarterly* 3 (Winter 1976):337-50.

280. Mackay, H.B. "Taft's Early Life in Cincinnati," *The Independent* 70 (Feb. 2, 1911):227-29.

281. Smith, Bessie White. *The Boyhoods of the Presidents*. Boston: Lothrop, Lee and Shepart, 1929.

282. "Valedictory, Poem and Oration, June 25, 1878." New Haven: Morehouse and Taylor, Printers, 1878. Contains Taft's valedictory speech at Yale University.

5
Early Career, 1878-1888

Court reporter for the *Cincinnnati Commercial* while completing the Cincinnati Law School, 1878-1880; Assistant Prosecuting Attorney, Hamilton County, 1880; Collector of Internal Revenue, First District of Ohio, 1882; private law practice and marriage, 1883-1886; Judge of the Superior Court of Ohio, 1887, and elected to full term, 1888.

283. Dingilian, Arlene. "The Political Education of a Saloonkeeper," *Cincinnati Historical Society Bulletin* 24 (1966):311-20. Life and work of George Barnsdale Cox, the political leader in Cincinnati in the 1880s and 1890s.

284. Downes, Randolph C. "Joseph B. Foraker," Maumee Valley Historical Society, *Ohio Cues* 17 (Jan. 1968):2, 6.

285. Foraker, Joseph Benson. *Notes of a Busy Life*, 2 vols. Cincinnati: Ohio Historical Society, 1917. Taft in vol. 1.

286. Miller, Zayne L. *Boss Cox's Cincinnati: Urban Politics in the Progressive Era.* New York: Oxford University Press, 1968. Good for the Taft family and the Cincinnati of W. H. Taft's day.

287. ———. "Boss Cox's Cincinnati: A Study in Urbanization and Politics, 1880-1914," *Journal of American History* 44 (1968):832-88.

288. Ross, Ishbel. *An American Family: The Tafts*, Chapters 8 and 9. No. 275.

289. Taft. W.H. "The Right of Private Property." No. 112.

290. ———. *The Annual Address by William H. Taft . . . at the Eighteenth Annual Meeting at Detroit, Michigan, on August 28, 1895.* No. 113.

291. Taft, Mrs. Helen Herron (William Howard). *Recollections.* Taft on almost every page through 1912. No. 256.

292. *Weekly Law Bulletin and Ohio Law Journal*, 1887-1890. Contains quite dull reading in Taft's decisions as the Judge of the Superior Court of Cincinnati.

293. See also: Foraker, *Notes of a Busy Life*. No. 285.

294. Ross, *An American Family: The Tafts*. No.275.

6
Mature Years, 1888-1908

A. Introduction

Judge of the Superior Court of Ohio, 1888-1890; Solicitor General of the United States, 1890; appointed Judge of the Sixth Federal Circuit Court, 1892; President of the Second Philippine Commission, 1900; First Governor of the Philippines, 1901; Secretary of War, 1904-1908.

295. Asbury, Eslie Asbury. "The Literary Club," *Filson Club History Quarterly* 44 (July 1970):209-26. Highlights of the Literary Club in Cincinnati, founded in 1839. Among its most prominent members were Presidents Rutherford B. Hayes and William H. Taft.

296. Curl, Donald. *Murat Halstead of the CINCINNATI COMMERCIAL*. Boca Raton: University Presses of Florida, 1980.

297. Foraker, Joseph Benson. *Notes of a Busy Life*. No. 285.

298. Foraker, Julia B. *I Would Live it Again*. New York: Harper, 1932. Mrs. Joseph Benson Foraker speaks of Taft's early days in Ohio, including his appointment as Solicitor General of the United States. See pp. 307-31.

299. Lyle, Eugene, P. "Taft: A Career of Big Tasks. The Beginnings of Public Service," *The World's Work* 14 (July-Nov. 1907):9135-44, 9224-31, 9349-60, 9434-44, 9513-18.

300. Miller, Zayne L. *Boss Cox's Cincinnati*. Taft, pp. 186-87, 195, 209, 227-30. No. 286.

301. Ross, Ishbel. *An American Family: The Tafts*. Chapters 10-15. No. 275.

302. Taft, William H. "Recent Criticism of the Federal Judiciary. . .", Aug. 18, 1895. No. 113.

303. "Turning Points in Taft's Career," *The Century Magazine* 77 (Mar. 1909):685-89.

304. Zink, Howard. *City Bosses in the United States*. Durham: Duke University Press, 1930. Includes Boss Cox of Cincinnati.

B. Solicitor General and Circuit Court Judge, 1890-1900

305. Caplan, Lincoln. *The Tenth Justice: The Solicitor General and the Rule of Law*. New York: Knopf, 1987. On the Supreme Court and the politics of the Justice Department.

306. Fahy, Hon. Charles. "The Office of the Solicitor General," *American Bar Association Journal* 28 (Jan. 1942):201.

307. Anderson, Judith I. *William Howard Taft*, Chapter 4. No. 226.

308. Pringle, *Taft*, 1:92-147. No. 248.

C. In the Philippines, 1900-1904

309. Alfonso, Oscar M. *Theodore Roosevelt and the Philippines, 1897-1909*. Quezon City: University of the Philippines, 1970. Covers Taft's service in the islands.

310. Anderson, Judith I. *William Howard Taft*, Chapter 5. No. 226.

311. Beale, Howard K. *Theodore Roosevelt and the Rise of America to World Power*. Baltimore: Johns Hopkins Press, 1956. Though dated, this work remains one of the best on Roosevelt's diplomacy and has much to say about Taft's part in it.

312. Dennis, Alfred L.P. *Adventures in American Diplomacy, 1896-1906*. 1928; rept. New York: Johnson Reprint Corp., 1969. Chapter 8, The Open Door; 9, Cuba and the Caribbean; and *passim* for Taft as Secretary of War.

313. Farrell, John T. "Background of the Taft Mission to Rome," *Catholic History Review* 37 (1951):1-22. On Taft's negotiations for the American purchase of the Friar Lands in the Philippines.

314. Minger, Ralph Eldin. "Taft, MacArthur, and the Establishment of Civil Government in the Philippines," *Ohio Historical Quarterly* 70 (Oct. 1961):308-31.

315. ———. *William Howard Taft and United States Foreign Policy: The Apprenticeship Years, 1900-1908*. Urbana: University of Illinois Press, 1975.

316. Morris, Edmund. *The Rise of Theodore Roosevelt*. New York: Coward, McCann, Geohegan, 1979. Includes material on Taft and Roosevelt from their first meeting through 1901.

317. Mowry, George E. *The Era of Theodore Roosevelt, 1900-1912*. New York: Harper & Row, 1958. The concluding chapters cover Taft as Roosevelt's secretary of war—and more.

318. Ness, Gary. "Proving Ground for a President: William Howard Taft and the Philippines, 1900-1905," *Cincinnati History Society Bulletin* 34 (1976):7-23.

319. Patterson, Raymond. *Taft's Training for the Presidency*. No. 247.

320. Pier, Arthur S. *American Apostles to the Philippines*. Boston: Beacon, 1950, 1971. Taft, pp. 29-38. Taft established civil government and initiated the era of good will between Americans and Filipinos.

321. Pringle, Henry F. *The Life and Times of William Howard Taft*. No. 248. In vol. I, pp. 187-295, Pringle deals with Taft's successful weight reduction program; travels with a Congressional Party to the Far East in the summer of 1905; and his campaigning for Roosevelt in 1906, with Roosevelt saying that his speech at Bath, Maine, on Sept. 5, 1906, was the best yet delivered in the campaign.

322. Roosevelt, Theodore. *The Letters of Theodore Roosevelt*, 8 vols. Elting E. Morison and others, eds. Boston: Houghton Mifflin, 1951-1954. These volumes contain many letters exchanged between Roosevelt and Taft.

323. Solvick, Stanley D. "The Pre-Presidential Political and Economic Thought of William Howard Taft," *Northwest Ohio Quarterly* 43 (1971):87-96. An excellent study.

324. *Decisions Rendered by Hon. William H. Taft in Cases Coming Before Him as Judge in Which Were Involved Questions Affecting Boycotts*. No. 37.

325. Taft, William H. "Education in the Philippines." No. 36.

326. ———. "Administration of Criminal Law . . . June 26, 1905." No. 115.

327. ———. "Philippines." No. 114.

328. ———. "Some Recent Instances of National Altruism: The Efforts of the United States to Aid the Peoples of Cuba, Puerto Rico, and the Philippines." No. 123.

329. ———. "Ten Years in the Philippines." No. 108.

330. ———. "Philippines Revisited," No. 117.

331. ———. "Panama Canal." No. 118.

332. ———. "Panama Canal." No. 119.

333. ———. "U.S. National Coast Defense Board. *Report*. . . . 1906. No. 121.

334. ———. "Power Permits Under the Burton Law," *Chautauqua* 47 (Aug. 1907):365-79.

335. "Taft in the Orient," *Overland Magazine*, n.s. 51 (Jan 1908):34-41.

336. "Taft Party's Reception in Japan," *The Outlook* 81 (Sept. 9, 1905):67-69.

337. Taft, William Howard. "Inaugural Address as Civil Governor of the Philippines," No. 114.

338. U.S. Philippine Commission. *Report of the Philippine Commission to the President of the United States, January 31, 1900*, 4 vols. Washington: GPO, 1900. Taft was the president of the commission.

339. U.S. Congress. House. Committee on the Philippines. *Affairs in the Philippines, Hearings before the Philippine Committee*. 57th Cong., 1st Sess. Sen. Doc. No. 331. Washington: GPO, 1902. Includes Taft's testimony.

340. Wellman, Walter, "Trained to Be President," *Review of Reviews* 37 (June 1908):675-81.

341. Williams, Daniel Roderick. *The Odyssey of the Philippine Commission*. Chicago: McClurg, 1913.

D. Secretary of War, 1904-1908

With Taft in Roosevelt's cabinet were George M. Cortelyou, Commerce and Labor; John Hay, State; Ethan A. Hitchcock, Interior; Philander C. Knox, Attorney General; John D. Long and several others, Navy; Leslie Shaw, Treasury; James A. Wilson, Agriculture; and Robert J. Wynne, Post Office.

342. Abel, Christopher A. LT, USCG. "Controlling the Big Stick: Theodore Roosevelt and the Cuban Crisis of 1906," NWCR 40 (Summer 1987):88-98. Roosevelt objected to committing the nation to a major military occupation of the island while the Navy's field commanders wished to play a starring role in the exercise of his foreign policy. Taft supported Roosevelt in avoiding military occupation.

343. Anderson, Judith I. *William Howard Taft*, Chapter 6. No. 226.

344. Bailey, Thomas A. *Theodore Roosevelt and the Japanese-American Crises*. Stanford: Stanford University Press, 1934. Taft helped Roosevelt by reaching several agreements with the Japanese that at least on paper provided security for U.S. possessions in the Pacific.

345. ―――. "The Root-Takahira Agreement," *Pacific Historical Review* 9 (Mar. 1940):19-35. An executive agreement that bound only the existing administration to protect the territorial integrity of China.

346. Braisted, William R. *The United States Navy in the Pacific, 1897-1909*. Austin: University of Texas Press, 1958. As Secretary of War, Taft was involved with the Navy in providing defenses for the Philippines.

347. ―――. "The United States Navy's Dilemma in the Pacific, 1906-1909," *Pacific Historical Review* 26 (Aug. 1957):235-44. How to defend American interests in both the Atlantic and Pacific with a one-ocean navy?

348. ―――. "The Philippine Naval Base Problem, 1898-1909," *Mississippi Valley Historical Review* 41 (June 1954):21-40. The Navy and War Departments disagreed on Philippine defenses, with the result that little was done about them.

349. Callcott, Wilfrid H. *The Caribbean Policy of the United States, 1890-1920*. 1942; rept. Octagon, 1967. Though dated, this work is still among the best written on the period covered.

350. Chay, Jongsuk, "The Taft-Katsura Memorandum Reconsidered," *Pacific Historical Review*, 37 (1968):321-26. Holds that the memorandum was merely an exchange of views, an "understanding" that was not quite an "agreement."

351. Clinard, Outten J. *Japan's Influence on American Naval Power, 1897-1917*. Berkeley: University of California Press, 1947. Somewhat overrates the Japanese influence. Includes Taft's visits to Japan.

352. Coletta, Paolo E. *William Jennings Bryan: Political Evangelist, 1860-1908*. Lincoln: University of Nebraska Press, 1964. Includes Bryan's objections to American imperialism and demands that the Philippines be granted independence.

353. ———. "The Diplomacy of Theodore Roosevelt and William Howard Taft." In Gerald K. Haines and J. Samuel Walker, eds. *American Foreign Relations: A Historiographical Review*. Westport, Conn.: Greenwood Press, 1981, pp. 91-113. An evaluation of the scholarship, objectivity, and literary qualities of works written on the subject.

354. Dennett, Tyler. *Americans in East Asia*. New York: Macmillan, 1922. Contains background information on American interests in the Far East.

355. Dinwiddie, W. "Return of Secretary Taft," *Harper's Weekly* 49 (Oct. 7, 1905):1442-45. From his visit to Japan.

356. Doris, A. Graber. *Crisis Diplomacy: A History of U.S. Intervention Policies and Practices*. Washington: Public Affairs Press, 1959. Includes Taft's attempts to solve problems in Cuba and with Japan.

357. Esthus, Raymond A. "The Taft-Katsura Agreement: Reality or Myth?" *Journal of Modern History* 31 (1959):46-51. Holds that the conversations merely affirmed Roosevelt's early "agreement" that Japan would not menace the Philippines and the United States would let Japan acquire suzerainty in Korea.

358. ———. *Theodore Roosevelt and Japan*. Seattle: University of Washington Press, 1966. Includes Taft's two visits to the Far East, 1905 and 1907.

359. ———. *Theodore Roosevelt and the International Rivalries*. Waltham, Mass.: Ginn-Blaisdell, 1970. As above.

360. Fitzgibbon, R.H. *Cuba and the United States, 1900-1935*. Menasha, Wis: George Banta Pub. Co., 1935. Includes Taft's temporary governorship of Cuba.

361. Iriye, Akira. *Pacific Estrangement: Japanese and American Expansion, 1897-1911*. Cambridge, Mass.: Harvard University Press, 1972. Despite promises to respect each other's interests in the Far East, the United States and Japan drifted farther and farther apart.

362. "Judge Taft's Decisions Affecting Labor Organizations." Remarks of F.W. Stevens, June 30, 1908. *Ohio Law Bulletin and Reporter* 7 (1908):217-61. Taft was anti-labor.

363. Marks, Frederick W. III. *Velvet on Iron: The Diplomacy of Theodore Roosevelt*. Lincoln: University of Nebraska Press, 1979. Includes Taft's services as Secretary of War.

364. Minger, Ralph E. "Taft's Missions to Japan: A Study in Personal Diplomacy," *Pacific Historical Review* 30 (1961):179-84. In two visits, of 1905 and 1907, Taft was somewhat naive regarding Japan's expansionist designs.

365. ———. "William Howard Taft and the United States Intervention in Cuba in 1906," *Hispanic American Historical Review* 41 (1961):75-89. Taft was reluctant to intervene even though Americans had $150 million invested in Cuba.

366. ———. "William Howard Taft's Forgotten Visit to Russia," *Russian Review* 22 (1963):149-59. Kindly disposed toward Russia during his visit in 1907 while Secretary of War, Taft was able to obtain a broadened view of events in the Far East.

367. Munro, Dana G. *Intervention and Dollar Diplomacy in the Caribbean, 1900-1921*. Princeton, N.J.: Princeton University Press, 1965. Covers Taft's seeking of peace and use of dollar diplomacy in the region.

368. Murphy, G.M.P. "Another Chance for Cuba," *Harper's Weekly* 52 (Feb. 1, 1908):15. Roosevelt directed that a new president for Cuba be elected by Feb. 1, 1909.

369. Murray, Robert H. *Around the World with Taft*. Detroit: F.B. Dickerson Co., 1909. By a newspaper reporter who accompanied Taft in 1907.

370. Neu, Charles E. *An Uncertain Friendship: Theodore Roosevelt and Japan, 1906-1909.* Cambridge, Mass.: Harvard University Press, 1967. Includes Taft's visits to Japan.

371. ———. *The Troubled Encounter: The United States and Japan.* New York: John Wiley & Sons, 1975. As above.

372. ———. "Theodore Roosevelt and Involvement in the Far East, 1901-1909," *Pacific Historical Review* 35 (Nov. 1966):433-69. As above.

373. Reid, John Gilbert, ed. "Taft's Telegram to Root," *Pacific Historical Review* 9 (Mar. 1940):70-7. Taft notified Root about the Taft-Katsura "agreed memorandum."

374. Rowe, Joseph Milton. "William Howard Taft: Diplomatic Trouble-Shooter," Ph. D. diss., Texas A&M University, 1977. How Secretary of War Taft helped President Roosevelt in the diplomatic field.

375. *Secretary Taft's Visit to Shanghai.* Shanghai: American Association of China, 1907.

376. Snowbarger, W.E. "Pearl Harbor in Pacific Strategy, 1898-1908." *The Historian* 19 (1957):361-84. The war scare with Japan in 1907 and inability of the U.S. Army, Navy, and Congress to agree on fortifying the Philippines provoked the decision to make Pearl Harbor the major naval base in the Pacific.

377. "Taft Talks to Yuan Shi-Kai," *Current Literature* 43 (Dec. 1907):602-5. Taft's meeting with Yuan, who would be a leader in the Chinese Revolution of 1911.

378. Taft, William Howard. "The Panama Canal." At the Meeting of the Ohio State Bar Association, Put-in-Bay, July 11, 1906. No. 119.

379. ———. "A Republican Congress and Administration, and Their Work from 1904 to 1906." No. 120.

380. ———. "The Legislative Policies of the Present Administration . . . August 19, 1907." No. 124.

381. ———. "Southern Democracy and Republican Principles . . . August 22, 1907." No. 125.

382. ———. "The Inauguration of the Philippine Assembly . . . October 16, 1907." No. 126.

383. ———. "China and Her Relations with the United States . . . October 8, 1907." No. 108.

384. ———. "Japan and Her Relations with the United States . . . September 30, 1907." No. 108.

385. ———. "The Panic of 1907 . . . December 30, 1907." No. 108.

386. ———. "Labor and Capital . . . January 10, 1908." No. 108.

387. ———. "The Achievements of the Republican Party . . . February 10, 1908." No. 108.

388. ———. "An Appreciation of General Grant . . . May 30, 1908." No. 108.

389. ———. "The Army of the United States . . . April 1, 1908." No. 108.

390. ———. "Delays and Defects in the Enforcement of Law in This Country." No. 108.

391. ———. "Civilizing the Work of Missions." No. 108.

392. ———. *Address of William Howard Taft in Response to Notification Speech . . . July 28, 1908.* No. 108.

393. ———. "Republican Party's Appeal." No. 108.

394 ———." Four Aspects of Civic Duty." No. 107.

395. ———. "What the United States Has Done for the Philippines." No. 120.

396. Terrell, M.C. "Taft and the Negro Soldiers," *The Independent* 65 (July 23, 1908):189-90. On Roosevelt's order, Taft dismissed from the service all companies of Negro soldiers allegedly involved in the murder of a man in Texas.

397. Wright, T.P., Jr. "United States Electoral Intervention in Cuba," *Inter-American Economic Affairs* 13 (1959): 50-71. In both interventions, those of 1906-1909 and of 1917-1922, intervention by a democratic country failed where democracy did not prevail.

For Taft's part as Secretary of War in the building of the Panama Canal, see:

398. Du Val, Miles P. *And the Mountains Will Move*. Stanford: Stanford University Press, 1947.

399. Liss, Sheldon. *The United States and the Panama Canal*. Notre Dame, Ind.: University of Notre Dame Press, 1967.

400. McCullough, David. *The Path Between the Seas: The Creation of the Panama Canal, 1870-1914*. New York: Simon and Schuster, 1977. Thoroughly researched and at this writing the last word on the subject.

401. McGinney Brian. "The Land Divided: The World United," *American History Illustrated* 12 (May 1977):11-18.

For the rapprochement of the United States and Great Britain that permitted the United States to build and fortify the canal, see:

402. Campbell, Alexander E. *Great Britain and the United States, 1895-1903*. London: Longmans, Green & Co., 1960.

403. ———. *America Comes of Age: The Era of Theodore Roosevelt*. New York: American Heritage Press, 1971.

404. Campbell, Charles S. *Anglo-American Understanding, 1898-1903*. Baltimore: Johns Hopkins Press, 1957.

405. Perkins, Bradford. *The Great Rapprochement: England and the United States, 1895-1914*. New York: Atheneum, 1968.

406. Grenville, John A.S. "Great Britain and the Isthmian Canal, 1898-1901," *American Historical Review* 61 (Oct. 1955):48-69.

7
The Election of 1908

407. Anderson, Judith I. *William Howard Taft*, Chapters 7 and 8. No. 226.

408. "The Archbold-Foraker Letters," *The World's Work* 17 (Nov. 1908):10851-53. How Standard Oil paid Foraker to kill objectionable legislation.

409. Baker, H.L. "Taft and the Presidency," *The Nation* 84 (Jan. 17, 1907):56. This conservative journal of opinion preferred Taft to Bryan.

410. Barber, J.D. *The Presidential Character: Predicting Performance in the White House.* Englewood Cliffs, N.J.: Prentice-Hall, 1972. The author classified four character types which form in childhood and become entrenched by the time of the leader's first political success. These are: world view, style, power situation, and climate of expectations. Presidents are rated as active negative, passive negative, passive positive, and active positive. Taft was passive positive. "Taft's winning smile and unfailing cheerfulness concealed his friendlessness, personal agony, and his disgust with politics."

411. ———. "Strategies for Understanding Politicians," *American Journal of Political Science* 18 (Spring 1974):443-67. The author explains his procedures for classifying presidential character and style.

412. Bishop, Joseph B. *Our Political Drama: Conventions, Campaigns, Candidates.* . . . New York: Scott, Thaw, 1904.

413. Boller, Paul F., Jr. *Presidential Campaigns.* New York: Oxford University Press, 1984. Crammed with anecdotes and often forgotten dirty tricks of every campaign. Taft, pp. 187-90, 191-92, 194, 196, 197, 200, 247, 250.

414. Bolt, Robert. "William Howard Taft: A Frustrated and Fretful Unitarian in the White House," Cincinnati: *Queen City Heritage* 42 (Spring 1984):39-48. Only after he left the presidency did Taft answer charges by orthodox evangelicals that he looked upon Jesus Christ as a bastard and imposter by saying that while he did not believe in the virgin birth and Christ's divinity he believed in God and therefore was no infidel.

415. Brooks, Sydney. "Presidential Possibilities," *Fortnightly Review* 89 (June 1908):766-82. Profiles of the leading candidates.

416. Bryan, Martin. "A Study of the Speaking of William Howard Taft in the 1908 Presidential Campaign." Ph.D. diss., Northwestern University, 1953.

417. Bryan, William Jennings. "How Could the United States, if Necessary, Give Up Its Colonies." *World Today* 14 (Feb. 1908):151-54.

418. ———. "Why the Philippines Should be Independent." *Everybody's Magazine* 19 (Nov. 1908):640d-f. A republic can have no subjects.

419. Burner, David. "The Democratic Party, 1910-1932." In *History of U.S. Political Parties*, 4 vols. Arthur M. Schlesinger, Jr., General Editor. New York: Chelsea House, 1973, 3:1811-2068.

420. Burton, Theodore. "Presidential Candidates: William Howard Taft," *North American Review* 187 (May 1908):677-83. Taft has been identified with many of the important events of his time, knows his way about the government, and has "a rare union of judicial temperament with a remarkable gift for administrative management."

421. Butt, Archibald. *The Letters of Archie Butt*. Lawrence F. Abbott, ed. Garden City, N.Y.: Doubleday, Page, 1924. Contains valuable insights on both Roosevelt and Taft by their military aide.

422. "Campaign Fund Publicity: Before or After," *The World's Work* 17 (Nov. 1908):10851. Bryan would publicize contributions prior to election; Taft, after the election.

423. "Campaign: Taft in the West," *The Outlook* 90 (Oct. 10, 1908):175-76.

424. "Canvass of Mr.Taft," *Current Literature* 44 (Feb. 1908):117-22.

425. "[Grover] Cleveland for Taft," *Current Literature* 45 (Oct. 1908):358-62. Even as he neared death, Cleveland could not forgive Bryan's taking the Democratic Party from him.

426. Coletta, *William Jennings Bryan: Political Evangelist*, Chapters 15 and 16. No. 352.

427. ———. "The Election of 1908." In *History of Presidential Elections, 1789-1968*, 4 vols. Arthur M. Schlesinger, Jr., and Fred L. Israel, eds. New York: Chelsea House, 1971, 3:1049-2134.

428. ———. "The Democratic Party, 1884-1910." In *History of U.S. Political Parties*. Arthur M. Schlesinger, Jr., General ed. 1:987-1140.

429. Daniels, Josephus. "Mr. Bryan's Third Campaign" *Review of Reviews* 38 (Nov. 1908):423-31.

430. Davis, Oscar King. *William Howard Taft, The Man of the Hour. . . .* Philadelphia: P.W. Ziegler Co., 1908. A long campaign biography.

431. Dawes, Charles Gates. *A Journal of the McKinley Years, 1893-1913*. Chicago: Lakeside Press, 1950. Although Dawes had known Bryan when he was another fledgling lawyer in Nebraska, he had no use for his politics.

432. "Differences Between Taft and Bryan as President." *The World's Work* 16 (Oct. 1908):10739-40. Bryan had no administrative experience while Taft had much of it.

433. "Down the Years with Taft: Photographs," *Harper's Weekly* 51 (June 27, 1908): 11.

434. Dunn, Arthur W. *From Harrison to Harding: A Personal Narrative, Covering a Third of a Century, 1888-1921*, 2 vols. New York: G.P. Putnam's Sons, 1922. Memoirs of a newspaper reporter who closely followed political affairs.

435. Ewing, Cortez A.M. *Presidential Elections from Abraham Lincoln to Franklin D. Roosevelt*. Norman: University of Oklahoma Press, 1940.

436. Fitch, G. "Summing Up of Taft," *American Magazine* 67 (Mar. 1909):519-24. A favorable sketch.

437. Foraker, *Notes of a Busy Life*. Foraker's troubles with Standard Oil and loss of political power to Taft in Ohio. Taft, s.v.

438. "Foraker's Fight Against Taft," *Current Literature* 42 (May 1907):469-74.

439. Gillias, A. "Plain Man's Impressions of Taft," *The Outlook* 90 (Oct. 17, 1908):337-38.

440. Ginger, Ray. *The Bending Cross: A Biography of Eugene Victor Debs*. New Brunswick, N.J.: Rutgers University Press, 1949. The labor leader and Socialist presidential candidate.

441. Gompers, Samuel. *Seventy Years of Life and Labor: An Autobiography*, 2 vols., 1925; rept. New York: A. M. Kelley, 1966. From laboring in a cigar factory to longtime head of the American Federation of Labor.

442. Haney, James E. "Blacks and the Republican Nomination of 1908," *Ohio History* 84 (Aug. 1975):207-21. Foraker had supported the black soldiers who, on Roosevelt's order, Taft dismissed from the service in the Brownsville, Texas, affair of 1906. Blacks supported Foraker rather than Taft for the presidential nomination in 1908, but black journalists turned the black vote toward Taft in hope of expecting political rewards.

443. Harbaugh, William Henry. *The Life and Times of Theodore Roosevelt*, rev. ed. New York: Oxford University Press, 1975. Contains much on Taft as well.

444. ———. "The Republican Party, 1893-1932." In *History of Political Parties*. Arthur M. Schlesinger, Jr., General Editor. 3:2069-2258.

445. Harvey, Roland Hill. *Samuel Gompers*. Stanford: Stanford University Press, 1935.

446. Hitchcock, Frank Harris. "Campaign Chauffeurs of 1908," *Current Literature* 45 (Oct. 1908):387-91.

447. H.J.H. "The Democratic Convention," *The Outlook* 89 (July 1908):649-50.

448. Hornig, Edgar A. "The Indefatigable Mr. Bryan in 1908," *Nebraska History* 37 (Sept. 1956):183-99. During the long campaign Bryan made as many as thirty speeches a day.

449. ———. "Campaign Issues in the Presidential Election of 1908," *Indiana Magazine of History* 54 (Sept. 1958):236-64. Especially tariff reform, banking and currency reform, and the labor injunction.

450. ———. "The Religious Issue in the Taft-Bryan Duel of 1908," *Proceedings of the American Philosophical Society* 105 (Dec. 1961):530-37. Taft kept as quiet as he could about his Unitarianism and Bryan did not push the issue.

451. Kohlsaat, Herman H. *From McKinley to Harding*. New York: Charles Scribner's Sons, 1923. Personal recollections of the presidents he knew. Taft mentioned *passim*.

452. Leroy, J.A. "Taft as Administrator," *The Century Magazine* 77 (Mar. 1908):691-98. Gives Taft high marks especially for his work in the Philippines and as Secretary of War.

453. McBee, Silas. *The South and Mr. Taft.* Sewanee, Tenn.: University Press at the University of the South, 1908. The Southern Republican machine supported Taft but could expect little reward in return because of the race issue.

454. McMaines, Howard F. "The Road to George Ade's Farm: Origins of the Taft's First Campaign Rally, September 1908," *Indiana Magazine of History* 67, No. 4 (1971):317-34. Candidate Taft made the first speech of his campaign against Bryan at George Ade's farm, near Brook, Indiana, and showed that he favored taking the stump over a front porch campaign.

455. Morgan, Howard Wayne. "Red Special, Eugene V. Debs and the Campaign of 1908," *Indiana Magazine of History* 54 (Sept. 1958):211-36.

456. ———. *Eugene V. Debs: Socialist for President.* Syracuse, N.Y.: Syracuse University Press, 1962.

457. ———. "The Republican Party, 1876-1893." In *History of U.S. Political Parties.* Arthur M. Schlesinger, Jr., General Editor, 2:1411-1548.

458. Mowry. *The Era of Theodore Roosevelt*, Chapter 11. No. 317.

459. Odegard, Peter H., ed. *Religion and Politics.* Dobbs Ferry, N.Y.: Oceana, 1960.

460. Oulahan, R.V. "Taft As a Judge on the Bench," *Review of Reviews* 36 (Aug. 1908):208-11. Gives Taft good marks except on his labor record.

461. Pringle. *Theodore Roosevelt*, Book II, chapter 15. No. 249.

462. ———. *William Howard Taft*, 1: 321-75. No. 248.

463. Porter, Kirk H., and Donald B. Johnson. *National Party Platforms, 1840-1956.* Urbana: University of Illinois Press, 1956. Repubican Party platform, pp. 157-63.

464. Rhodes, James Ford. *The McKinley and Roosevelt Administrations, 1897-1909.* 1922; rept. Port Washington: Kennikat Press, 1965.

465. Robinson, Edgar E. *The Presidential Vote, 1896-1932.* Stanford: Stanford University Press, 1934-1947.

466. Roosevelt, Theodore. "Candidacy of Taft," *The Outlook* 90 (Sept. 19. 1908):108-12. Many kind words.

467. Roseboom, Eugene H. *A History of Presidential Elections*, 3rd ed. New York: Macmillan, 1970.

468. Salvatore, Nick. *Eugene V. Debs: Citizen and Socialist.* Urbana: University of Illinois Press, 1982.

469. "Secretary Taft Prefers the Bench," *The Independent* 65 (Oct. 22, 1908):914-16. That is, he would rather be a Supreme Court Justice than President.

470. Shaw, Albert. "Bryan and His Future," *Review of Reviews* 38 (Dec. 1908):656. Perhaps now Bryan will retire from active politics and serve as an elder statesman.

471. Shibley, G.H. "Taft as Upholder of Machine Rule," *The Arena* 38 (Nov. 1907):515-17. Taft needed the support of the southern Republican machine in order to be nominated and elected as president.

472. Steffens, Lincoln. "Roosevelt-Taft-La Follette on What the Matter Is in America and What To Do About It," *Everybody's Magazine* 18 (June 1908):731-36. Roosevelt is guided by the public interest; Taft will follow Roosevelt's policies and regularize them without seeking additional laws; La Follette wants to get rid of special privilege in government.

473. Stickley, G. "Man Of Inspired Common Sense," *Craftsman Magazine* 13 (Feb. 1908):605-8. The reference is to Taft.

474. Sumberg, Alfred D. "A History of the Presidential Campaign of 1908." Ph.D. diss, University of Wisconsin, 1960.

475. ———. "William Howard Taft and the Ohio Endorsement Issue." In *Some Pathways in Twentieth-Century History: Essays in Honor of Reginald Charles McGrane.* Daniel R. Beaver, ed. Published for the University of Cincinnati by The Wayne State University Press, Detroit, 1969, pp. 67-94. With Bryan already named for president by Ohio's Democrats, brother Charles P. Taft and Rep. Theodore E. Burton overcame the Boss Cox machine and the

older Republican state bosses, Joseph E. Foraker and Charles W. F. Dick, and won an endorsement for Taft.

476. "Taft Is Notified: Cincinnati Joyful," *New York Times*, July 29, 1908, pp. 1-3. Taft said that the chief function of his administration would be to clinch what Roosevelt had already done.

477. "Mr. Taft and the Presidency," *The Outlook* 17 (Dec. 1908):10962. Taft had been well schooled to assume the office.

478. Taft, William Howard. "The People Rule." No. 127.

479. ———. *Speeches Delivered between August 1908 and February 1909*. No. 109.

480. Tugwell, Rexford G. *How They Became President*. New York: Simon and Schuster, 1964. Taft, pp. 323-38.

481. Wellman, Walter, "The Management of the Taft Campaign," *Review of Reviews* 38 (Nov. 1908):432-38.

482. White, William Allen, "Taft: A Hewer of Wood," *American Magazine* 66 (May 1908):19-32. An unfavorable portrait of a shadow of Roosevelt.

483. Williams, Hon. George Fred. "The Political Outlook for the Coming Election," *The Arena* 39 (May 1908):552-53. Wrongly concluded that Taft would lose because of his attitude toward labor and the Brownsville affair.

484. Winkler, John K. *W.R. Hearst: An American Phenomenon*. New York: Simon & Schuster, 1928. Includes Hearst's attempt to win the Democratic presidential nomination in 1908.

8
The Presidency

A. Bibliographic Guides

Obtaining information about the office of the president, about which many thousands of titles have been published, is facilitated by reference to the bibliographical guides that follow.

485. *The American Presidency: A Historical Bibliography.* Gail Schlacter, ed. Santa Barbara, Calif.: ABC-Clio Information Services, 1984. Abstracts of 3,489 periodical articles from the ABC-Clio database.

486. Bailey, Harry A., Jr., ed. *Classics of the American Presidency.* Oak Park, Ill.: Moore Pub. Co., 1980. Selected periodical articles and books on the presidency.

487. Burch, Philip H. *Elites in American History.* New York: Holmes and Meier, 1981. Vol. 2. A biased but interesting work with good footnotes. Taft, 2:166-74.

488. Davison, Kenneth E. *The American Presidency: A Guide to Information Sources.* Detroit, Mich.: Gale Research Co., 1983. The most comprehensive study of the scholarship on the presidency, with emphasis particularly since 1945 and after 1960.

489. Durant, John, and Alice Durant. *The Presidents of the United States: With an Encyclopedic Supplement on the Office and Powers of the Presidency, Chronologies, and Records of Presidential Elections*, 2 vols. Miami: A.A. Gache, 1976. Taft, s.v.

490. Greenstein, Fred I. *Evolution of the Modern Presidency: A Bibliographical Survey.* Washington: American Enterprise Institute for Policy Research, 1977. Contains 2,504 entries, most of them from F.D. Roosevelt through Gerald Ford.

491. Martin, Fenton S., and Robert U. Goehlert. *The American Presidents: A Bibliography*, 2 vols. Washington: Congressional Quarterly Books, 1987. Contains more than 21,000 entries dealing with English-language works covering the years 1885 to 1896. A thorough survey covering the office of the president, including its history, development, powers, and relations with the

other branches of the government. Cites books, articles, dissertations, essays, and research reports, but not government documents.

492. Mugridge, Donald H., comp. *The President of the United States, 1789-1962*. Washington: GPO, 1963. A selected bibliography with emphasis upon autobiographies, biographies, memoirs, and writings of the presidents.

493. Sobel, Robert, Editor-in-Chief. *Biographical Directory of the United States Executive Branch*. Westport, Conn: Greenwood Press, 1977.

494. For all of Taft's messages, and the daily work of the Congress, see *Congressional Record*, 1909-1913.

B. Presidential Studies

Monographs

495. Ambruster. Maxim Ethan. *The Presidents of the United States and their Administrations from Washington to Nixon*. New York: Horizon Press, 1981. Short essays on each incumbent. Taft, s.v.

496. *The American Heritage Pictorial History of the Presidents of the United States*, 2 vols. Kenneth W. Leish, Editor-in-Chief. New York: American Heritage Publishing Co., 1968. Taft, s.v.

497. "An Index to Presidential Election Campaign Biographies 1824-1972." Ann Arbor, Mich.: University Microfilms International, 1981.

498. Bach, Stanley, and George Sulzner, comps. *Perspectives on the Presidency*. Lexington, Mass.: D.C. Heath, 1974. A collection of essays combining description and analysis.

499. Bailey, Thomas A. *Presidential Greatness: The Image and Man from George Washington to the Present*. 1966; rept. New York: Irvington Publishers, 1978. Arranged topically; has an excellent bibliography.

500. ———. *Presidential Saints and Sinners*. New York: Free Press, 1981. Taft, pp. 162-67.

501. ———. *The Pugnacious Presidents: White House Warriors on Parade*. New York: Free Press, 1980. Taft, "Apostle of Dollar Diplomacy," pp. 337-49.

502. Barger, Harold M. *The American Presidency: Myths and Realities.* New York: Robert A. Taft Institute of Government. Written for the Institute.

503. Beard, Charles A. *The Presidents in American History.* New York: Messner, 1935. Taft, pp. 121-24.

504. Blaidsell, T.C., Jr., and others. *The American Presidency in Political Cartoons: 1776-1976.* St. Lake City, Utah: Peregrine Smith, 1976.

505. Boller, Paul F. Jr. *Presidential Campaigns.* No. 413.

506. Bonnell, John Sutherland. *Presidential Profiles: Religion in the Life of American Presidents.* Philadelphia: Westminster Press, 1971. Taft, pp. 174-77.

507. Brown, Stewart Gerry. *The American Presidency: Leadership, Partisanship, and Popularity.* New York: Macmillan, 1966.

508. Brownlow, Louis. *The President and the Presidency.* Chicago: Public Administration Service, 1949. By a journalist and knowledgable public administrator. Prefers a strong president, one who has a sense of history.

509. Buchanan, Bruce. *The Presidential Experience: What the Office Does to the Man.* Englewood Cliffs, N.J.: Prentice-Hall, 1978. Bureaucratic red tape frustrates a president's ability to work with Congress, the media, and the public to get things done.

510. Burns, James MacGregor. *Presidential Government: The Crucible of Leadership.* Boston: Little, Brown, 1965. Taft's abilities were clouded by the events of 1912.

511. Commager, Henry. *The Defeat of America: Presidential Power and the National Character.* New York: Simon and Schuster, 1974.

512. Cornwell, Elmer E. *Presidential Leadership of Public Opinion.* Bloomington: Indiana University Press, 1965. Taft, pp. 26-30, on his failure to get along well with journalists.

513. ———. *The American Presidency: Vital Center.* Chicago: Scott, Foresman, 1966. Basic readings on the presidency.

514. Coyle, David Cushman. *Ordeal of the Presidency.* 1960; rept. Westport, Conn.: Greenwood Press, 1973. About the personal abuse suffered by presidents.

515. Cronin, Thomas E. ed. *Rethinking the Presidency.* Boston: Little Brown, 1982. Essays by experts.

516. Cunliffe, Marcus, and the Editors of American Heritage. *The American Heritage History of the Presidency.* 1968; rev. and enl ed. New York: McGraw-Hill, 1976. Colorful illustrations and text.

517. DeClerico, Robert E. *The American President.* Englewood Cliffs, N.J.: Prenctice-Hall, 1979. Stresses personality and leadership.

518. DeGregorio, William A. *The Complete Book of U.S. Presidents.* New York: Dembner Books; distributed by W.W. Norton, 1984. Short essays on each incumbent.

519. Dumond, Dwight L. *Roosevelt to Roosevelt.* New York: Holt, 1937. Taft mentioned *passim.*

520. Edwards, George. *The Public Presidency: The Pursuit of Popular Support.* New York: St. Martin's Press, 1983.

521. Edwards, George C. III, and Stephen J. Wayne, eds. *Studying the Presidency.* Knoxville: University of Tennessee Press, 1983. Taft, pp. 23-26. As in the study above, Taft denigrated the powers of the presidential office.

522. ———. *The Presidential Leadership: Politics and Policy Making.* New York: St. Martin's Press, 1985. Taft is not mentioned.

523. Egger, Rowland Andrews. *The President of the United States*, 2d ed. New York: McGraw-Hill, 1972. Taft's presidential term was characterized by "congressionalism" (p. 160).

524. Filler, Louis, ed. *The Presidents in the 20th Century. Vol. I: The Ascendant President: From William McKinley to Lyndon B. Johnson.* Englewood N.J.: Ozer, 1983. Collected documents with introductory essays.

525. Fischer, Robert A. *Tippecanoe and Trinkets Too: The Material Culture of American Presidential Campaigns, 1828-1984.* Champaign: University of Illinois Press, 1987. Buttons, pins, banners, plates, and other memorabilia offer insights into campaign strategies and the campaigners themselves.

526. Freidel, Frank. *The President of the United States of America*, 5th ed. Washington: White House Historical Association, 1973, 1982. Good illustrations with text. Taft, pp. 58. Photograph and short essay.

527. Graff, Henry F., ed. *The Presidents: A Reference History*. New York: Charles Scribner's Sons, 1984. Essays on presidents by specialists. Taft, pp. 413-43.

528. Hargrove, Erwin C. *Presidential Leadership: Personaliity and Political Style*. New York: Macmillan, 1966. Taft, 77-96, is given poor marks as a president but high grades as a judge. Compares men of "action," such as the two Roosevelts, with "presidents of restraint," such as Taft.

529. Hathaway, Esse Virginia. *The Book of American Presidents*, 2d ed., 1933; rept. Freeport, N.Y.: Books for Libraries Press, 1970. Taft, pp. 274-86.

530. Heclo, Hugh, and Salamon Lester. *The Illusion of Presidential Government*. Boulder, Colo.: Westview Press, 1981.

531. Heller, Francis H. *The Presidency: A Modern Perspective*. New York: Random House, 1960. Doubts that a leader's presidential qualities can be predetermined. Notes that polls rated Taft as "average" rather than "great."

532. Heslop, David Alan. *The Presidency and Political Science: A Critique of the Work of Political Scientists in Three Areas of Presidential Politics*. Ann Arbor, Mich: University Microfilms, 1969. Matter dealing with the president as chief legislator, chief administrator, and party leader.

533. Hoopes, Roy. *What the President of the United States Does*. New York: John Day, 1974. An introduction for the general reader.

534. Hurd, C. *The White House Story*. New York: Hawthorn Books, 1966. The White House is, "at one and the same time, the name of a building, the nerve center of American government, the example of the nation's constant and evergrowing aspirations, the focal point of the social and political life of the United States, and the expression of a national personality."

535. Hyman, Sidney. *The American President*, 1954; rept. Westport, Conn.: Greenwood Press, 1974. Taft mentioned on pp. 22, 26, 65, 66, 105, 185, 219, and 221.

536. Johnson, Donald Bruce, and Jack L. Walker, comps. and eds. *The Dynamics of the American Presidency*. New York: Wiley, 1964; pp. 137-39 on Taft's limited view of the presidency.

537. Johnson, Richard Tanner. *Managing the White House: An Intimate Study of the Presidency*. New York: Harper & Row, 1974.

538. Juergens, George. *News From the White House: The Presidential Press Relationships in the Progressive Era*. Chicago: University of Chicago Press, 1981. Taft was badly hurt by his inability to get along with journalists and his problems with the tariff and conservation.

539. Kallenbach, Joseph E. *The American Executive: The Presidency and the Governorship*. New York: Harper and Row, 1966. Covers Taft's presidential career, views on presidential power, and subsequent career.

540. Kanes, J.N. *Facts about the Presidents*. New York: H.H. Wilson, 1974. Taft, s.v.

541. Kellerman, Barbara. *The Political Presidency: Practice of Leadership*. New York: Oxford University Press, 1984. Taft, s.v.

542. Koenig, Louis W. *Official Makers of Public Policy: Congress and the President*. Glenview, Ill.: Scott, Foresman, 1967. A brief study with several documented examples.

543. ———. *The Chief Executive*, 6th ed. New York: Harcourt, Brace Jovanovich, 1986. Rather than presidential powers, stresses the importance of a strong presidency counterbalanced by a strong Congress and strong Supreme Court. Concludes that Taft deferred to the other branches of the government.

544. Laski, Harold Joseph. *The American Presidency: An Interpretation*. 1940; rept. New York: Grosset and Dunlap, 1958. Taft mentioned *passim*.

545. McConnell, Grant. *The Modern Presidency*, 2d ed. New York: St. Martin's Press, 1976; pp. 14-17 on Taft's limited view of the power of the presidency.

546. Mansfield, Harvey C., Sr., ed. *Congress Against the President*. New York: Academy of Political Science, 1975; p. 93 on Taft's development of the institution of the special message to Congress. Notes the inevitable battle between Congress and President, especially when the Congress is controlled by the opposition party.

547. Merrill, Samuel, and Marion Galbraith Merrill. *The Republican Command, 1897-1913*. Lexington: University Press of Kentucky, 1971. Contains a broadbrush but neat synthesis of the Taft administration.

548. Nevins, Allan. *American Press Opinion: Washington to Coolidge. A Documentary Record of Editorial Leadership and Criticism, 1785-1927*, 2 vols., 1928; rept. Port Washington: N.Y.: Kennikat Press, 1969. Comments on Taft's handling of the tariff, arbitration, trusts, and the League of Nations.

549. Paolucci, Henry. *War, Peace, and the Presidency*. New York: McGraw-Hill, 1968. The difficulty a president has in dealing with war when Congress alone has the power to declare it, and the Senate must agree to treaties. Has nothing on Taft.

550. Paolucci, Henry. *The South and the Presidency: From Reconstruction to Carter, a Long Day's Task*. Whitestone, N.Y.: Published for the Bagehot Council by Griffin House Publishers, 1978.

551. Patterson, Caleb Perry. *Presidential Government in the United States: The Unwritten Constitution*. Chapel Hill: University of North Carolina Press, 1947. Taft, s.u.

552. Pious, Richard M. *The American Presidency*. New York: Basic Books, 1979. A text with heavy emphasis on recent information. Taft, pp. 43, 49, 94, 122, 230, 257, 339, 351, 356. Taft was a follower of the delegated powers theory.

553. Polsby, Nelson W. *Congress and the Presidency*, 4th ed. Englewood Cliffs, N.J.: Prentice-Hall, 1986. How to resolve the conflict between a president and his Congress?

554. *Presidential Elections Since 1789*, 3d ed. Washington: Congressional Quarterly, 1983. Maps and tables.

555. Reedy, George E. *The Presidency in Flux*. New York: Columbia University Press, 1973. By a press secretary knowledgable of White House affairs since the John F. Kennedy administration.

556. Rossiter, Clinton. *The American Presidency*, rev. ed. New York: Harcourt, Brace and World, 1960. A fine blend of history and political science.

557. Russell, Francis. *President Makers of the Twentieth Century: From Mark Hanna to Joseph P. Kennedy*. Boston: Little, Brown, 1976. A popular account.

558. Schultz, Louis P. "William Howard Taft: A Constitutionalist's View of the Presidency." Ph.D. diss., Northern Illinois University, 1979.

559. Small, Norman Jerome. *Some Presidential Interpretations of the Presidency*, 1932; rept. New York: Da Capo Press, 1970. Contrasting views of various presidents prior to F.D. Roosevelt.

560. Stanwood, Edward. *A History of the Presidency*, 2 vols., 1928; rept. New and rev. ed. Clinton, N.J.: A.M. Kelley, 1975. By an historian who had personal contacts with many of the presidents he wrote about.

561. Stein, Meyer L. *When Presidents Meet the Press*. New York: Julian Messner, 1969. Brief, popular sketches of presidential press relations throughout American history.

562. Taylor, Tim. *The Book of the Presidents*. Taft, pp. 310-22. No. 210.

563. Tebbell, John, and Sarah Miles Watts. *The Press and the Presidency: From George Washington to Ronald Reagan*. New York: Oxford University Press, 1985. The press relations of each president from Washington to F.D. Roosevelt. Has more on Taft than on Thomas Jefferson!

564. Tourtello, Arthur Benson. *The Presidents on the Presidency*. 1964; rept. New York: Russell and Russell, 1970. Quotations from presidents about various aspects of the presidental role and the experience of being president. Taft mentioned *passim*.

565. Tugwell, Rexford G. *The Enlargement of the Presidency*. 1960; rept. Octagon. Growth of presidential power at the expense of Congress especially since the administrations of F.D. Roosevelt.

566. ———. *How They Became President: Thirty-Six Ways to the White House*. New York: Simon and Schuster, 1968. Vignettes of the career patterns and the path to office of all presidents from Washington through Lyndon Johnson. Taft mentioned *passim* but especially on pp. 323-38.

567. Vinyard, Dale. *The Presidency*. New York: Charles Scribner's Sons, 1971; pp. 15-16 for Taft as a "literalist" rather than strong or middle-of-the-road president.

568. Vivian, James F. *A Pretty Thin Salami: A History of the President's Salary.* New York: Vantage Press, 1987. Shows when and why the president's salary has undergone only four upward revisions.

569. Warren, Sidney. *The American Presidency: Readings.* Englewood Cliffs, N.J.: Prentice-Hall, 1967; pp. 26-28 on Taft's restricted view of the presidency.

570. Whitney, David C. *The American Presidents*, 6th ed. Garden City, N.Y.: Doubleday, 1975. Taft, s.v.

571. Wildavsky, Aaron, ed. *The Presidency.* Boston: Little, Brown, 1969. A collection of essays containing documents suitable as subjects for social science analysis.

572. Wilson, V. *The Book of the Presidents.* Brookeville, Md.: American History Research Associates, 1973. Only 79 pages long.

573. Wilson, Woodrow. *Constitutional Government in the United States.* New York: Columbia University Press, 1908, 1961. Wilson defended decisive leadership by a president who held himself directly responsible to public opinion.

574. Wise, Sidney, comp. Ed. by Sidney Wise and Richard F. Schier. *The Presidential Office.* New York: Crowell, 1968. Essays by experts on the presidency.

Articles and Essays

575. "The American Presidency," *American Heritage* 15 (August 1964): entire issue; 16 essays.

576. Baker, R.S. "Signs of the Times as Seen by Mr. Taft," *Harper's Weekly* 58 (May 9, 1914):7-8.

577. Barilleux, Ryan. "Toward an Institutionalist Framework for Presidency Studies," *Presidential Studies Quarterly* 12 (Spring 1982):154-58. The elaborate inauguration, salute, popular acclaim upon seeing him, and other happenings of the "elective kingship."

578. Binkley, Wilfred E. "The President as a National Symbol," *Annals* 283 (Sept. 1952):86-93.

579. Boller, Paul F., Jr., "Religion and the U.S. Presidency," *Journal of Church and State* 21 (Winter 1979):5-21.

580. Burton, Agnes Rose. "Political Parties: Effect on the Presidency," *Presidential Studies Quarterly* 11 (Spring 1981):289-98.

581. Carleton, William G. "Six Year Term for the President?" *South Atlantic Quarterly* 71 (Spring 1972):165-76. Among many others, Bryan and Taft favored a six-year term.

582. Chamberlain, Charles W. F. "Organizing a National Convention: A Lesson from Senator Dick." Ed. by Thomas E. Felt. *Ohio Historical Quarterly* 67 (Jan. 1958):50-62. Dick, b. 1858, was an Akron, Ohio, lawyer who served in the House of Representatives for three terms before being elected U.S. Senator, 1904-1911, and played a role in getting Taft renominated for president in 1912.

583. Chamberlain, Lawrence H. "The President As Legislator," *Annals* 283 (Sept. 1952):94-103. The president's success as a legislator depends upon his philosophy of government, relationship with Congress and the press, and power in Congress.

584. Congressional Quarterly Service. "Presidential Candidates from 1788 to 1964, including Third Parties, 1832-1964, and Popular and Electoral Vote: Historical Review." Rev. ed. Washington: 1964.

585. Coletta, Paolo E. "William Howard Taft." In Graff, Henry F., ed. *The Presidents: A Reference History*. No. 293.

586. Eleazar, D.J. "Which Road to the Presidency?" *Southwestern Social Science Quarterly*, June 1965, pp. 37-46. Career backgrounds of presidents statistically analyzed.

587. Fredman, L.E. "Why Great Men Are, or Are Not, Elected President: Some British Views of the Presidency," *Presidential Studies Quarterly* 10 (Summer 1980):296-305. Men who could be great presidents are busy in areas other than politics, especially in money-making.

588. Graber, Doris A. "Personal Qualities in Presidential Images: The Contribution of the Press," *Midwestern Journal of Political Science* 16 (Feb. 1972):467-76.

589. Halsey, Edwin A. "The Procedure and Protocol of Presidential Elections," *American Bar Association Journal* 27 (Jan. 1941):17-22.

590. Helms, E.A. "The President and Party Politics," *Journal of Politics* 11 (1949):42-64. Presidents should be gifted party politicians in order to be better able to bridge the separation of powers.

591. Hockstra, Douglas J. "The Textbook Presidency Revisited," *Presidential Studies Quarterly* 12 (Spring 1982): 159-67.

592. Hyman, Sidney, ed. "The Office of the American Presidency," *Annals* 307 (Sept. 1956):entire issue. Contains essays by fourteen authorities on the presidency.

593. Loss, Richard. "Dissolving Concepts of the Presidency," *Presidential Studies Quarterly* 6 (Winter-Spring 1976):64-84. A review essay.

594. Maranell, G.M. "The Evaluation of Presidents: An Extension of the Schlesinger Polls," *Journal of American History* 57 (June 1970):104-13. A measure of the greatness of America's presidents. In the original polls, Taft ranked quite low but not among the worst. See Schlesinger, A.M., Sr. No. 600.

595. Mowry, George E. "The Uses of History by Recent Presidents," *Journal of American History* 35 (1966):5-18. Studies seven presidents of whom F.D. Roosevelt and John Kennedy were the most historically aware.

596. Patterson, C.P. "The President as Chief Administrator," *Journal of Politics* 11 (1949):213-35. Inventory of presidential administrative powers and responsibilities largely drawn from Supreme Court decisions.

597. Peabody, R.L. and E. Lubalin. "The Making of the Presidential Candidates." In *The Future of the American Presidency*. Charles W. Dunn, ed. Morristown, N.H.: General Learning Press, 1975. An analysis of career patterns that have led to presidential nominations.

598. Pious, R.M. "The Evolution of the Presidency, 1789-1932," *Current History* 66 (June 1974):242-45, 271-72. Until the advent of F.D. Roosevelt, congressional rather than presidential leadership prevailed.

599. Putney, Bryant. "The President, the Constitution, and the Supreme Court," *Editorial Research Reports* 12 (1935): 449-70.

600. Schlesinger, Arthur M., Sr. "Historians Rate U.S. Presidents," *Life* 25 (Nov. 2, 1948):65-66. Taft was rated a bit below average.

601. Spracher, William C. "Some Reflections on Improving the Study of the Presidency," *Presidential Studies Quarterly* 9 (Winter 1979):71-80.

602. Thompson, Carol. "Controlling the Presidency." *Current History* 25 (Sept. 1952):162-66. The most important check on the president is the fact that he has to win the next election.

603. Warren, Sidney. "The President in the Constitution," *Current History* 25 (Sept. 1953):133-37. Over time, the president has become the driving force in the government.

C. Presidential Elections

Bibliographic Guides

604. Agranoff, Robert. *Elections and Electoral Behavior: A Bibliography*. De Kalb, Ill.: Northern Illinois State University, 1972.

605. ——————. *The Political Campaigns: A Bibliography*. DeKalb: Center for Governmental Studies, North Illinois University, 1972.

606. Brown, William B. *The People's Choice: The Presidential Image in the Campaign Biography*. No. 215.

607. Coppa and Avery Consultants. *The Administration of Presidential Political Campaigns*. Monticello, Ill.: Vance Bibliographies, 1981.

608. *Choosing the President*. Ottie K. Sutton, ed. Colorado Springs, Colo.: Air Force Academy, 1974.

609. Congressional Quarterly. *National Party Conventions, 1831-1980*. Washington: Congressional Quarterly, 1983. The votes, fight over the platforms, the platforms, and brief biographies of the candidates.

610. *The Democratic and Republican Parties in America: A Historical Bibliography*. Santa Barbara, Calif.: ABC-Clio, 1983.

611. Mauer, Donald J. *United States Politics and Elections: A Guide to Information Sources*. Detroit: Gale, 1971.

612. Neals, Thomas H. *The American Electoral College: Origins, Development, Proposal for Reform or Abolition: A Selected and Annotated Bibliography.* Washington: Congressional Research Service, 1979.

613. Szekely, Kalman. *The Electoral College: A Selective Annotated Bibliography.* Littleton, Colo.: Libraries Unlimited, 1970.

614. Wynar, Lubomyr, comp. *American Political Parties: A Selective Guide to Parties and Movements of the Twentieth Century.* Littleton, Colo.: Libraries Unlimited, 1969.

Monographs

615. Alexander, Herbert E. *Financing Politics: Money, Elections and Political Reforms*, 3d. ed. Washington: Congressional Quarterly Press, 1984.

616. Aly, Bower, ed. *Selecting the President*, 2 vols. Columbia, Mo.: Artcraft Press, 1953. Much on the importance of a candidate's ability to speak in public.

617. Bain, Richard C., and Judith Parris. *Convention Decisions and Voting Records*, 2d ed. Washington: Brookings Institution, 1973.

618. Bishop, Joseph B. *Presidential Nominations and Elections.* New York: Charles Scribner's Sons, 1916.

619. *Choosing the President.* James David Barber, ed. Englewood Cliffs, N.J.: Prentice-Hall, 1987.

620. Congressional Quarterly. *Historical Review of Presidential Candidates from 1788 to 1868: Including Third Parties, 1832 to 1968, with Popular and Electoral Vote*, 5th ed. Washington: Congressional Quarterly, 1969.

621. David, Paul T., Ralph M. Goldman, and Richard C. Bain. *The Politics of National Party Conventions.* Washington: Brookings Institution, 1960.

622. Dunn, Delmer D. *Paying for Politics: Highlights of Financing Presidential Campaigns.* Washington: Brookings Institution, 1972.

623. Eaton, Herbert A. *Presidential Timber: A History of Nominating Conventions, 1868-1960.* New York: Free Press, 1964.

624. Ewing, Cortez A.M. *Presidential Elections from Abraham Lincoln to Franklin D. Roosevelt*, 1940; rept. Westport, Conn.: Greenwood Press, 1972.

625. Fishel, Jeff. *The President Promises: From Campaign Pledge to Presidential Performance*. Washington: Congressional Quarterly, 1985.

626. Heard, Alexander. *The Cost of Democracy*. Chapel Hill: University of North Carolina Press, 1960. How money was raised and spent in presidential campaigns.

627. Johnson, Donald Bruce, and Kirk, H. Porter, comps. *National Party Platforms, 1840-1972*, 5th ed. Urbana: University of Illinois Press, 1940; rept. Greenwood Press, 1972. The Progressive platform of 1912, pp. 175-82; the Republican National platform of 1912, pp. 183-88.

628. Kessel, John H. *Presidential Campaign Politics*, 2d ed. Homewood, Ill.: Dorsey Press, 1984.

629. Moos, Malcolm. *The Republicans: A History of Their Party*. New York: Random House, 1956.

630. ———. *Politics, Presidents, and Coattails*. 1932; rept. Westport, Conn.: Greenwood Press, 1969.

631. Myers, William Starr. *The Republican Party: A History*. New York: The Century Co., 1928. Includes Taft's nomination, election, inauguration, cabinet choices, policies, renomination, and defeat, pp. 376-412.

632. *100 Years of Presidential Elections, 1864-1964, Covered in the Evening and Sunday Star*. Washington: Evening Star Newspaper Co., 1968.

633. Overacker, Louise. *Presidential Campaign Funds*. Boston: Boston University Press, 1946. Very critical of how such funds are raised and spent.

634. Petersen, Svend. *A Statistical History of American Presidential Elections*. New York: Frederick Ungar Pub. Co., 1963. For the elections of 1912, see pp. 74-79.

635. Roseboom, Eugene H. *A History of Presidential Elections*, 2d ed. New York: Macmillan, 1964.

636. ———., and Alfred E. Eckes, Jr. *A History of Presidential Elections From George Washington to Richard M. Nixon*, 3rd ed. New York: Macmillan, 1970.

637. Rosewater, Victor. *Back Stage in 1912: The Inside Story of the Split Republican Convention*. Phila: Dorrance, 1932.

638. Russell, Francis. *The President Makers: From Mark Hanna to Joseph P. Kennedy*. Boston: Little, Brown, 1976.

639. Schlesinger, Arthur M., Jr., ed. *The Coming to Power: Critical Presidential Elections in American History*. New York: Chelsea House, 1972.

640. Stoddard, Henry L. *Presidential Sweepstakes: The Story of Political Conventions and Campaigns (1840-1944)*. Ed. by Francis W. Leary. New York: G.P. Putnam's Sons, 1948. By a newspaper reporter who covered many of the conventions he discusses.

641. Strum, Philippa. *Presidential Power and American Democracy*, 2d ed. Santa Monica, Calif.: Goodyear Publishing Co., 1979.

642. Warren, Sidney. *The Battle for the Presidency*. Philadelphia: J.B. Lippincott, 1968.

Articles

643. Butler, Nicholas M. "Fourteen Republican Convention," *Scribner's Magazine* 99 (Jan. 1936):13-17, 78-81, 225-29. When Taft's vice president, James S. Sherman, died just prior to the election of 1912, Butler succeeded him as the candidate.

644. Hahn, Harland. "The Republican Party Convention of 1912 and the Role of Herbert S. Hadley in National Politics," *Missouri Historical Review* 59 (July 1965):407-13.

645. Jones, Charles A. "Ohio in the Republican National Conventions," *Ohio Archaeological and History Society Publications* 38 (Jan. 1929):1-46.

646. Walton, Haynes, Jr., and C. Vernon Gray. "Black Politics at the National Republican and Democratic Conventions, 1868-1972," *Phylon* 36 (Sept. 1975):269-78.

D. Presidential Power

Such matters as the system of checks and balances, whether the President or Congress should take the lead in policy-making, and whether Taft was right in restricting rather than expanding executive power are covered in many studies. A representative selection follows.

Bibliographical Guides

647. *Background Information on the Use of United States Armed Forces in Foreign Countries.* Library of Congress for the House Committee on Foreign Affairs. Committee Print and revision, 94th Cong., 1st Sess., 1975. Includes a list of instances of the use of American armed forces abroad.

648. Smith, S.C. *Bibliography: Executive Privilege.* New Haven: Yale Law Library, 1973,

Monographs

649. Bell, Jack. *The Presidency: Office of Power.* Boston: Allyn & Bacon, 1967. A general discussion of the presidency by a Washington journalist.

650. Berdahl, Clarence A. "War Powers of the Executive in the United States." Ph.D. diss., University of Illinois, 1921.

651. Bell, Jack. *The Presidency: Office of Power.* Boston: Allyn & Bacon, 1967. A general discussion of the presidency by a Washington journalist.

652. Bessette, Joseph M., and Jeffrey Tulis, eds. *The Presidency in the Constitutional Order.* Baton Rouge: Louisiana State University Press, 1981. Taft is not mentioned.

653. Binkley, Wilfred Ellsworth. *The Man in the White House: His Powers and Duties*, 1958; rev. ed., New York: Harper & Row, 1968. The president as party leader, legislator, administrator, commander in chief, chief diplomat, and national symbol. Notes Taft's adherence to limited presidential power.

654. Corwin, Edward S. *The President, Office and Powers: History and Analysis of Practice and Opinion*, 4th rev. ed. New York: New York University Press, 1962. By an outstanding student of the Constitution who uses the reasoning in key constitutional law decisions. Covers Taft as Theodore

Roosevelt's secret diplomatic agent, as having a limited view of the office of president, and as a "constitutional caretaker."

655. Dolce, Philip C., and George H. Skau, eds. *Power and the Presidency.* New York: Charles Scribner's Sons, 1976. The historical evolution of presidential power.

656. Fisher, Louis. *Presidential Spending Power.* Princeton, N.J.: Princeton University Press, 1975. How a president can control expenditures.

657. ———. *Constitutional Conflicts between Congress and President.* Princeton, N.J.: Princeton University Press, 1985. These can occur over the separation of powers, nominations, removal power, vetoes, Congressional investigations, budget, treaties, and the war power.

658. Funderbunk, Charles. *Presidents and Politics: The Limits of Power.* Monterey, Calif.: Brooks Cole Pub. Co., 1982.

659. Goldsmith, William M. *The Growth of Presidential Power (A Documented History),* 3 vols. Edgemont, Pa.: Chelsea House, 1974.

660. Hargrove, Erwin C. *The Power of the Modern Presidency.* Philadelphia: Temple University Press, 1974. The interplay between the presidency, Congress, courts, bureaucracy, public opinion, ideology, political party, military, and foreign affairs. Taft is not mentioned.

661. Hart, James. *The Ordinance Making Powers of the President of the United States.* 1925; rept. N.Y.: Da Capo Press, 1970. How administration officials execute the legislative powers granted to them.

662. Hirschfield, Robert S., comp. *The Power of the Presidency: Concepts and Controversy,* 2d ed. Chicago: Adline, 1973. Readings on such matters as whether the president has sufficient power to meet current needs and the danger that the presidency will become a dictatorship. A citation from Taft is from his *Our Chief Magistrate and his Powers.*

663. Humbert, Willard. *The Pardoning Power of the President.* Washington: American Council on Public Affairs, 1941.

664. Jackson, Carlton. *Presidential Vetoes, 1791-1945.* Athens: University of Georgia Press, 1967.

665. Kallenbach, Joseph E. *The American Chief Executive: The Presidency and the Governorship*. New York: Harper & Row, 1966. Presidential styles in such matters as chief administrator, chief legislator, party chief, conservator of public order and safety, commander in chief, and head of foreign affairs.

666. Kessler, Frank. *The Dilemmas of Presidential Leadership: Of Caretakers and Kings*. Englewood Cliffs, N.J.: Prentice-Hall, 1982.

667. Klein, Mary, comp. *The Presidency: The Power and the Glory*. Minneapolis: Winstron Press, 1973.

668. Koenig, Louis. *The Chief Executive*. New York: Harcourt Brace and World, 1984. The president as party chief, legislative leader, administrative chief, maker of public opinion, chief diplomat, commander in chief, voice on economy and social justice, and handling of crises. Barely mentions Taft.

669. Laski, Harold. *The American Presidency: An Interpretation*. New York: Harper & Row, 1940. The President and his cabinet, Congress, and foreign relations.

670. Lease, Martin Harry, Jr. "William Howard Taft and the Powers of the President." Ph.D. diss., Indiana University, 1961. On his limited conception of presidential power.

671. Longacre, Richard P. *The Presidency and Individual Liberties*. Ithaca: Cornell University Press, 1961.

672. Miller, Arthur Selwyn. *Presidential Power in a Nutshell*. St. Paul, Minne.: Est Pub. Co., 1977.

673. Milton, George Fort. *The Use of Presidential Power, 1789-1943*. 1944; rept. New York: Octagon Books, 1965. The power of the president must match the severity of the crises he faces. Taft is covered in part.

674. Morganston, Charles E. *The Appointing and Removal Power of the President of the United States*. Washington: GPO, 1929.

675. Mullen, William F. *Presidential Power and Politics*. New York: St. Martin's Press, 1976.

676. Neustadt, Richard E. *Presidential Power: The Politics of Leadership with Reflections on Johnson and Nixon.* New York: Wiley, 1976. The president's power is more one of persuasion than of command, even within the executive branch of the government. Much depends upon the avidity with which the president seizes and wields the reins of power.

677. Nikolaieff, George A., comp. *The President and the Constitution.* New York: H.W. Wilson Co., 1974. A series of essays on executive power.

678. Congress. Senate Library. *Presidential Vetoes.* Washington: GPO, 1969.

679. Roberts, Charles, ed. *Has the President Too Much Power?* New York: Harper's Magazine Press, 1974. Transcript of conference held by journalists.

680. Schaffter, Dorothy, and Dorothy M. Mathews. *The Powers of the President as Commander in Chief of the Army and Navy of the United States.* 1956; rept. Da Capo, 1974.

681. Small, Norman J. *Some Presidential Interpretations of the Presidency.* 1932; rept. New York: Da Capo, 1970. Includes Taft's version of limited presidential power.

682. Warren, Sidney. *The President as World Leader.* Philadelphia: Lippincott, 1964. Case studies of activities by presidents from Theodore Roosevelt through John F. Kennedy. Chapter 4 is on Taft: "A Restricted View of Office."

683. Withers, John Lovell. "The Administrative Theories and Practices of William Howard Taft." Ph.D. diss., University Chicago, 1956. Available on microfilm from the University of Chicago.

Articles

684. Ballard, Rene N. "The Administrative Theory of William Howard Taft," *Western Political Quarterly* 7 (Mar. 1954):65-74.

685. Binkley, Wilfred E. "The President as Chief Legislator," *Annals* 307 (Sept. 1956):92-105. Strong presidents recommend and seek to obtain legislation from Congress; Taft refused to pressure Congress.

686. Chambers, Raymond I. "The Executive Power: A Preliminary Study of the Concept and Efficacy of Presidential Directives," *Presidential Studies Quarterly* 7 (Winter 1977):21-37.

687. Cohn, M.B. "Impoundment of Funds Appropriated by Congress," *Ohio State Law Journal* 34 (1973):416-27.

688. Damon, Allan L. "Veto," *American Heritage* 25 (Feb. 1974):12-15. Reviews past presidents' use of the veto and summarizes them in tabular form. Taft used 30 regular vetoes and 9 pocket votes, a small number compared with most presidents.

689. ―――. "Presidential Availability," *American Heritage* 25 (Apr. 19745):60-3. William Howard Taft: "I have come to the conclusion that the major part of the work of a president is to increase the gate receipts of expositions and fairs and bring tourists into town."

690. ―――. "Presidential Expenses," *American Heritage* 25 (June 1974):64-67. There is no way of knowing exactly because the expenses are spread through a dozen accounts.

691. Driggs, Don W. "The President as Chief Educator on Foreign Affairs," *Western Political Quarterly* 11 (Dec. 1958):813-19.

692. Edwards, George C. III. "The President and Congress: The Inevitability of Conflict," *Presidential Studies Quarterly* 8 (Summer 1978):245-57.

693. ―――. "Presidential Influence in the House: Presidential Prestige as a Source of Presidential Power," *American Political Science Review* 70 (Mar. 1976):10-13.

694. Goldman, Eric F. "The Presidency as Moral Leadership," *Annals* 280 (Mar. 1952):37-45.

695. Gunstein, Nathan D. "Presidential Power, Administration, and Administrative Law," *George Washington Law Review* 18 (Apr. 1950):285-326.

696. Hamilton, Lee H., and Michael H. Van Dusen. "Making the Separation of Powers Work," *Foreign Affairs* 57 (Fall 1978):17-39.

697. Hoxie, R. Gordon. "The Office of Commander in Chief: An Historical and Projective View," *Presidential Studies Quarterly* 6 (Fall 1976):10-36.

698. Jacob, C.E. "Limits of Presidential Leadership," *South Atlantic Quarterly* 62 (Autumn 1963):461-73.

699. Lea, James S. "The Presidency: Auxiliary and Primary Limits," *Southern Quarterly* 14 (Jan. 1976):133-49.

700. Lee, John R. "Presidential Vetoes From Washington to Nixon," *Journal of Politics* 37 (May 1975):522-46.

701. Mikell, William E. "The Extent of the Treaty-making Power of the President and Senate of the United States," *University of Pennsylvania Law Review* 57 (Apr. 1909):435-528, and 57 (May 1909):528-88. Congress not only has a part in making treaties but enforces them by appropriate legislation.

702. Potter, P.B. "Power of the President of the United States to Utilize its Armed Forces Abroad," *American Journal of International Law* 48 (July 1954):458-59.

703. "Power of the President," *The Outlook* 95 (May 14, 1910):54; (July 2, 1910):464-68; (Aug. 6, 1910):789-92.

704. Ringelstein, Albert C. "Presidential Vetoes: Motivation and Classification," *Congress and the Presidency* 12 (Spring 1985):43-55.

705. Rose, Richard. "The President: A Chief But Not an Executive," *Presidential Studies Quarterly* 7 (Winter 1977):5-20.

706. Rossiter, Clinton. "The Presidents and the Presidency," *American Heritage* 7 (Apr. 1956):28-33, 94. On the growth of power in the presidential office. Taft is not mentioned.

707. Schick, Allen. "The Battle of the Budget," *Proceedings of the Academy of Political and Social Science* 32, No. 1 (1975):51-70. President vs. Congress.

708. Towle, K.A. "The Presidential Veto Since 1889," *American Political Science Review* 31 (Feb. 1937):51-56.

E. The Inauguration, March 4, 1909

Bibliographical Aid

709. Freitag, Ruth S. *Presidential Inaugurations: A Selected List of References*, 3d ed. Washington: Library of Congress, 1969.

Monographs

710. Anderson, Isabel (Perkins). *Presidents and Pies: Life in Washington, 1897-1919*. Boston: Houghton Mifflin, 1920. For the inauguration of Taft, see pp. 98-103.

711. Colman, Edna M. *White House Gossip, from Andrew Johnson to Calvin Coolidge*. New York: Doubleday, Page, 1927. Contains descriptions of inaugural days.

712. Durbin, Louise. *Inaugural Cavalcade*. New York: Dodd, Mead, 1971. Inaugural ceremonies from Washington to Nixon.

713. Fersh, Seymour H. *The View from the White House: A Study of the Presidential State of the Union Messages*. Washington: Public Affairs Press, 1961.

714. Germino, Dante L. *The Inaugural Addresses of American Presidents: The Public Philosophy and Rhetoric*. Lanham, Md.: University Press of America, 1984.

715. Hurja, Emil E. *History of Presidential Inaugurations*. New York: New York Democratic Pub. Co., 1933.

716. *Inauguration of William Howard Taft, as President of the United States, and James Schoolcraft Sherman*. Washington: Press of W.F. Roberts, Co., 1909.

717. Kittler, Glenn D. *Hail to the Chief: Inaugural Days of Our Presidents*. Philadelphia: Chilton Books, 1965.

718. Lott, Davis Newton, ed. *The Inaugural Addresses of the American Presidents, from Washington to Kennedy*. New York: Holt, Rinehart and Winston, 1961.

719. Owsley, Clifford C. *Inaugural*. New York: Olympic Press, 1964.

720. Potts, E. Daniel, comp. *List of Motion Pictures and Sound Recordings Relating to Presidential Inaugurations*. Washington: National Archives, 1960.

721. United States. President. *Inaugural Addresses of the Presidents of the United States from George Washington to Richard Milhous Nixon, 1973.* Washington: GPO, 1974.

722. Woodward, William. *A Memorial of the First Inauguration of William Howard Taft.* Worcester, Mass.: Priv. Print, 1909.

Articles

723. Christensen, Bonniejean. "Style is the Man: A Sampling of Prose from Presidential Inaugural Addresses," *North Dakota Quarterly* 48 (Winter 1980):5-27.

724. "Greetings to William Howard Taft, March 6, 1909," *North American Review* 221 (Mar. 1925):385-87. Reprint of an article from *Harper's Weekly* of March 6, 1909, that was critical of Taft on tariff reform.

725. "The Historic Ball Upon Inauguration Day," *Harper's Weekly* 53 (Mar. 6, 1909):29.

726. "The Inauguration of Taft," *The Outlook* 91 (Mar. 13, 1909):565-67.

727. "The Inauguration of President Taft," *The Independent* 66 (Mar. 11, 1909):503-6.

728. Lafontaine, Charles V.S.A. "God and Nation in Selected U.S. Presidential Inaugural Addresses, 1789-1945." Part II. *Church and State* 18 (Autumn 1976):503-21.

729. Macdiarmid, John. "Presidential Inaugural Addresses," *Public Opinion Quarterly* 1 (July 1937):79-82.

730. Moore, Barbara. "When Presidents Take Office," *American Heritage* 4 (Spring 1953):5-7. Mrs. Taft threw precedent to the winds by insisting upon riding in the same carriage with her husband on the return from the inaugural.

731. Taft, Helen. "Inaugural of 1909." In her *Recollections of Full Years*, pp. 325-33.

732. "Mr. Taft's Excellent Address,"*Review of Reviews* 39 (Apr. 1909):392.

733. West, H.L. "Incoming of Taft's Administration," *The Forum* 41 (Mar. 1909):199-205.

734. Weir, H.C. "Inaugurating a President in a Blizzard," *World To-Day* 16 (Apr. 1909):359-62.

F. The Cabinet

Bibliographic Guides

735. Bell, Christopher, comp. *Vice Presidents of the United States, 1789-1961*. Washington: Library of Congress Legislative Reference Service, 1962.

736. Laird, Archibald. *The Near Great: A Chronicle of the Vice President: A Collection of Photographs and Inscriptions and a Record of Historical Events*. North Quincy, Mass.: Christopher Pub. House, 1908. James Sherman, pp. 248-55.

737. Tompkins, Dorothy L.C. *The Office of Vice President: A Selected Bibliography*. Berkeley, Calif.: Bureau of Public Administration, University of California, 1957.

738. ———., comp. *Selection of the Vice President*. Berkeley, Calif.: University of California Press, 1974.

739. Vexler, Robert I., ed. *The Vice-Presidents and Cabinet Members: Biographies Arranged Chronologically by Administration*, 2 vols. Dobbs Ferry, N.Y.: Oceana Publications, 1975. Sketches of Taft's vice president and cabinet members in 2:452-68.

Monographs

740. Barzman, Sol. *Mad Men and Geniuses: The Vice President of the United States*. Chicago: Follett, 1974.

741. Clymer, Ernest Fletcher. *Cabinets of the Presidents and the Speakers of the House of Representatives, Presidential Votes by States, 1900-1916. Special Notes on the Presidents*. New York: W.E. Rudge, 1920.

742. Curtis, Richard, and Maggie Wells. *Not Exactly a Crime: Our Vice Presidents from Adams to Agnew*. New York: Dial Press, 1972.

The Presidency 79

743. DiSalle, Michael V., and Lawrence G. Blochman. *Second Choice*. New York: Hawthorn, 1966.

744. Hindsdale, Mary L. *A History of the President's Cabinet*. Ann Arbor, Michigan: Wahr, 1911.

745. Kessel, John Howard. *The Domestic Presidency: Decision-Making in the White House*. North Scituate, Mass.: Duxbury Press, 1975.

746. Koenig, Louis W. *The Invisible Presidency*. New York: Rinehart, 1960. On presidential advisers.

747. Patterson, Bradley H. *The President's Cabinet: Issues and Questions*. Washington: American Society for Public Administration, 1976. On the relationships of cabinet members with each other and with the White House.

Articles

748. "A Gallery of Vice Presidents," *American Heritage* 15 (Aug. 1964):78-80. James S. Sherman on p. 80.

749. "Cabinet Choosing and Golf," *Collier's* 42 (Feb. 6, 1909):24. Taft spent more time golfing than in choosing his cabinet members.

750. Beveridge, Albert J. "The Fifth Wheel in Our Government," *Century Magazine* 79 (Dec. 1909):208-14. The vice president.

751. Hoxie, R. Gordon. "The Cabinet in the American Presidency," *Presidential Studies Quarterly* 14 (Spring 1984): 209-30.

752. "President Taft's Cabinet," *The World's Work* 17 (Apr. 1909):11411-12. Good choices—but wait and see.

G. Taft as Administrator

Under this title are considered a president's administrative, legislative, emergency, appointing, veto, pardon, and financial impoundment powers.

Bibliographical Guide

753. White, Anthony G. *Public Executives' Teams; Presidential Appointments: Selected Bibliographies*. Monticello, Ill.: Vance Bibliographies, 1981.

Monographs

754. Corwin, Edward S. *Presidential Removal Power Under the Constitution.* New York: National Municipal League, 1927.

755. Goldstein, Sidney M. *The Growth of Executive Power in the United States.* Washington: Georgetown University Press, 1938.

756. Humbert, Willard H. *The Pardoning Power of the President.* Washington: American Council on Public Affairs, 1941.

757. Jackson, Carlton L. *Presidential Vetoes, 1792-1945.* Athens: University of Georgia Press, 1967.

758. Johnson, Haynes. *The Working White House. A WASHINGTON POST BOOK.* New York: Praeger, 1974. The White House as a home for the presidents and their families, and as a place of employment for the servants, secretaries, and guards who attend them.

759. Mackenzie, George C. *The Politics of Presidential Appointments.* New York: Free Press, 1980.

760. Milton, George F. *The Use of Presidential Power, 1789-1943.* Boston: Little, Brown, 1944.

761. Morganston, Charles E. *The Appointing and Removal Power of the President of the United States of America.* Washington: GPO, 1929.

762. Nathan, Richard P. *The Administrative Presidency.* New York: John Wiley and Sons, 1983.

763. U.S. Congress. House. Committee on the Judiciary. *The Veto Power of the President.* Washington: GPO, 1952.

764. Wann, Andrew J. *The President as Chief Administrator.* Washington: Public Affairs Press, 1968.

Articles

765. Binkley, Wilfred E. "The President as Chief Legislator," *Annals* 307 (Sept. 1956):92-105.

766. Brigman, William E. "The Executive Branch and the Independent Regulatory Agencies," *Presidential Studies Quarterly* 11 (Spring 1981):244-61.

767. Brooks, Sidney. "Eight Months of President Taft," *Fortune* 92 (Dec. 1909):903-13.

768. "Busiest Man of a Busy Government," *Current Literature* 40 (Apr. 1909): 375-76.

769. Christman, Kenneth W. "Limits of Presidential Removal Power," *Ohio State Law Journal* 35 (1974):513-31.

770. Cohn, Mark B. "Impoundment of Funds Appropriated by Congress," *Ohio State Law Journal* 34 (1973):416-27.

771. Culp, Maurice S. "Executive Power in Emergencies," *Michigan Law Review* 31 (June 1933):1066-96.

772. Dauncey, E.C. "Impressions of Mr. Taft," *Cornhill Magazine* 99 (Mar. 1909):351-55.

773. Hart, James. "Ordinance Making Power of the President," *North American Review* 218 (July 1923):59-66.

774. "Has President Taft Made Good?" *Current Literature* 47 (Sept. 1909):232-38. Questionable, particularly with reference to tariff reform.

775. "Is Taft To Be a Reactionary?" *Current Literature* 46 (June 1909):579-82.

776. Kenski, Henry C. "The Impact of Economic Conditions on Presidential Popularity," *Journal of Politics* 39 (Aug. 1977):764-73.

777. McCarran, Patrick A. "The Growth of Federal Executive Power," *American Bar Association Journal* 19 (Oct. 1933): 587-92.

778. Nagel, Charles. "Helping Hand to Commerce," *The Independent* 73 (Oct. 31, 1912):989-90.

779. ———. "Prevention of Industrial Accidents," *Annals* 38 (July 1911):71-73.

780. Oh, John C.H. "The Presidency and Public Welfare Policy," *Presidential Studies Quarterly* 8 (Fall 1978):377-90.

781. "Personality of the New President," *The Century Magazine* 77 (Mar. 1909):680-4.

782. Turner, George Kibbe. "Daughters of the Poor," *McClure's Magazine* 34 (Nov. 1909):45-61.

783. Wilcox, M. "Harmonizer's Outlook: International Problems Confronting the Taft Administration," *Putnam's Magazine* 6 (Sept. 1909):657-62.

H. Taft as Commander in Chief

Bibliographic Guides

Research on this subject is facilitated by reference to various bibliographical guides and texts. Broader studies of military and naval matters, including those of Taft's tenure, follow.

784. Coletta, Paolo E., comp. *A Bibliography of American Naval History*. Annapolis, Md.: Naval Institute Press, 1981. Chapter 9.

785. ―――., comp. *An Annotated Bibliography of U.S. Marine Corps History*. Lanham, Md.: University Press of America, 1986. Chapter 5.

786. ―――. *The American Naval Heritage*, 3d ed. Lanham, Md.: University Press of America, 1987, pp. 209-14.

787. Miller, William M., and Others. *Chronology of the United States Marine Corps*, 2 vols. Washington: Headquarters, U.S. Marine Corps, 1965. Vol. 1 for Taft's employment of the Corps, especially in Central America.

Monographs

788. Braisted, William R. *The United States Navy in the Pacific, 1909-1922*. Austin: University of Texas Press, 1970. Skillfully evaluates Taft's hesitant efforts to provide for an adequate Navy.

789. Coletta, Paolo E. *Bradley A. Fiske and the American Navy*. Lawrence: Regents Press of Kansas, 1979. Fiske served in the General Board of the Navy in 1910 and was Secretary of the Navy Meyer's Aide for Inspections and then Aide for Operations, 1912-1913.

790. Costello, Comdr. Daniel J., U.S. Navy. "Planning for War: A History of the General Board of the Navy, 1900-1914." Ph.D. diss., Fletcher School of Diplomacy, 1968. Advice from the General Board was offered to the Secretary of the Navy for transmission to the President.

791. Cummings, Capt. Damon, USN. *Rear-Admiral Richard Wainwright, USN*. Washington: GPO, 1962. Wainwright was the first Aide for Operations to Secretary of the Navy George von L. Meyer.

792. Fiske, Rear Adm. Bradley A., USN. *From Midshipman to Rear-Admiral*. New York: The Century Co, 1919. The Navy's greatest inventor of his generation, Fiske also attempted to reform the organization of the Navy so that it could be better prepared for war.

793. Grenville, John A.S., and George B. Young. *Politics, Strategy, and American Diplomacy, 1873-1917*. New Haven: Yale University Press, 1966. Relate Taft's ideas with respect to diplomacy worldwide, but especially to Central America and China.

794. Hassler, Warren W. *The President as Commander in Chief*. Reading, Mass.: Addison Wesley, 1971.

795. Hyman, Harold M. *Quiet Past and Stormy Present? War Powers in American History*. Washington: American Historical Association, 1986. The nature and limits of constitutional war and emergency powers.

796. Kanter, Arnold. *Presidential Leadership of the Military Services*. Ann Arbor, Mich.: Institute of Public Policy Studies, 1973.

797. Huidekoper, Frederick. *The Military Unpreparedness of the United States: A History of the American Land Forces from Colonial Times until June 1, 1915*. New York: Macmillan, 1916. Under Taft, agreement was reached upon how best to reorganize the Army with the men and materials at hand, and what could be done to improve the Army in the future.

798. May, Ernest R., ed. *The Ultimate Decision: The President as Commander in Chief*. New York: Braziller, 1960. Taft is not included.

799. Millett, Allan R. *Semper Fidelis: The History of the United States Marine Corps*. New York: Macmillan, 1980. Includes three chapters on Taft's Caribbean interventions.

800. Nelson, Maj. Gen. Otto. *National Security and the General Staff.* Washington: Infantry Journal Press, 1946. Gen. Leonard Wood's reforms as Chief of Staff of the Army.

801. *Powers of the President as Commander in Chief of the Army and the Navy of the United States.* Washington: Library of Congress, 1956.

802. Rappaport, Armin. *The Navy League of the United States.* Detroit: Wayne State University Press, 1962. The influence of this group was generally ineffectual.

803. Records of the General Board of the Navy. Naval Historical Center, Operational Archives Branch.

804. "Report of the Joint Board of the Army and Navy, Nov. 8, 1909," General Board Records, File 405. The fleet was strong enough to permit the basing of some battleships in the Pacific.

805. Schaffter, Dorothy, and Dorothy M. Matthews. *The Powers of the President as Commander in Chief of the Army and Navy of the United States.* Washington: GPO, 1956.

806. Sprout, Harold and Margaret. *The Rise of American Naval Power, 1776-1918.* 1946; rept. Annapolis, Md.: Naval Institute Press, 1980. Uses many primary documents, especially Congressional hearings, to tell of the development of naval policy for the period covered.

807. Sweetman, Jack. *American Naval History: An Illustrated Chronologly of the U.S. Navy and Marine Corps, 1775 to the Present.* Annapolis, Md.: NIP, 1984.

808. Tracy, R.G. "History of the Naval Petroleum Reserves."8383 Ms. compiled in 1937. Copy in Josephus Daniels Papers, Manuscript Division, Library of Congress, Box 264.

809. See also Leonard James Bates, *The Origins of Teapot Dome: Progressive Parties and Petroleum, 1901-1921.* Urbana: University of Illinois Press, 1963. Under Taft, oil resources in California and Wyoming were reserved for naval use because by 1911 major warships began using oil rather than coal for propulsion purposes.

Articles

810. Braisted, William R. "The United States Navy's Dilemma in the Pacific, 1906-1909," *Pacific Historical Review* 26 (Aug. 1957):235-44. How could the United States protect its two-ocean interests with a one-ocean navy?

811. Coletta, Paolo E. "George von Lengerke Meyer, 6 March 1909–4 March 1913." In Coletta, Paolo E., Robert G. Albion, and K. Jack Bauer, eds. *American Secretaries of the Navy*, 2 vols. Annapolis, Md.: Naval Institute Press, 1980, 1:495-522. Meyer's reforms as Taft's naval secretary.

812. Destler, I.M. "National Security Management: What Presidents Have Wrought," *Political Science Quarterly* 95 Winter 1980-1981):573-88.

813. Dunn, A.W. "The Fundamental Cause of Waste in the Army and Navy," *The World's Work* 22 (May 1912):14364-77. Blames the "porkbarrel" and gives many examples of how it operated to the detriment of the services.

814. Featherton, LCdr. Frank H., USN, "P.G. School," USNIP 89 (Dec. 1963):61-71. The Naval Postgraduate School was established at Annapolis, Md., in 1911 to give officers the knowledge they needed to operate technologically advanced machinery and to design new ships and mechanisms.

815. Grenville, John A.S. "Diplomacy and War Plans in the United States, 1898-1917," Royal Historical Society *Transactions*, 5 Ser. 11 (1961):1-21. Traces the deterioration of German-American relations and the rapprochement in British-American relations during this period.

816. Hemphill, J.C. "The Charleston Navy Yard," *Harper's Weekly* 53 (Sept. 4, 1909):11-12. A yard that most probably should have been closed was kept open by the influence of Southern senators.

817. Livermore, Seward W. "The American Navy as a Factor in World Politics, 1903-1913," *American Historical Review* 63 (July 1958):863-79. American naval cruises during this decade showed friendship for Britain and France and by snubbing Germany increased the latter's ill will.

818. Luce, RAdm. Stephen B., USN, "The U.S. Naval War College," USNIP 36 (June 1910):559-86 and 36 (Sept. 1910):68-96. Rather than increase their efficiency as technicians, a War College education should enable officers to see the Navy in relation to world affairs.

819. Marsch, Comdr. C.C., USN, "Wanted: A First Aid," USNIP 37 (Mar. 1911):59-81. That is, a Naval Reserve.

820. "The Naval Appropriations," *Army and Navy Journal* 47 (25 July 1910):1282. Taft cut the Navy's appropriations by $38 million less than in 1908.

821. "The Naval Program," *Army and Navy Journal* 47 (12 Mar. 1910):817. Taft got Congress to fund two battleships.

822. "The Navy Gets One Battleship," *Army and Navy Journal* 50 (Mar. 8, 1913):834-35.

823. "Oil Lands Withdrawn," *The Outlook* 93 (Dec. 11, 1909):796. Taft ordered oil producing areas in Wyoming and California reserved for naval use.

824. "Ousting General Wood," *Literary Digest* 44 (June 22, 1912):1287. When Wood sought to close eighteen Army installations, affected Congressmen wrote legislation that engineered his ouster as Army Chief of Staff.

825. Paullin, Charles Oscar, "The American Navy in the Orient in Recent Years," USNIP 37 (Sept. 1911):2237-76. U.S. warships showed the flag and protected American lives and property but had no American overseas support facilities closer than U.S. West Coast ports.

826. Potter, P.B. "Power of the President of the United States to Utilize Its Armed Forces Abroad," *American Journal of International Law* 48 (July 1954):458-59.

827. "Program of Naval Increase," *Army and Navy Journal* 50 (5 Oct. 1912):145. The Navy wanted three battleships but got only one.

828. Smith, Capt. Roy C., USN, "Some Considerations Affecting the Navy Personnel," USNIP 37 (Sept. 1911):1913-17. In addition to more personnel the Navy needed men able to handle machinery rather than sails.

829. "Substituting the Pruning Hook for the Big Stick," *Literary Digest* 39 (July 17, 1909):78-80. Taft failed to follow Roosevelt with respect to the naval building program.

830. Wainwright, RAdm. Richard, USN, "The Fleet and Its Readiness for Service," *Scientific American* 105 (9 Dec. 1911):514-15. As Aide for Operations to

Secretary of the Navy Meyer, Wainwright reorganized both the battleship and torpedo fleets so that the load of repair work in the navy yards was evened out and in addition brought war plans and strategic studies up to date.

831. Wiegand, Wayne A. "The Lauchheimer Controversy: A Case of Group Political Pressure during the Taft Administration," *Military Affairs* 40 (1976):54-59. Col. Charles Lauchheimer, USMC, was transferred from a post in Washington because he had held it too long rather than because he was a Jew.

I. Progressivism: General

Despite his portrayal as a champion of privilege, Taft was able to obtain a greater number of progressive reforms in four years than Theodore Roosevelt obtained in seven years. Among the subjects to be reformed were: liberalize the Rules Committee of the House of Representatives; obtain a Tariff Commission; simplify and speed up court procedures; place a limit upon the issue of labor injunctions; admit Arizona and New Mexico as states; provide ship subsidies, postal savings banks, parcel post, a federal budget, and a commerce court; the federal incorporation of corporations; railroad regulation; economy and efficiency in government; the direct election of U.S. Senators; banking and currency reform; improve the civil service; and obtain a federal income tax amendment. In addition, many persons sought a federal prohibition amendment.

Monographs

832. Abrams, Richard M. *Conservation in a Progressive Era: Massachusetts Politics, 1900-1912*. Cambridge: Harvard University Press, 1964.

833. ———— ed. *The Issue of Federal Regulation in the Progressive Era*. Chicago: Rand McNally, 1965.

834. Bryan, William Jennings, and Mary Baird Bryan. *The Memoirs of William Jennings Bryan*, 1925; rept. Haskell House. Useful for Bryan's motivation and objectives.

835. Croly, Herbert. *The Promise of American Life*. rept. of 1914 ed., Da Capo, 1986. The duty of the individual citizen in the process of the fulfillment of the promise of American life.

836. ————. *Progressive Democracy*. New York: Macmillan, 1914. His second significant commentary on the Progressive Movement.

837. De Witt, Benjamin Parke. *The Progressive Movement: A Non-partisan, Comprehensive Discussion of Current Tendencies in American Politics.* 1915; rept. Seattle: University of Washington Press, 1968. Chapter and verse on every needed progressive reform on the national, state, and local level. Criticism of Taft for failing to carry out Roosevelt's policies, control corporations, and the Winona speech.

838. Faulkner, Harold U. *The Quest for Social Justice, 1898-1914.* 1931; rept. Chicago: Quadrangle Books, 1971. In Chapter 13, Faulkner deals with Taft's opposition to the recall of judges, advocacy of a federal income tax, sidestepping of the woman suffrage issue, and his attitude toward China and the Philippines.

839. Filler, Louis. *Crusaders for American Liberalism.* Yellow Springs, Ohio: Antioch Press, 1950. Biographical sketches of reform leaders.

840. Forcey, Charles. *The Crossroads of Liberalism: Croly, Weyl, Lippmann and the Progressive Era, 1900-1925.* New York: Oxford University Press, 1961.

841. Haber, Samuel. *Efficiency and Uplift: Scientific Management in the Progressive Era, 1890-1920.* Chicago: University of Chicago Press, 1964. The attempt to "Taylorize" social matters as well as industrial production.

842. Hays, Samuel P. *The Response to Industrialism: 1885-1914.* Chicago: University of Chicago Press, 1957. How the nation tried to adjust to the industrialization of the nation, including novel modes of competition, a new urban culture in which city folk were indifferent to each other, new industrial production methods, and the striving after wealth. If Americans were able to participate in great economic achievements and enjoy a higher standard of living, they were also forced to make drastic changes in their lives.

843. Hofstadter, Richard. *The Age of Reform: From Bryan to F.D.R.* New York: Alfred A. Knopf. 1955. Has little sympathy for those like Bryan who wished to return to the simple democracy of earlier days.

844. Ickes, Harold L. *Autobiography of a Curmudgeon*, 1943; rept. Westport, Conn.: Greenwood Press, 1985. Contains the story of the Insurgent revolt and Progressive Republican politics.

845. Johnson, Tom Loftus. *My Story.* New York: B.W. Hubsch, 1911. The autobiography of the reform mayor of Cleveland, Ohio, 1901-1909.

846. Kirkpatrick, Ivy Eugene. "The Struggle for Industrial Democracy: Croly, Lippmann, and Weyl, 1912-1917." Ph.D. diss., Fort Worth, Tex.: Texas Christian University, 1974. How these perceptive writers tried to realize the Promise of American Life.

847. Lippmann, Walter. *Drift and Mastery: An Attempt to Diagnose the Current Unrest*, 1914; rept. Englewood Cliffs, N.J.: Prentice-Hall, 1961. On Progressive theory.

848. Mann, Arthur, ed. *The Progressive Era: Liberal Renaissance or Liberal Failure?* New York: Holt, Rinehart and Winston, 1966.

849. Mowry, George E. *Theodore Roosevelt and the Progressive Movement.* Madison: University of Wisconsin Press, 1946. In order to win support from the old Guard, Roosevelt went slow on reform until elected in his own right.

850. Norris, George W. *Fighting Liberal: The Autobiography of George W. Norris*, 1945; rept. New York: AMS Press, 1983. The U.S Senator from Nebraska who clipped the wings of Speaker Joseph G. Cannon and supported many progressive reforms.

851. Nye, Russell B. *Midwestern Progressive Politics: A Historical Study of its Origins and Development, 1870-1958.* East Lansing, Michigan: Michigan State University Press, 1958. Has much on the Roosevelt and Taft presidencies.

852. Phillips, David Graham. *Contemporaries: Portraits in the Progressive Era.* Louis Filler, ed. Westport, Conn.: Greenwood Press, 1981. A collection of Phillips' articles dealing with progressive reforms.

853. Noble, David W. *The Progressive Mind, 1890-1917.* Chicago: Rand McNally, 1970. Among other things, Roosevelt and Taft refused to try to improve the political climate for the Southern Negro.

854. Regier, Cornelius C. *The Era of the Muckrakers.* 1932; rept. Gloucester, Mass.: Peter Smith, 1957. Journalists who exposed bad conditions and so helped to correct them.

855. Ross, Edward A. *Seventy Years of It: An Autobiography.* New York: D. Appleton Century, 1937. Sin takes many forms including the forcing by employers of employees to "vote right."

856. Sander, Aldred D. "The Political and Social Views of William Howard Taft." Ph.D. diss., The American University, 1955.

857. Solvick, Stanley Donald. "William Howard Taft and the Progressive Movement: A Study in Conservative Thought and Politics." Ph.D. diss., University of Michigan, 1963.

858. Steffens, [Joseph] Lincoln. *The Autobiography of Lincoln Steffens*, 2 vols., 1931; rept. New York: Harcourt, Brace Jovanovich, 1968. Among the best of the muckraking journalists of the Progressive Era.

859. Sullivan, Mark. *Our Times: The United States, 1900-1925*, 6 vols. New York: Charles Scribner's Sons, 1926-1935. Journalistic accounts of problems and their correction during the Progressive Era.

860. Warner, Hoyt L. *Progressivism in Ohio, 1897-1917*. Columbus: Ohio State University Press, 1965. A fine study of the subject in Taft's home state.

861. Wiebe, Robert H. *Businessmen and Reform: A Study of the Progressive Movement*. 1962; rept. Chicago: Quadrangle Books, 1968. In the search for stability while still making profits, businessmen supported progressive reforms.

862. ———. *The Search for Order, 1877-1920*. New York: Hill and Wang, 1967. A seminal work on ways sought to balance ambitions against ambitions.

863. Winter, Ella, and Granville Hicks, eds. *The Letters of Lincoln Steffens*, 2 vols. 1938; rept. Westport, Conn.: Greenwood Press, 1974. Having witnessed the Russian and Mexican revolutions and the Fascist movement in Italy, toward the end of his life Steffens leaned toward approving undemocratic methods.

Articles

864. Allen, Howard W. "Geography and Politics: Voting on Reform Issues in the United States Senate, 1911-1916," *Journal of Southern History* 27 (May 1961):217-28.

865. "A Body Blow for Cannonism," *La Follette's Magazine* 2 (Jan. 15, 1910): 1. To let the members rather than the Speaker of the House of Representatives determine the membership of important committees.

866. Leupp, Francis E. "President Taft's Own View: An Authorized Interview," *The Outlook* 99 (Dec. 2, 1911):811-18. How Taft had fought especially for a railroad regulation bill, postal savings banks bill, and conservation measures.

867. Norris, George W. "A History of the Insurgent Movement in the House of Representatives," *La Follette's Weekly Magazine* 2 (Jan. 8, 1910): 7-9.

868. "The President and His Administration," *The Outlook* 100 (Feb. 10, 1912):300-1. Taft should learn that human rights must be made to fit the Constitution rather than trying to fit the Constitution to human rights.

869. "Senator Cummins' Bill of Particulars," *The Outlook* 99 (Sept. 16, 1911):177-83. Taft had aligned himself with reactionaries rather than with progressives.

870. Solvick, Stanley D. "The Conservative as Progressive: William Howard Taft and the Politics of the Square Deal," *Northwest Ohio Quarterly* 39 (Summer 1967):38-48. Argues that Taft did not turn his back on the Progressive philosophy of the Square Deal after becoming president but that the American public demanded more drastic concepts of reform.

871. Taft, William Howard. "Parcel Post." No. 871.

872. Turner, George Kibbe. "An Interview with the President," *McClure's Magazine* 35 (June 1910):220-1. Taft had appointed a Commission on Economy and Efficiency in June 1911 in part because, he admitted, as Secretary of War he had not known what went on in his own department.

873. Wiebe, Robert H. "Business Disunity and the Progressive Movement, 1901-1914," *Mississippi Valley Historical Review* 44 (Mar. 1958):664-85.

1. The Antitrust Crusade

Monographs

874. Allen, Frederick Lewis. *The Great Pierpont Morgan.* New York: Harper, 1949.

875. Bringhurst, Bruce. *Antitrust and the Oil Monopoly: The Standard Oil Cases, 1890-1911.* Westport, Conn.: Greenwood Press, 1979. An indictment of federal anti-trust policy, "which has never worked."

876. Chessman, G. Wallace. *Theodore Roosevelt and the Politics of Power*, 1969; rept. Boston: G.K. Hall, 1976. See pp. 149-50 for Roosevelt on the U.S. Steel Corporation antitrust case.

877. Clark, James D. *The Federal Trust Policy*. Baltimore: Johns Hopkins Press, 1931.

878. Gordon, David. *The Beef Trust: Antitrust Policy and the Meat Packing Industry, 1902-1922*. Claremont, Calif: Claremont Graduate School, 1983.

879. Griffin, Appleton P.C., comp. *List of Books, with References to Periodicals, Relating to Trusts*. Washington: GPO, 1907.

880. Harvey, George B.M. *Henry Clay Frick, The Man*. N.p., Priv. print, 1936.

881. Jones, Eliot. *The Trust Problem in the United States*. New York: Macmillan, 1921.

882. Letwin, William. *Law and Economic Policy in America: The Evolution of the Sherman Anti-trust Act*. New York: Random House, 1965.

883. McLaughlin, James Angell. *Cases on the Federal Anti-Trust Laws of the United States*. New York: The Ad Press, 1930.

884. Seager, Henry Roberts, and Charles A. Gulick, Jr. *Trust and Corporation Problems*. New York: Harper & Bros., 1929.

885. Sharfman, Isiah Lee. *The Interstate Commerce Commission: A Study in Administrative Law and Procedure*, 5 vols. New York: The Commonwealth Fund, 1931-1937. Still the authoritative work on the subject.

886. Standard Oil Co. of New Jersey, Defendants. United States, Petitioner. *The Great Standard Oil Monopoly Case: The United States of America v. Standard Oil Co. of New Jersey*. Arlington, Va.: University Publications of America, 1975. Microfilm, 6 reels.

887. Taft, William Howard. *The Anti-Trust Act and the Supreme Court*. No. 172.

888. [Taft, W.H.] *Opinion of the Hon. William H. Taft on Cincinnati Freight Rate Discriminations*. No. 166.

889. Tarbell, Ida M. *The Life of Elbert H. Gary: The Story of Steel.* New York: D. Appleton, 1923. On whether Roosevelt approved of U.S. Steel's acquiring of the Tennessee Coal, Iron, and Railroad Company in 1907.

890. Thacher, Thomas. *Mr. Taft and the Sherman Act.* New York: The North American Review Publishing Co., 1909.

891. Thorelli, Hans B. *Federal Antitrust Policy: Organization of an American Tradition.* Baltimore: Johns Hopkins Press, 1954.

892. Van Hise, Charles R. *Concentration and Control: A Solution of the Trust Problem in the United States.* New York: Macmillan, 1914.

893. Walker, Albert Henry. *History of the Sherman Law of the United States of America.* New York: The Equity Press, 1910.

894. ―――. *President Taft and the Railroads: A Historical Sketch.* New York: The author, 1912.

895. ―――. *President Taft and the Sherman Law: A Historical Sketch.* New York: The author, 1912.

896. Wickersham, George W. *Recent Interpretations of the Sherman Act: An Address before the Michigan State Bar Association, July 6, 1911.* Washington: GPO, 1911.

Articles

897. Alderson, William T., ed. "Taft, Roosevelt, and the U.S. Steel Case: Letter of Jacob McGavock Dickinson," *Tennessee Historical Quarterly* 18 (Sept. 1959):266-72.

898. Bryan, W.J. "A Remedy for Trusts," *Public Opinion* 39 (1905):645-48. Extirpate them or bring them under federal control.

899. Dix, George E. "Commerce Court," *American Journal of Legal History* 8 (1964):238.

900. German, James C., Jr. "The Taft Administration and the Sherman Anti-Trust Act," *Mid-America* 54 (July 1972): 172-86. Since no one really knew what Taft's position on the trust question was, how could he expect Congress to enact his program?

901. ———. "Taft, Roosevelt, and United States Steel," *The Historian* 34 (1972):598-613. Taft's instituting of an antitrust suit against U.S. Steel and naming former President Roosevelt in it became one of the major causes of the split between Roosevelt and Taft and the victory of Woodrow Wilson in 1912.

902. "The Government and the Steel Corporation," *The Outlook* 99 (Nov. 4, 1911):547. Had Roosevelt in 1907 blessed U.S. Steel's acquisition of the Tennessee Coal, Iron, and Railroad Co.?

903. "The Growth of a Great Monopoly," *The Outlook* 98 (June 10, 1911):272-73. The American Tobacco Co.

904. "How Business Conditions Determine Presidential Elections," *Current Literature* 52 (Apr. 1912):4311-13.

905. Johnson, Arthur M. "Anti-trust Policy in Transition, 1908: Ideal and Reality," *Mississippi Valley Historical Review* 48 (1961):415-34.

906. Johnston, Charles. "Attorney General [Wickersham] and the Trusts," *Harper's Weekly* 55 (Apr. 22, 1911):8.

907. "Need to Amend the Sherman Law," *The Outlook* 97 (Jan. 1, 1909). Amend it so as to destroy "bad" trusts only.

908. "President Taft on the Interstate Commerce Law," *The Outlook* 99 (Jan. 15, 1910):97-98. On the need to change it so that businessmen could understand it.

909. "Mr. Roosevelt's Attack on the Taft Trust Policy," *Literary Digest* 43 (Nov. 25, 1911):959-61. TR would leave "good" trusts alone.

910. "Mr. Roosevelt and the Harvester Trust," *The Outlook* 101 (May 4, 1912):1-2. Taft's administration brought suit against the Harvester Co., which Roosevelt had had investigated but not sued.

911. "Mr. Roosevelt's Statement on the Harvester Trust," *The Outlook* 101 (May 4, 1912):2. Roosevelt's charge that Taft waited three years before filing suit against the company and then did so for political purposes.

912. Roosevelt, Theodore. "The Steel Corporation and the Panic of 1907," *The Outlook* 98 (Aug. 19, 1911):865-88.

913. ———. "The Trusts, the People and the Square Deal," *The Outlook* 99 (Nov. 18, 1911):649-56. In this article and the one above TR defended himself against Taft's charges that he let U.S. Steel monopolize the steel industry and that he was friendly toward trusts.

914. Rublee, George, "The Original Plan and Early History of the Federal Trade Commission," *Proceedings of the Academy of Political Science* 11 (1926):114-20.

915. "The Rule of Reason," *The Outlook* 98 (July 8, 1911): 513. In the Standard Oil antitrust case, the Supreme Court read the "rule of reason" into its decision. It would decide case by case whether a given restraint of trade was a "reasonable" or "unreasonable" one, thus portending chaos in the business world.

916. "Standard Oil Loses a Customer," *Literary Digest* 40 (Jan. 1, 1910):4. Secretary of War Dickinson barred the Army from making contracts with such trusts as the Standard Oil Co. and the American Tobacco Co.

917. "The Steel Corporation and the Panic of 1907," *The Outlook* 98 (Aug 19, 1911): 849. Had Roosevelt in 1907 blessed U.S. Steel's acquisition of the Tennessee Coal, Iron, and Railroad Co.?

918. Stephens, George A. "Recent Federal Trust Regulation," *South Atlantic Quarterly* 14 (Apr. 1915):154-67. Two schools battle over the issue: those who hold that monopoly is the inevitable outcome of the industrial revolution, and those who would regulate competition and overthrow private monopoly. Praises the creation of the Interstate Commerce Commission and of the Federal Trade Commission.

919. "The Supreme Court Decision," *North American Review* 194 (July 1911):1095. The "rule of reason" introduced by the Supreme Court in the Standard Oil antitrust case portended chaos in the business world.

920. "Taft Policy and the Trusts," *Current Literature* 48 (Feb. 1910):131-4.

921. "Mr. Taft's Firm Antitrust Stand," *Literary Digest* 43 (Sept. 30, 1911):518-19. On Taft's wish to "exterminate" Big Business.

922. "President Taft on the Trusts and the Tariff," *The Outlook* 99 (Sept. 30, 1911):249-50.

923. "The President and the Trusts," ibid., 99 (Nov. 11, 1911):595-96. This article and the one above discuss Taft's call for legislation for the federal incorporation of corporations engaged in interstate commerce with supervision over that business by an executive bureau of the government.

924. Thacher, Thomas. "Mr. Taft and the Sherman Act," *North American Review* 189 (Apr. 1909):513. Per Taft, the Sherman Act should be amended to make every combination of capital in interstate commerce illegal and tell businessmen exactly what they could do rather than use the words "reasonable" and "unreasonable."

925. Urofsky, Melvin I. "Proposed Federal Incorporation in the Progressive Era," *American Journal of Legal History* 26 (Apr. 1982):160-83.

926. Wickersham, George. "Administration's Theory of a Constructive Policy Concerning Combinations," *Annals* 42 (July 1912):277-83.

927. ———. "Enforcement of the Antitrust Law," *The Century Magazine*, 83 (Feb. 1912):616-22.

928. ———. "How Shall the Sherman Law Be Amended?" *The Independent* 77 (June 11, 1912):88-90.

929. Wiebe, Robert H. "The House of Morgan and the Executive, 1905-1913," *American Historical Review* 65 (Oct. 1959):49-60, shows that Taft rejected the *modus vivendi* Roosevelt had achieved with J.P. Morgan.

2. Banking and Currency Reform

930. Brandeis, Louis D. *Other People's Money, and How the Bankers Use It*. New York: Frederick A. Stokes, 1914. A severe indictment of the current monetary system.

931. Glass, Carter. *An Adventure in Constructive Finance*. 1927; rept. New York: Ayer, 1975. Some background on the money question and on who wrote the Federal Reserve Act.

932. Kemmerer, Edwin W. "The Aldrich Plan of Banking Reform," *South Atlantic Quarterly* 10 (Jan. 1911):201-11. Aldrich relies almost exclusively on national banks.

933. Krooss, Herman E., ed. *Documentary History of Banking and Currency in the United States*, 4 vols. New York: Chelsea House, 1969.

934. Laughlin, J. Laurence. *The Federal Reserve Act, Its Origins and Problems*. New York: Macmillan, 1933. By an economist and strong gold standard man who opposed a central banking system.

935. McCully, Richard T. "The Origins of the Federal Reserve Act of 1913: Banks and Politics during the Progressive Era, 1897-1913." Ph.D. diss., University of Texas, 1981.

936. Meyer, George von Lengerke. "Our Inelastic Currency," *Atlantic Monthly* 98 (July 1906):126-31.

937. Meyer, Herman H.B., and W. A. Slade. *Select List of References on the Monetary Question*. Washington: Library of Congress, 1913.

938. Owen, Robert Latham. *The Federal Reserve Act*. New York: The Century Co., 1919. Has some background on the money question during Taft's term.

939. United States. *National Monetary Commission*. 62d Cong., 2d Sess. Washington: GPO, 1912. Sen. Doc. 243. Sen. Nelson A. Aldrich, who headed the commission, investigated banking and currency systems world wide and recommended a central banking system to replace the old national banks. When House Insurgents opposed, Taft supported them, as did Senate Insurgents. The law Taft signed on June 25, 1910, placed deposits in local banks under the supervision of a government Board of Trustees, thus pleasing the Insurgents. However, in time of emergency the deposits could be used to purchase government bonds, thus pleasing conservatives.

940. U.S. Congress. House. Committee to Investigate the Concentration of Control of Money and Credits. *Report* 62d Cong., 3rd Sess., 1913. (The Pujo Committee.)

941. Willis, H. Parker. *The Federal Reserve System*, 1923; rept. New York: Arno Press, 1975. In 1,765 pages, Willis provides ample background on the money question and the creation of the Federal Reserve system.

3. Children's Bureau

942. Coletta, *Taft*, pp. 250, 255. No. 231.

943. Mangold, George B. *Problems of Child Welfare*. New York: Macmillan, 1914.

944. U.S. Bureau of Labor Statistics *Bulletin* No. 175, *Summary of the Report on Conditions of Women and Child Wage Earners in the United States*. Washington: 1915; and *Bulletin* No. 5, 1916.

945. Sumner, Helen L., and Ella A. Merritt, *Child Labor Legislation in the United States*. Washington: U.S. Bureau of Labor, Children's Bureau, Industrial Series, No. 1, 1915.

946. Tobey, J.A. *The Chidren's Bureau*. Baltimore: Johns Hopkins Press, 1925.

4. Civil Service

947. Hahn, H. "President Taft and the Discipline of Patronage," *Journal of Politics* 18 (May 1966):368-90.

948. Hill, John P. *The Federal Executive*. Boston: Houghton Mifflin, 1916.

949. Rodabaugh, Karl. "Congressman Henry D. Clayton and the Dothan Post Office Fight: Patronage and Politics in the Progressive Era," *Alabama Review* 33 (Apr. 1980):125-49. Postmaster Byron Trammel of Dothan, Alabama, had supported Roosevelt in 1912. Despite Alabama's Sen. Henry Clayton, Taft removed Trammel in the name of civil service reform.

950. Sayer, Wallace S., ed. *The Federal Service*. Englewood Cliffs, N.J.: Prentice-Hall, 1965.

951. "Mr. Taft's Southern Appointments," *Literary Digest* 38 (June 5, 1909):952-54.

952. Van Riper, Paul P. *History of the United States Civil Service*. Evanston, Ill.: Row, Peterson, 1958.

5. Conservation

Were conservationists progressives who sought to counter corporate wealth? Pinchot was certainly one of these, and Roosevelt adopted the crusade as part of his battle to obtain efficiency in government. Taft and Secretary of the Interior Ballinger held differing views on the subject, with many authors questioning the latter's sincere devotion to the cause.

Bibliographical Guides

953. Carstensen, Vernon, ed. *The Public Lands: Studies in the History of the Public Domain*. Madison: University of Wisconsin Press, 1963. More than 20 articles on the management and distribution of federally owned public lands from historical journals during the last half century.

954. Davis, Richard C., ed. *Encyclopedia of American Forest and Conservation History*, 2 vols. New York: Macmillan, 1983. Contains more than 400 entries by more than 200 contributors. The first complete guide and reference "to the history of forestry, conservation, forest industries and other forest-related subjects of the United States."

955. Cutright, Paul Russell. *Theodore Roosevelt: The Making of a Conservationist*. Urbana: University of Illinois Press, 1985. Roosevelt heeded Gifford Pinchot's push for sustained yields in timber management yet forged ahead with a program of wildlife refuges.

Monographs

956. Haber, *Efficiency and Uplift*. No. 841.

957. Havemeyer, Loomis, and others, eds. *Conservation of Our Natural Resources*. 1910; rept. New York: Macmillan, 1930.

958. Hays, Samuel P. *Conservation and the Gospel of Efficiency: The Progressive Conservation Movement, 1890-1920*. Cambridge, Mass.: Harvard University Press, 1959. Hayes shows that conservation was originally sponsored by scientific and technical men rather than by anti-corporation crusaders.

959. Hibbard, Benjamin H. *A History of the Public Lands*. 1924; rept. New York: Peter Smith, 1939.

960. Ickes, Harold L. *Not Guilty: An Official Inquiry into the Charges Made by Glavis and Pinchot against Richard A. Ballinger, Secretary of the Interior, 1909-1911*. Washington: GPO, 1940.

961. Mason, Alpheus Thomas. *Bureaucracy Convicts Itself: The Ballinger-Pinchot Controversy of 1910*. New York: Viking Press, 1941. Steers a middle course between the principals even though Pinchot would not let him use his papers.

962. Ogden, Gerald R. *"Forestry for a Nation": The Making of a National Forest Policy Under the Weeks and Clarke-McNary Acts, 1900-1924*. Albuquerque: University of New Mexico Press, 1980.

963. Peffer, E. Louise. *The Closing of the Public Domain: Disposal and Reservation Policies, 1900-1950*. 1951; rept. New York: Ayer Press, 1972.

964. Penick, James, Jr. *Progressive Politics and Conservation: The Ballinger-Pinchot Affair*. Chicago: University of Chicago Press, 1968. As the title indicates, the work relates the conservation crusade to progressivism.

965. Pinchot, Gifford. *Breaking New Ground*. New York: Harcourt, Brace, 1947. The former Chief Forester told his own story.

966. Pinkett, Harold T. *Gifford Pinchot: Private and Public Forester*. Urbana: University of Illinois Press, 1970. Upholds his subject vs. Ballinger.

967. Richardson, Elmo R. *The Politics of Conservation: Crusades and Controversies, 1897-1913*. Berkeley: University of California Press, 1962, provides a well-balanced account that includes thorough research into the attitude of the West on conservation.

968. Robbins, Roy M. *Our Landed Heritage: The Public Domain, 1776-1936*. Princeton, N.J.: Princeton University Press, 1942, 1976.

969. Ross, Thomas Richard. *Jonathan Prentiss Dolliver: A Study in Political Integrity and Independence*. Iowa City: State Historical Society of Iowa, 1960. Dolliver was one of the Senators of the Progressive Era who equated conservation with progressivism.

970. U.S. President [Taft]. *Letter from President William H. Taft to the Governors of the States on Land and Agricultural Credit in Europe*. Washington: Department of State, 1912.

971. Gould, Alan Brant. "Secretary of the Interior Walter L. Fisher and the Return to Constructive Conservation: Problems and Policies of the Conservation Movement, 1909-1913." Ph.D. diss., West Virginia University, 1969. Fisher followed Ballinger in office.

Articles

972. "Alaska as Seen by Secretary Fisher," *The Outlook* 99 (Nov. 4, 1911):548-49.

973. "American Dreyfus Case," *Collier's Magazine* 45 (May 7, 1910):22-23.

974. Ballinger, Richard A. "Water-power Sites on the Public Domain," *Review of Reviews* 41 (Jan. 1910):47-48.

975. "Ballinger: A Killer of Snakes," *Current Literature* 47 (Nov. 1909):503-5.

976. "Ballinger and the Cunningham Claims," *Current Literature* 48 (Feb. 1910):119-27.

977. "Ballinger as Administrator," *The Outlook* 94 (Apr. 21, 1910):735-36.

978. "Ballinger Case: A Review," *The Outlook* 95 (June 11, 1910):288-95.

979. "Ballinger Cross-Examined by Mr. Brandeis," *The Outlook* 95 (May 21, 1910):96-99.

980. "Ballinger Resigns," *The Outlook* 97 (Mar. 18, 1911): 566-67.

981. "Ballinger's Side of the Case," *The Outlook* 94 (Apr. 9, 1910):778-80.

982. Bates, J. Leonard. "Fulfilling American Democracy: The Conservation Movement, 1907-1921," *Mississippi Valley Historical Review* 44 (June 1957):29-57.

983. Bennett, A.L. "Profile of a Year: 1910," *American Forests* 66 (Sept. 1960):30-3.

984. "Burden of Ballinger," *The World's Work* 20 (July 1910):131-8.

985. "Can This Be Whitewashed Also: New Quagmires for Ballinger," *Collier's Magazine* 44 (Dec. 18, 1909):8-9.

986. Connolly, C.P. "Ballinger—Shyster," *Collier's Magazine* 45 (Apr. 2, 1910):16-17.

987. ———. "Who Is Behind Ballinger?" *Collier's Magazine* 45 (Apr. 2, 1910):16-17.

988. "Conservation in Dispute," *Review of Reviews* 40 (Oct. 1909):398-400.

989. "The Dismissal of Mr. Pinchot," *The Outlook* 94 (Jan. 25, 1910):107-8. Pinchot forced his own dismissal.

990. "Famous Controversy," *Review of Reviews* 41 (Feb. 1910):131-38.

991. Fichen, Robert E. "Gifford Pinchot Men: Pacific Northwest Lumbermen and the Conservation Movement, 1902-1910," *Western History* 13 (1982):165-78.

992. Fisher, Walter Lourie. "Alaska's Needs," *The Independent* 72 (May 23, 1912):1094-96.

993. Ganoe, John T. "Some Constitutional Aspects of the Ballinger-Pinchot Controversy," *Pacific Historical Review* 3 (1934):323-33. How the Bureau of Forestry and the Reclamation Service in the Department of Agriculture disagreed on conservation with the Department of the Interior.

994. Glavis, Louis R. "Whitewashing of Ballinger," *Collier's Magazine* 44 (Nov. 13, 1909):15-17.

995. Gould, Alan B. "'Trouble Portfolio' to Constructive Conservation: Secretary of the Interior Walter L. Fisher, 1911-1913," *Forest History* 16 1973):4-12. After Pinchot's ouster as Chief Forester, Fisher restored confidence in the Interior Department and undertook a policy known as "constructive conservation."

996. Ickes, Harold L. "Not Guilty! Richard A. Ballinger," *Saturday Evening Post* 212 (May 25, 1940):9.

997. "Lawler Memorandum" *The Outlook* 95 (May 28, 1910): 136-37. On Taft's predating of the memorandum.

998. McCardle, Richard E., with Elwood R. Maunder. "Wilderness Politics: Legislation and Forest Service Policy," *Journal of Forest History* 19 (Oct. 1975):166-79.

999. "Mr. Ballinger and Mr. Pinchot," *The Independent* 67 (Sept. 9, 1909):563-64.

1000. "Mr. Taft's Hand in the Pinchot Fray," *Literary Digest* 39 (Oct. 9, 1909):560-2.

1001. Page, Arthur W. "The Fight for Conservation," *The World's Work* 21 (Nov. 1910):13607-10. Report on enthusiasm for conservation at the Second National Conservation Congress, St. Paul, Minn.

1002. Page, Walter H. "Gifford Pinchot: The Awakener of the Nation," *The Outlook* 99 (Mar. 1910):12662-68.

1003. Pinchot, Gifford, U.S. Forester. "The ABC of Conservation," *The Outlook* 93 (Dec. 4, 1909):770-72. Spells out the Pinchot-Roosevelt attitude toward conservation.

1004. "Pinchot-Ballinger Controversy," *The Outlook* 93 (Sept. 25, 1909):131-33.

1005. "Pinchot vs. Ballinger," *The Nation* 89 (Sept. 23, 1909):270.

1006. "The Power Site Controversy," *The Independent* 67 (Sept. 30, 1909):725-26.

1007. "The President and Ballinger," *Literary Digest* 39 (Sept. 25, 1909):525-26.

1008. "President Taft and Secretary Ballinger," *The Independent* 70 (Mar. 16, 1911):575-76.

1009. Rakestraw, Lawrence. "Conservative Historiography; An Assessment," *Pacific Historical Review* 41 (Aug. 1972): 271-88. Takes issue with Penick (q.v.) for the manner in which he dealt with Ballinger.

1010. "Secretary Ballinger and Conservation," *The Outlook* 94 (Dec. 1, 1909):748-49.

1011. "Secretary Ballinger and Our Natural Resources," *The Outlook* 93 (Nov. 20, 1909):617-18.

1012. "Secretary Ballinger and the Cunningham Claims" *The Outlook* 93 (Oct. 2, 1909):246-47.

1013. "Secretary Ballinger's Acquittal," *The Independent* 67 (Sept. 23, 1909):713-14.

1014. "Secretary Fisher and Alaska," *The Outlook* 99 (Sept. 16, 1911):96.

1015. Stahl, Rose. "The Ballinger-Pinchot Controversy." In *Smith College Studies in History*. Northampton, Mass., 1915., 11 (1926):65-126. Established the theme that conservationists were part of the Progressive Movement and sought to counter corporate wealth. She supported Pinchot and his associates.

1016. "State of National Conservation," *Literary Digest* 41 (Sept. 17, 1910):525-26.

1017. Wert, S.T. "Transmutation of Fact into Fancy" *Collier's Magazine* 45 (Mar. 26, 1910):34.

1018. White, S.E. "Ballinger Case," *American Magazine* 69 (Mar. 1910):686-89.

1019. "Who Is Behind Ballinger?" *Collier's Magazine* 45 (Apr. 9, 1910):16-17.

6. The Direct Election of Senators

1020. The Senate had long been known as the "Millionaires' Club" because so many men of great wealth were in it; moreover, they represented such special interests as steel, sugar, and railroads. The Populists had called for direct elections since 1892 and the Democrats since 1900. By that time, many state legislatures were in effect ratifying the results of popular referendums, and Taft looked upon direct elections as a nonpartisan issue. With the Senate agreeable to the Seventeenth Amendment in 1912 and its implementation on May 31, 1913, the government was made more directly responsive to voters.

1021. Bryce, James. *The American Commonwealth*, 3 vols. 1888; rept. New York: AMS Press, 1973, 1:158.

1022. Burns, James MacGregor, and Jack Walter Peltason. *Government by the People: The Dynamics of American National, State, and Local Government*, 6th ed. Englewood Cliffs, N.J.: Prentice-Hall, 1966, pp. 76-77, 214.

1023. Coletta, *Taft*, pp. 38, 133, 147, 250. No. 231.

1024. Faulkner, Harold Underwood. *The Quest for Social Justice, 1898-1914.* 1931; rept. Chicago: Quadrangle Books, 1959, pp. 87-88.

1025. Tarr, Joel Arthur. *A Study in Boss Politics: William Lorimer of Chicago.* Urbana: University of Illinois Press, 1971.

7. A Federal Budget

1026. "Report of Economy and Efficiency Commission on Need for a National Budget, with Recommendations." *CIS*, 62-2. H. Doc. 854. 6300.

1027. Arnold, Peri E. *Making the Managerial Presidency: Comprehensive Reorganization Planning, 1905-1979.* Princeton, N.J.: Princeton University Press. 1986. From the Keep Commission of Theodore Roosevelt to Jimmie Carter.

1028. Coletta, *Taft*, pp. 124, 130-31, 253. No. 231.

1029. Collins, Charles Wallace. "The Coming of the Budget System," *South Atlantic Quarterly* 15 (Oct. 1916):309-18. How the system works, and the hope that it will abolish logrolling and "invisible government."

1030. Hill, Kim Q., and John P. Plumlee. "Presidential Success in Budgetary Policymaking: A Longitudinal Analysis," *Presidential Studies Quarterly* 12 (Spring 1982):174-85.

1031. Ramsey, John W. "The Director of the Bureau of the Budget as a Presidential Aide, 1921-1952, with Emphasis on the Truman Years." Ph.D. diss., University of Missouri, 1967.

1032. Rockoff, Hugh. "The Origins of a Federal Budget," *Journal of Economic History* 45 (June 1985):377-82.

1033. Tucker, Robert H. "The Budget System and Popular Control," *South Atlantic Quarterly* 17 (Jan. 1918):96-112. Traces the development of the U.S. budget from British practices and the legislative history of Taft's budget program.

1034. U.S. Bureau of the Budget (now Office of Management and Budget). *The Federal Budget.* Washington: GPO, annual since 1921.

8. A Federal Corporation Tax

1035. Bayne, Hugh A. "Is the Federal Corporation Tax Constitutional?" *The Outlook* 94 (Jan. 1, 1910):20-25.

1036. "The Corporation Tax," *The World's Work* 18 (Aug. 1909):11858. To raise revenue to replace that lost by reducing the tariff rates.

1037. "The New Federal Corporation Tax Law, *The Outlook* 93 (Nov. 20, 1909):622-23.

1038. Johnson, Alvin S. "The Incidence of the Federal Corporation Tax," *South Atlantic Quarterly* 9 (Jan. 1910): 35-42. Because the time has passed when protective and sumptuary excise taxes can meet the burden of the federal expenditures, a corporation tax is needed.

1039. Wilson, William L. "An Income Tax on Corporations," *North American Review* 158 (Jan. 1894):1-7.

9. A Federal Income Tax

Such a tax was collected during the Civil War and for several years thereafter before being abandoned. In 1895 the Supreme Court found an income tax law of 1894 to be unconstitutional. In his platform for 1896, 1900, and 1908 Bryan called for a constitutional amendment on the subject which Taft also supported.

Monographs

1040. Black, Henry C. *A Treatise on the Law of Income Taxation*, 2d ed. Kansas City: Vernon, 1916.

1041. Blakey, Roy G., and Gladys C. Blakey. *The Federal Income Tax*. New York: Longmans, Green, 1939.

1042. Comstock, Alzada P. *Taxation in the Modern State*. New York: Longmans, Green, 1929.

1043. Dewey, Davis R. *Financial History of the United States*, 11th ed. New York: Longmans, Green, 1931.

1044. Haig, Robert M., ed. *The Federal Income Tax*. New York: Columbia University Press, 1921.

1045. Kennan, Kossuth K. *Income Taxation*. Milwaukee: Burdick and Allen, 1910.

1046. McGuffy, Richard T. "The Origins of the Federal Reserve Act of 1913: Banks and Politics during the Progressive Era." Ph.D. diss., University of Texas, 1981.

1047. National Bureau of Economic Research. *Income in the United States, 1909-1919*. New York: Harcourt, Brace, 1921.

1048. Noyes, Alexander D. *Forty Years of American Finance*. 1909; rept. New York: Ayer, 1981.

1049. Ogg, Frederic. *National Progress, 1907-1917*. 1918; rept. Arden Library, 1978.

1050. Ratner, Sidney. *American Taxation: Its History as a Social Force in Democracy*. New York: W. W. Norton, 1942.

1051. Seidman, J.S. *Legislative History of Federal Income Tax Laws*. New York: Prentice-Hall, 1938.

1052. Seligman, Edwin R.A. *The Income Tax: A Study of the History, Theory, and Practice of Income Taxation at Home and Abroad*, 2d ed. rev. and enl. New York: A.M. Kelley, 1970.

1053. Simons, Henry. *Personal Income Taxation*. Chicago: University of Chicago Press, 1938.

1054. Studenski, Paul, and Herman E. Krooss, *Financial History of the United States*. New York: McGraw-Hill, 1952.

1055. Walker, Albert Henry. *The Income Tax Law of the United States of America*. New York: The Author, 1913.

1056. ———. *The Unconstitutional Character and the Illegal Administration of the Income Tax Law*. New York: The Author, 1914.

1057. Waltman, Jerold L. *Political Origins of the U.S. Income Tax.* Jackson: University Press of Mississippi, 1985. The legislative history and principal provisions of the first five federal revenue acts, 1913-1921.

1058. White, Eugene Nelson. *The Regulation and Reform of the American Banking System, 1900-1929.* Princeton, N.J.: Princeton University Press, 1983.

1059. White, John. *The Politics and Development of the Federal Income Tax.* Madison: University of Wisconsin Press, 1985.

1060. Witte, John F. *The Politics and Development of the Federal Income Tax.* Madison: University of Wisconsin Press, 1985.

Articles

1061. Baack, Bennett D., and Edward, John Ray. "Special Interests and the Adoption of the Income Tax in the United States." *Journal of Economic History* 45 (Sept. 1985):607-26. An income tax was supported by the low income South and opposed by the industrial states of the Northeast. Both Roosevelt and Taft supported it because of the need to pay for growing expenditures for military services and veterans pensions and, in Taft's case, lower income from tariff duties.

1062. Boutwell, George S. "The Income Tax," *North American Review* 160 (May 1895):589-601.

1063. Carson, Gerald. "The Income Tax and How It Grew," *American Heritage* 25 (Dec. 1973):4-9.

1064. Ellis, Elmer. "Popular Opinion and the Income Tax, 1860-1900," *Mississippi Valley Historical Review* 27 (Sept. 1940):225-42.

1065. Seligman, Edwin R.A. "Is the Income Tax Constitutional and Just?" *The Forum* 18 (Mar. 1895):48-56.

1066. Wells, David A. "Is the Existing Income Tax Constitutional?" *The Forum* 16 (Oct. 1893):537-42.

10. Governmental Reorganization

1067. Arnold, Peri E. *Making the Managerial Presidency: Comprehensive Reorganization Planning.* Princeton, N.J.: Princeton University Press, 1986.

Attempts made since 1905 to make administration more subordinate to the president and more coherent than it had been under Congressional authority.

1068. Gould, Lewis L. *Reform and Regulation: American Policy from Roosevelt to Wilson*, 2d ed. New York: Knopf, 1986.

1069. Kraines, O. "The President versus Congress: The Keep Commission, 1905-1909. First Comprehensive Presidential Inquiry into Administration," *Western Political Quarterly* 23 (1970):5-54. A major step was taken in ending congress's full legislative authority in the management of the public business.

1070. Marcy, Carl Milton. *Presidential Commissions*. New York: King's Crown Press, 1945.

1071. "President's Message December 1909," *The Outlook* 93 (Dec. 12, 1909):803-4. Taft suggested the adoption of a federal budget.

1072. "President's Message December 1909," *The Independent* 67 (Dec. 16, 1909):1333-35, 1388-89.

11. Immigration

Despite the demands of American labor, Taft on February 14, 1913, vetoed a law providing for a literacy test for immigrants.

1073. Freidel, Frank, ed. *Harvard Guide to American History*, rev. ed., 2 vols. Cambridge, Mass.: Belknap Press of Harvard University Press, 1974. Chapter 20 has an extensive list of titles on immigration and ethnicity.

1074. Abbot, Edith. *Immigration: Select Documents and Case Records*. 1924; rept. New York: Arno Press, 1967.

1075. ———. *Historical Aspects of the Immigration Problem*. 1914; rept. New York: Arno Press, 1969.

1076. Handlin, Oscar. *Race and Nationality in American Life*. Boston: Little, Brown, 1950.

1077. ———. *The Uprooted: The Epic Story of the Great Migrations that Made the American People*. Boston: Little, Brown, 1952.

1078. Higham, John. *Strangers in the Land: Patterns of American Nativism, 1900-1925*. New Brunswick, N.J.: Rutgers University Press, 1955. Much empathy for the newcomer.

12. The Judicial System

Bibliographic Guide

1079. Miller, Arthur A. "The Supreme Court of the United States: A Bibliographic Essay," *American Studies International* 16 (Winter 1977):5-14.

Monographs

1080. Abraham, Henry Julian. *Justices and Presidents: A Political History of Appointments to the Supreme Court*, 2d ed. New York: Oxford University Press, 1985. An attempt to explain the presidential motives behind every nomination for a post on the Supreme Court since 1789.

1081. ———. *The Judiciary: The Supreme Court in the Governmental Process*, 5th ed. Boston: Allyn & Bacon, 1980.

1082. Baum, Lawrence, *The Supreme Court*, 2d ed. Washington: Congressional Quarterly Books, 1985. How the Supreme Court works.

1083. Beard, Charles A. *The Supreme Court and the Constitution*. Englewood Cliffs, N.J.: Prentice-Hall, 1962.

1084. Boudin, Louis B. *Government by Judiciary*. 1932. rept. New York: Russell and Russell, 1968.

1085. Rossiter, Clinton. *The Supreme Court and the Commander in Chief*. Expanded and ed. by Richard P. Longaker. Ithaca: Cornell University Press, 1976.

1086. Schubert, Glendon A., Jr. *The Presidency and the Courts*. Minneapolis: University of Minnesota Press, 1957.

1087. ———. *Judicial Policy-making: The Political Role of the Courts*. Chicago: Scott, Foresman, 1965.

1088. Scigliano, Robert G., *The Courts: A Reader in the Judicial Process*. Boston: Little, Brown, 1962.

1089. ———. *The Supreme Court and the Presidency*. New York: Free Press, 1971. Denies that presidents tend generally to dominate the Supreme Court.

1090. *United States Reports: The Decisions of the United States Supreme Court Organized According to the Terms of the Court*. Washington: GPO, various dates.

Articles

1091. Kahn, M.A. "The Politics of the Appointment Process: An Analysis of Why Learned Hand was Never Appointed to the Supreme Court," *Stanford Law Review* 25 (Jan. 1973):251-85.

1092. ———. "On the Appointment of Justices to the Supreme Court," *Stanford Law Review* 26 (Feb. 1974):689-715.

1093. Kurland, P.B. "The Appointment and Disappointment of Supreme Court Justices," *Arizona State University Law Journal* 2 (1972):183-207.

1094. "Remaking the Supreme Court," *The Outlook* 90 (Sept. 1910):13347. Of the nine justices, Taft has appointed two; a third vacancy exists; and the resignation of Moody will leave a fourth place open. Taft will appoint men of his own type. [Actually, the death or resignation of five of the justices during his term gave Taft the unusual opportunity to reconstitute the Court with a majority of new men he hoped would help him protect the Constitution from the Insurgents if not from Roosevelt's New Nationalism.]

1095. Swindler, William F. "The Selling of the Constitution," Supreme Court Historical Society. *Yearbook* 5 (1980):49-54.

1096. Timbers, Edwin. "The Supreme Court and the President as Commander in Chief," *Presidential Studies Quarterly* 16 (Spring 1986):224-36.

13. Labor

Monographs

1097. Beard, Mary. *The American Labor Problem*, 1928; rept. New York: Arno Press, 1969.

1098. Berman, Edward. *Labor Disputes and the President of the United States*. 1914; rept. New York: AMS Press, 1968.

1099. Commons, John R. and others. *History of Labor in the United States*. 1924. rept. New York: A.M. Kelley, 1966. Especially good for child labor legislation.

1100. *Decisions Rendered by Hon. William Howard Taft in Cases Coming Before Him as Judge in Which Were Involved Questions Affecting Boycotts, Labor Organizations, Injunctions, and Antitrust Law*. Washington: Sudworth Co, 1908.

1101. Dubofsky, Melvyn. *Industrialism and the American Worker, 1865-1920*, 2d ed. Arlington Heights, Ill.: Harlan Davidson, 1987.

1102. Fink, Gary M., ed. *Biographical Dictionary of American Labor Leaders*. Westport, Conn.: Greenwood Press, 1974. See entries for Gompers, Strasser, and others.

1103. Frankfurter, Felix, and Nathan Green. *The Labor Injunction*. 1930; rept. Peter Smith, 1978. Gives useful background material on relations between Taft and organized labor.

1104. Gompers, Samuel. *Seventy Years of Life and Labor: An Autobiography*, No. 441.

Articles

1105. Alger, George W. "Taft and Labor," *McClure's Magazine* 31 (Sept. 1908):597-602.

1106. Hilles, Charles D. "Socialism and Its Menace: Why Government Ownership Would Not Help the Wage Earner," *The Century Magazine* 84 (Oct. 1912):943-48.

1107. Judson, F.N. "Labor Decisions of Judge Taft," *Review of Reviews* 36 (Aug. 1907):212-17.

14. Black Americans

Bibliographic Guides

1108. *Bibliographic Guide to Black Studies: 1979.* Boston: G.K. Hall, 1975.

1109. Logan, Rayford, and Michael R. Winston, eds. *Dictionary of American Negro Biography.* New York: W.W. Norton, 1982.

1110. Low, W. Augustus, and Virgil A. Clift, eds. *Encyclopedia of Black America.* New York: McGraw-Hill, 1981. Eighty-nine prominent contributors and 33 consultants interpret the life and history of Afro-Americans in the United States from their African roots to 1977.

1111. Miller, Elizabeth W. *The Negro in America: A Bibliography*, 2d rev. ed. Cambridge, Mass.: Harvard University Press, 1970.

1112. Porter, Dorothy B. *The Negro in the United States: A Selected Bibliography.* Washington: Library of Congress, 1970.

Monographs

1113. Aptheker, Herbert ed. *A Documentary History of the Negro People of the United States*, 2 vols. New York: Citadel Press, 1951, 1969-1970.

1114. Baker, Ray Stannard. *Following the Color Line: American Negro Citizenship in the Progressive Era.* New York: Doubleday, Page, 1908. Also issued as a Torchbook: New York: Harper & Row, 1964.

1115. Broderick, Francis L. *Negro Protest Thought in the Twentieth Century.* Indianapolis: Bobbs-Merrill, 1966.

1116. Casdorph, Paul D. *Republicans, Negroes, and Progressives in the South, 1912-1916.* University: University of Alabama Press, 1981. Includes the struggles of southern Republican delegates during 1912 to have a voice in the deliberations and how the national convention gave Taft rather than Roosevelt 166 of the 176 contested southern delegates and thus the nomination.

1117. Clark, Thomas D., and Albert D. Kirwan. *The South Since Appomatox: A Century of Regional Change.* New York: Oxford University Press, 1967.

1118. De Marco, Joseph P. *The Social Thought of W.E.B. Du Bois*. Washington: University Press of America, 1983. A study of Du Bois's nonfiction writing including his editorship of the *Crisis* and of the *Atlantic University Publications*.

1119. Fishel, Leslie H., Jr., and Benjamin Quarles, eds. *The Negro American: A Documentary History*. Glenview, Ill.: Scott, Foresman, 1967.

1120. Franklin, John Hope, and August Meier, eds. *Black Leaders of the Twentieth Century*. Urbana: University of Illinois Press, 1982.

1121. Grantham, Dewey W., Jr. *The Democratic South*. Athens: University of Georgia Press, 1963.

1122. ———. *Southern Progressivism: The Reconciliation of Progress and Tradition*. Knoxville, Tenn.: University of Tennessee Press, 1983. See especially Part Two: The Reform Movements.

1123. Harlan, Louis R. *The Making of a Black Leader: Booker T. Washington*. New York: Oxford University Press, 1972.

1124. ———. *Booker T. Washington: The Wizard of Tuskegee, 1915*. New York: Oxford University Press, 1983.

1125. ———. and Raymond H. Smock, eds. *Booker T. Washington Papers*, 13 vols. Urbana: University of Illinois Press, 1972-1984.

1126. Johnson, James Weldon. *Along This Way*. New York: Viking Press, 1969. Biography of a local black leader.

1127. Kellogg, Charles Flint. *NAACP: A History of the National Association for the Advancement of Colored People. Vol. 1: 1909-1920*. Baltimore: Johns Hopkins Press, 1967.

1128. Lewinson, Paul. *Race, Class & Party: A History of Negro Suffrage and White Politics in the South*. New York: Russell and Russell, 1932, 1963. Helpful on black participation and nonparticipation in the political process.

1129. Logan, Rayford Whittingham. *The Betrayal of the Negro: From Rutherford B. Hayes to Woodrow Wilson*, new enl. ed. New York: Collier Books, 1965. Originally published as *The Negro in American Life and Thought: Nadir, 1877-1901*.

1130. McDougall, William. *An Introduction to Social Psychology*. Boston: J.W. Luce & Co., 1908; 2d ed. enl. London: Methuen, 1931.

1131. Marable, Manning. *W.E.B. Du Bois: Black Radical Democrat*. Boston: Twayne, 1986. The scholar and activist who opposed Booker T. Washington in demanding full black rights and was editor of the *Crisis*, the newspaper of the NAACP, from 1910 to 1934.

1132. Meier, August. *Negro Thought in America, 1880-1915: Racial Ideologies in the Age of Booker T. Washington*. Ann Arbor: University of Michigan Press, 1963.

1133. ———, and John Hope Franklin. *Black Leaders in the Twentieth Century*. Urbana: University of Illinois Press, 1982.

1134. ———, and Elliott Rudwick, eds. *Along the Color Line: Explorations in the Black Experience*. Urbana: University of Illinois Press, 1976. Fourteen essays, many of which deal with the black's problems during Taft's lifetime.

1135. Miller, Kelley. *Out of the House of Bondage: Sourcebooks in Negro History*. 1914; rept. New York: Schocken Books, 1971. A collection of essays by a Howard University professor, many of them written during the Taft administration.

1136. Myrdal, Gunnar, with the Assistance of Richard Sterner and Arnold Rose. *An American Dilemma: The Negro Problem and Modern Democracy*, 2 vols. 1944; rept. Twentieth Century Anniversary Edition. New York: Harper & Row, 1962.

1137. Needham, David Charles, "William Howard Taft, the Negro, and the White South, 1908-1912." Ph.D. diss., University of Georgia, 1970.

1138. *Negro Year Book*. Tuskegee, Ala., 1912. Title varies, and published at irregular intervals.

1139. Ovington, Mary White. *The Walls Came Tumbling Down*. 1947; rept. New York: Arno Press, 1969.

1140. Ploski, Harry A., and James Williams, comps. and eds. *The Negro Almanac: A Reference Work on the Afro-American*, 4th ed. New York: Wiley, 1983.

1141. Pringle, *Taft*, 1:323-28. No. 248. Taft followed Roosevelt's order to dismiss black troops that allegedly killed a man in Texas.

1142. Rudwick, Elliott M. *W.E.B. Du Bois: A Study in Minority Group Leadership*. Philadelphia: University of Pennsylvania Press, 1960.

1143. ———. *W.E.B. Du Bois: Voice of the Black Protest Movement*. Champaign: University of Illinois Press, 1969, 1972.

1144. Scott, Emmet J., and Lyman Beecher Stowe. *Booker T. Washington: Builder of a Civilization*. Garden City, N.Y.: Doubleday, 1916.

1145. Sherman, Richard B. "In Troubled Waters: The Taft Administration." In Richard B. Sherman, *The Republican Party and Black America from McKinley to Hoover, 1896-1933*. Charlottesville: University of Virginia Press, 1973, pp. 83-112. Taft's failure to reconcile a conciliatory approach toward the white South with a positive program for the blacks.

1146. Shufeldt, Robert Wilson. *The Negro: A Menace to American Civilization*. Boston: R.G. Badger, 1907.

1147. Southern, David. *The Malignant Heritage: Yankee Progressives and the Negro Question, 1901-1914*. Chicago: Loyola University Press, 1968. Progressives did little to help the blacks.

1148. Spencer, Samuel R. Jr. *Booker T. Washington and the Negroes' Place in American Life*. Boston: Little, Brown, 1955.

1149. Taft, William Howard. Address. "Southern Democracy. . . ." No. 125.

1150. Tindall, George B. *The Emergence of the New South, 1913-1945*. Baton Rouge: Louisiana State University Press, 1967. Although he starts with 1913, the author gives many a backward look to earlier conditions in the South.

1151. White, John. *Black Leadership in America, 1895-1968*. London: Longmans, 1985.

1152. Woodward C. Vann. *The Origins of the New South, 1877-1913*. Baton Rouge: Louisiana State University Press, 1951; rev. ed. 1971. See especially Chapter 14: "Progressivism for Whites Only," and Chapter 17, "The Return of the South."

1153. ———. *The Strange Career of Jim Crow*, 2d rev. ed. New York: Oxford University Press, 1966.

1154. Zangrando, Robert L. *The NAACP Crusade Against Lynching. 1909-1950*. Philadelphia: Temple University Press, 1984.

Articles

1155. Baker, Ray Stannard. "The Negroes' Struggle for Survival in the North," *American Magazine* 65 (Feb. 1908):473-85.

1156. ———. "The Negro in a Democracy," *The Independent* 67 (Sept. 6, 1909):585-88. Pleads for the elevation of the blacks.

1157. Brown, William Garrott. "President Taft's Opportunity," *The Century Magazine* 81 (June 1909):256. Opportunity to end the Democratic monopoly in the South.

1158. Coulter, E. Merton. "The Attempt of William Howard Taft to Break the Solid South," *Georgia Historical Quarterly* 19 (June 1935):1-11.

1159. Du Bois, W.E.B., "The Dilemma of the Negro," *American Mercury* 3 (Oct. 1924):179-85. Whatever progress in black life was made in the last quarter century was made by blacks themselves, with little white help.

1160. Garner, James W. "New Politics for the South," *Annals* 35 (Jan. 1910):172-83.

1161. Gatewood, Willard B. "William D. Crum, a Negro in Politics," *Journal of Negro History* 53 (1968):301-20. A wealthy black physician of Charleston, S.C., Crum was appointed postmaster of Charleston by President Benjamin Harrison in 1892. A white backlash caused Harrison to withdraw Crum's name. Despite similar opposition, Theodore Roosevelt held fast in naming Crum the Collector of the Port of Charleston. Crum resigned after Taft was elected, but Taft appointed him as minister Resident and Consul General of Liberia.

1162. Grantham, Dewey W., Jr. "The Progressive Movement and the Negro," *South Atlantic Quarterly* 54 (1955):461-77. Progressives "passed over the Negro question."

1163. Link, Arthur S. "Theodore Roosevelt and the South in 1912," *North Carolina Historical Review* 25 (July 1946):313-24.

1164. ———. "The Negro as a Factor in the Campaign of 1912," *Journal of Negro History* 32 (Jan. 1947):81-99.

1165. Meier, August. "Booker T. Washington and the Rise of the N.A.A.C.P." *The Crisis* 61 (Feb. 1954):75-76, 117-21.

1166. Miller, Kelly. "The American Negro as a Political Factor," *Nineteenth Century* 88 (Aug. 1910):285-302.

1167. Milligan, Nancy Miller. "W.E.B. Du Bois' American Pragmatism," *Journal of American Culture* 8 (Summer 1985):31-37.

1168. "Mr. Taft and the South," *The World's Work* 17 (Feb. 1909):11187-88.

1169. "Negroes and Secretary Taft," *The Independent* 64 (Feb. 13, 1908):374-75.

1170. Osofsky, Gilbert. "Progressivism and the Negro: New York: 1900-1915," *American Quarterly* 16 (Summer 1964):153-68.

1171. Osborn, George C. "The Problem of the Negro in Government, 1913," *Historian* 23 (May 1961):330-47.

1172. "Taft on Race Discrimination," *The Independent* 65 (Oct. 22, 1908):960-2.

15. Parcel Post

1173. Coletta, *Taft*, pp. 124, 125, 255. No. 231.

1174. Meyer, George von Lengerke. "Parcel Post," *North American Review* 187 (Mar. 1908):330-6.

1175. Raper, Charles Lee. *Railway Transportation: A History of Its Economics and Its Relation to the State*. New York: G.P. Putnam's Sons, 1912. If light on the Sherman Antitrust Act, it is heavy on the anticipated success of parcel post.

1176. Taft, William Howard. "Parcel Post." No. 871.

1177. *U.S. Statutes at Large*, 37:557.

16. Postal Savings Banks

Bibliographic Guide

1178. Griffin, Appleton P.C., comp. *List of Books, with References to Periodicals, Relating to Postal Savings Banks*. Washington: GPO, 1904.

Book

1179. Kemmerer, Edwin Walter. *Postal Savings*. . . . Princeton, N.J.: Princeton University Press, 1917. The basic work on the subject.

Articles

1180. Hitchcock, Frank, "New Postal Savings Banks," *The Independent* 72 (Jan. 18, 1912):136-39. By the Postmaster General.

1181. Meyer, George von Lengerke. "Postal Savings Banks," *The Independent* 64 (Jan. 2, 1909):9-10. By Roosevelt's postmaster general, now Taft's Secretary of the Navy.

1182. "Need of a Postal Savings Bank," *Review of Reviews* 39 (Jan. 1909):47-48.

17. Public Health

1183. "Report of American Delegate to Second National Opium Conference." *CIS*, 63-1. S. Doc. 157.6536.

1184. "Abolition of Opium Evil." *CIS*. 63-1. H. Doc. 33.6548.

1185. Anderson, Oscar Edward. *Health of a Nation: Harvey W. Wiley and the Fight for Pure Food*. Chicago: University of Chicago Press, 1958. Includes Wiley's scrap with Secretary of Agriculture James Wilson.

1186. ———. "The Pure Food Issue: A Republican Dilemma, 1906-1912," *American Historical Review* 61 (1956):550-73. Crusader Harvey Washington Wiley sought enforcement of the Pure Food Act of 1906 and battled Secretary of Agriculture James Wilson. Wiley resigned and tried to persuade Taft to dismiss men in the administration whom he felt were incapable of handling their jobs.

1187. Dunn, Arthur Wallace, "Dr. Wiley and Pure Food: I," *The World's Work* 22 (Oct. 1911):14958-65. Part II. 23 (Nov. 1911):29-40.

1188. International Opium Commission. "Final Resolutions, February 26, 1909," *American Journal of International Law* 3, *Supplement* (1909):275-76. In several messages to Congress, Taft supported an international drive to get rid of the opium traffic.

1189. Smith, F.F. *The People's Health.* New York: Holmes & Meier, 1979.

1190. U.S. Department of State. *Communication of the Secretary of State Covering the Report of the American Delegation to the International Opium Conference Held at The Hague, from December 1, 1911, to January 23, 1912.* 62d Cong., 2d Sess. Sen. Doc. No. 733, in vol. 39.

1191. Wickersham, George. "Wiley Imbroglio," *The Nation* 93 (July 27, 1917):70.

1192. Wiley, Harvey Washington. *An Autobiography.* Indianapolis: Bobbs-Merrill, 1930. As Chief of the Bureau of Chemistry in the Department of Agriculture under Roosevelt, Wiley had done much of the research upon which Roosevelt based his demand for pure food and drug legislation. For a technical violation of a salary arrangement for an employee, Secretaries Wilson and Wickersham wanted Wiley fired. Trapped but anxious to enforce the pure food law, Taft exonerated Wiley, who had strong popular support. Taft, pp. 249, 258-59, 286, 291, 296.

1193. Wright, Hamilton, "The International Opium Commission (Part I)," *American Journal of International Law* 3 (July 1909):648-74; Part II), ibid. 3 (Oct. 1909):828-68.

18. Railroad Regulation

As president, Taft forced through Congress a law authorizing the Interstate Commerce Commission to make physical evaluations of railroad properties and to fix their tariffs, but he did not specify the method of determining their value.

Monographs

1194. Bernstein, Marver H. *Regulating Business by Independent Regulatory Commissions*. 1955; rept. Westport, Conn: Greenwood Press, 1977.

1195. Cunningham, William J. *American Railroads: Government Control and Reconstruction Policies*. Chicago: A.W. Shaw Co., 1922.

1196. Cushman, Robert E. *The Independent Regulatory Commissions*. 1941; rept. New York: Hippocrene (Octagon), 1972.

1197. Martin, Albro. *Enterprise Denied: Origins of the Decline of American Railroads, 1897-1917*. New York: Columbia University Press, 1971. Martin found that the railroads declined rapidly during Taft's term.

1198. Ripley, William Z. *Railroads: Rates and Regulation*. Rept. of 1915 ed., New York: Ayer, 1981.

Articles

1199. Dunn, Samuel O. "The Interstate Commerce Commission and the Railroads," *Annals* 29 (1907):155-72.

1200. Smalley, Harrison S. "Rate Control Under the Interstate Commerce Acts," *Annals* 29 (1907):292-309.

19. Shipping

1201. Bacon, Edwin M. *Manual of Ship Subsidies . . . of All Nations*. Chicago: McClurg, 1911. A chapter on subsidy legislation is devoted to each country.

1202. Hutchins, John G.B. *The American Maritime Industries and Public Policy, 1789-1914*. Cambridge, Mass.: Harvard University Press, 1941.

1203. McKee, Marguerite Miller, "The Ship Subsidy Question in United States Politics." In Northampton, Mass." *Smith College Studies in History* 8 No. 1, 1922. Entire issue.

1204. Morris, James M. *Our Maritime Heritage: Maritime Developments and Their Impact on American Life*. Washington: University Press of America, 1979.

1205. Renninger, W. Daub. "Government Policy in Aid of American Shipbuilding: A Historical Study of the Legislation Affecting Shipbuilding from Earliest Colonial Times to the Present." Ph.D. diss., University of Pennsylvania, 1911.

1206. "Third International Conference on Maritime Law," *American Journal of International Law* 4, Supplement (Apr. 1910):11525. Much on the subject of safety at sea.

20. Tariff Reform

Bibliographical Guides

1207. Collings, H.T. comp. "Brief Bibliography on Tariff and International Trade," *Annals* 141 (Jan. 1929):265-70.

1208. United States Tariff Commission. *The Tariff: A Bibliography: A Select List of References*. 1934; rept. Westport, Conn.: Greenwood Press, 1976.

Monographs

1209. Baker, Richard C. *The Tariff Under Roosevelt and Taft*. Hastings, Neb.: Democrat Printing Co. 1941. After their victory in 1910, Democrats in Congress would not follow Taft's advice on tariff reform.

1210. Cannon, Joseph Gurney. "Speech . . . Delivered at Kansas City, Missouri . . . November 26, 1909." Washington: GPO, 1909. On the Payne-Aldrich tariff.

1211. Dewey, Davis Rich. *Financial History of the United States*, 11th ed. New York: Longmans, 1931. Includes the tariff history of the United States.

1212. Dunne, Finley Peter. *Mr. Dooley Says*. New York: Charles Scribner's Sons, 1910. Contains a humorous monologue on "The Tariff," pp. 144-47.

1213. Kenkel, Joseph F. *Progressives and Protection: The Search for a Tariff Policy, 1886-1936*. Lanham: Md.: University Press of America, 1983. The failure to obtain "a stable and reasonable tariff policy . . . so as to promote the common good."

1214. Larkin, John Day. *The President's Control over the Tariff*. Cambridge, Mass.: Harvard University Press, 1936.

1215. McCall, Samuel Walker. *The Payne Tariff Law*. Washington: GPO, 1909.

1216. Page, Thomas Walker. *Making the Tariff in the United States*. New York: McGraw-Hill, 1924. A member of both Taft's and Wilson's tariff commissions suggests reforms in the procedure of tariff-making.

1217. Powell, John Harvey, "President Taft and the Payne-Aldrich Tariff," M.A. thesis, Swarthmore College, 1934.

1218. Rhodes, James Ford. *The McKinley and Roosevelt Administrations, 1897-1909*. 1922; rept. Port Washington, N.Y.: Kennikat Press, 1965. Valuable for background information on tariff legislation from 1897 to 1909.

1219. Stanwood, Edward. *A History of the Presidency from 1897 to 1909*. Boston: Houghton Mifflin, 1912. Includes the tariff views of McKinley and Roosevelt.

1220. Tarbell, Ida Minerva. *The Tariff in Our Times: A Study of Fifty Years' Experience with the Doctrines of Protection*. New York: Macmillan, 1911.

1221. Tedesco, Paul H. *Patriotism, Protection and Prosperity: James Moore Swank, The American Iron and Steel Association, and the Tariff, 1873-1913*. New York: Garland, 1985.

1222. U.S. Congress. Conference Committee. 61st Cong., 1st Sess. 1909, on H.R. 1438. *Statement on the Part of the House*. Washington: GPO, n.d. Conference report on the Payne-Aldrich tariff bill.

1223. U.S. Congress. House. Committee on Ways and Means. *Tariff Hearings*, 9 vols. 60th Cong., 1908-1909. Washington: GPO, 1909.

1224. U.S. President. *Address of President Taft at the Lincoln Birthday Banquet of the Republican Club of the City of New York, at the Waldorf-Astoria, Feb. 12, 1910*. Washington: GPO, 1910. Discussion of the Payne-Aldrich tariff bill.

1225. ———. *Annual Message to Congress, December 7, 1909*. Cong. Rec., 61st Cong., 1st Sess. Includes remarks on the maximum and minimum clauses in the Tariff Act of 1909 and on the uses of the new Tariff Board.

1226. ———. *Duties on Cotton. Special Message from the President . . . Returning without Approval H.R. 12812, An Act to Reduce the Duties on Manufactures of Cotton.* Washington: GPO, 1911.

1227. ———. *Articles on the Free List. Special Message from the President . . . Returning without Approval H.R. 4413, An Act to Place on the Free List Agricultural Implements, Cotton Bagging, Cotton Ties, Leather, Boots and Shoes, Fence Wire, Meats, Cereals, Flour, Bread, Timber, Lumber, Sewing Machines, Salt, and other Articles.* Washington: GPO, 1911.

1228. ———. *Duties on Wood. Special Message from the President . . . Returning without Approval H.R. 1109, an Act to Reduce the Duties on Wool and Manufactures of Wool.* Washington: GPO, 1911.

1229. Williams, Benjamin H. *Economic Foreign Policy of the United States.* New York: Howard Fertig, 1929, 1967.

Articles

1230. Bacon, Augustus Octavius. "The Democrats and the Tariff." Dec. 25, 1909. Washington: GPO, 1910. On the attitude of the Democratic Senators toward the current tariff law.

1231. Barfield, Claude E. "'Our Share of the Booty': The Democratic Party, Cannonism, and the Payne-Aldrich Tariff," *Journal of American History* 57 (Sept. 1970):308-23. Shows that many Democrats as well as Republicans favored tariff protection.

1232. Brossard, Edgar Bernard. "United States Tariff and Some of its International Aspects. Address . . . before the Foreign Relations Council, Syracuse, N.Y., Mar. 16, 1929." Typescript. A chairman of the Tariff Board among other things reviewed the work of the board Taft created.

1233. By the Editor [George Harvey]. "President Taft's 'Volte Face,' " *North American Review* 194 (Aug. 1911)177-83. Taft had veered from true Republican tariff policy and "blundered into a quagmire of apostasy" from which he could extract himself only with the greatest difficulty. The reference is the Payne-Aldrich tariff act.

1234. Child, Richard Washburn. "The Making of 'K,' The Wool Schedule," *Everybody's Magazine* 22 (Mar. 1910):338-49. The responsibility therefore rested with Aldrich and other conservatives.

1235. Crumpacker, E.D. "The Truth about the Payne-Aldrich Tariff Law." Speech in the House of Representatives. U.S. Congress, House, *Cong. Rec.* 70th Cong., 1st Sess., 69, pt. 10, pp. 10718-23.

1236. Dick, Reveror J.O. "Canadian Wheat Production and Trade 1896-1930," *Explorations in Economic History* 17 (July 1980):275-302.

1237. Dolliver, Jonathan. "The Downward Revision Hoax," *The Independent* 69 (Sept. 8, 1910):512-17. Excoriated Taft for his tariff policy and persecution of Insurgents.

1238. ———. "The Forward Movement in the Republican Party," *The Outlook* 96 (Sept. 24, 1910):161-72. Another blast at Taft.

1239. "Doubling the Tax on Print," *Literary Digest* 44 (1912):7. Opposition to this tax in the Payne-Aldrich tariff act by all who used newsprint.

1240. "Final Passage of the Tariff Bill," *The Independent* 67 (Aug. 17, 1909):329-30.

1241. Fraser, Herbert F. "Popular Tariff Fallacies," *Annals* 141 (Jan. 1929):53-60. Such as that the foreigner pays the tax.

1242. Gould, Lewis L. "Western Range Senators and the Payne-Aldrich Tariff," *Pacific Northwest Quarterly* 64 (1973):49-56. Western range Senators demanded a tariff on hides in the Payne-Aldrich tariff, thereby exposing an east-west sectionalism in the Republican Party.

1243. "How the Tariff Follows the Flag," *The Outlook* 18 (Aug. 1909):11859. U.S. sugar and tobacco interests sought help at the cost of the Filipinos.

1244. "Mistaken Veto: Wool Bill," *The Nation* 93 (Aug. 24, 1911):158-59.

1245. Myers, W.S. "The Republican Party and the Tariff," *Annals* 141 (Jan. 1929):243-48. The purposes, need for, and responsibility of tariffs.

1246. Post, Charles Johnson. "The Foreigner Pays the Tax," *Everybody's Magazine* 27 (Oct. 1912):459-61. Wrong: Americans paid more for many native products than did foreigners.

1247. "The President and the Duty on Paper," *The Outlook* 100 (Feb. 12, 1912):339-40. On the charge that Taft wanted only tariff reductions that would help the manufacturer at the expense of the farmer.

1248. "The President's Journey of Explanation and Programme-Making," *The World's Work* 19 (Nov. 1909):191-95. Taft must overcome opposition to tariff reform.

1249. "The Real Results of the Tariff Struggle," *The Outlook* 18 (Sept. 1909). Unsatisfactory because the rates were not lowered enough.

1250. Reed, Thomas B. "What Shall We do with the Tariff?" U.S. Cong., House, *Cong. Rec.* 60th Cong., 1st Sess., 42, pt. 2:1616-18. Feb. 5, 1908.

1251. "Republican Revolt against the Aldrich Tariff," *Literary Digest* 38 (May 15, 1909):830-2.

1252. Sanders, A.H. "The National Tariff Commission," *New Breeder's Gazette* 94 (July 1929):12. The vice chairman of President Taft's Tariff Board tells of the part the stockmen of America had in the creation of the tariff board in 1909.

1253. Solvick, Stanley. "William Howard Taft and the Payne-Aldrich Tariff," *Mississippi Valley Historical Review* 50 (Dec. 1963):424-42. Assesses Taft's thinking with respect to tariff reform.

1254. ———. "William Howard Taft and Cannonism," *Wisconsin Magazine of History* 48 (Autumn 1964):48-58. Assesses Taft's thinking with respect to the liberalization of the House Rules.

1255. "Taft on the Tariff," *The Nation* 89 (Sept. 23, 1909):27172.

1256. "Mr.Taft on the Tariff and on the Antitrust Law," *The World's Work* 17 (Feb. 1909):. On lowering the tariff rates and amending the Sherman Law.

1257. "Mr. Taft's Speech," *The Independent* 68 (Feb. 17, 1910):373. That is, at Winona, Minn.

1258. "Taft's Speech at Winona, Minn., Sept. 17, 1909," *New York Tribune*, Sept. 18, 1909. Also published by Washington: GPO, 1909. On Taft's saying that the Payne-Aldrich was "the best tariff bill that the Republican party has ever passed."

1259. "Tariff Revision," *Annals* 120 (1908): entire issue. Essays by experts on various aspects of tariff reform.

1260. Tompkins, D.A. "The Tariff and the Revenue," *South Atlantic Quarterly* 8 (Apr. 1909);143-49. The new tariff being drafted should provide enough revenue to defray governmental expenditures.

1261. "What the New Law Really Is," *Review of Reviews* 40 (Sept. 1909):259.

1262. Wilson, Woodrow. "The Tariff Make-Believe," *North American Review* 190 (Oct. 1909):535-56.

1263. ―――. "Hide-and-Seek Politics," *North American Review* 191 (May 1910):585-610. Both of Wilson's articles excoriate Republican tariff philosophy and the politics Republicans played to preserve protection.

21. Tariff Reciprocity with Canada

Bibliographic Guides

1264. Griffin, Appleton P.C., and H.H.B. Meyer, *List of References on Reciprocity*, 2d ed. Washington: Library of Congress, 1910.

1265. Meyer, Herman H.B., comp. *Additional References Relating to Reciprocity with Canada*. Washington: Library of Congress, 1911.

1266. Robbins, Edwin Clyde, comp. *Selected Articles on Reciprocity*. New York: H. H. Wilson Co., 1912.

1267. United States. Information Service. *A List of Selected Publications and Sources of Information on Canadian-American Relations*. Ottawa: 1966.

1268. United States. Library of Congress. Division of Bibliography. *Select List of References on the Commercial and Treaty Relations of the United States and Canada, with Special Reference to the Great Lakes*. Washington: 1910.

Monographs

1269. Bloomfield, Davis M., and Gerald F. Fitzgerald. *Boundary Waters Problems of Canada and the United States: The International Joint Commission, 1912-1958.* Toronto: Carswell, 1958.

1270. Chacko, Chirakaikaran J. *The International Joint Commission between the United States and the Dominion of Canada.* New York: Columbia University Press, 1932.

1271. Great Britain. Treaties, etc. *Handbook of Commercial Treaties, etc. with Foreign Powers*, 4th ed. London: HMSO, 1931.

1272. Glazebrook, G.P. deT. *A History of Canadian External Relations to 1914*, rev. ed. New York: Oxford University Press, 1950.

1273. Hornbeck, Stanley Kuhl. *"The Most-favored-nation" Clause in Commercial Treaties, Its Function in Theory and Practice and its Relations to Tariff Policies.* Madison: University of Wisconsin Press, 1910.

1274. Knox, P.C. *Reciprocity with Canada. Address before the Chicago Association of Commerce, February 1911.* U.S. Congress, House, 61st Cong., 2d Sess. Washington: GPO, 1911. House Doc. 1418.

1275. Norris, George W. "Criticism of the Proposed Canadian Reciprocity Agreement." Speech in the House of Representatives, February 14, 1911." U.S. Congress, House, *Cong. Rec.* 61st Cong., 3d Sess., 46, pt. 5, pp. 136-39.

1276. Poindexter, Miles. "The Canadian Reciprocity Agreement, although an Ill-made Agreement Is at Least a Beginning, not only of Reciprocity, but of Commerce with all the World." Speech in the House of Representatives, February 14, 1911. U.S. Congress. Senate, *Cong. Rec.*, 61st Cong., 3d Sess. 46, p. 5, pp. 51-52.

1277. Pringle, *Taft*, 2:582-602. No. 248.

1278. Taussig, Frank William. *Free Trade, the Tariff, and Reciprocity.* 1920; rept. Washington: National League of Women Voters, 1931. On the history of the tariff, tariff-making, the effects of a high tariff policy, and who benefits and loses by a tariff.

1279. *Treaties and Agreements Affecting Canada in Force Between His Majesty and the United States of America with Subsidiary Documents, 1914-1925*. Ottawa: 1927.

1280. U.S. Department of State. *Tariff Negotiations between the United States and Foreign Governments. Message from the President of the United States, Transmitting through the Secretary of State and the Secretary of the Treasury, Reports Relative to Recent Tariff Negotiations between the Government of the United States and other Governments, made Necessary by the Tariff Act of 1909.* U.S. Congress, House, 61st Cong., 2d Sess. Washington: GPO, 1910. House Doc. 956.

1281. U.S. President. *U.S. President. Reciprocity: Address . . . at the Banquet of the Marion Club, Indianapolis, Indiana, July 4, 1911, on Republican Reciprocity*. Washington: GPO, 1911.

1282. U.S. Tariff Commission. *Reciprocity with Canada: A Study of the Arrangement of 1911*. Washington: GPO, 1920. Brief but authoritative discussion.

1283. Walker, A.H. *"Reciprocity" of W.H. Taft*. New York: Published privately, 1912. A sharp attack.

1284. Poland, Eleanor, "Reciprocity Negotiations between Canada and the United States, 1866-1911." Radcliffe College. M.A. thesis, 1932.

Articles

1285. Beveridge, Albert J. "A Reciprocity Agreement with Canada Will Be the Beginning of a Policy of Mutual Trade Concessions and Commercial Friendliness." Remarks in the Senate, February 9, 1911. U.S. Congress, Senate, *Cong. Rec.* 61st Cong., 3d Sess., 46, pt. 3, pp. 12181-85.

1286. Jessup, Philip C. "Negotiating Reciprocity Treaties," *American Journal of International Law* 27 (Oct. 1933):738-43.

1287. Johnston, Richard, and Michael B. Percy. "Reciprocity, Imperial Sentiments, and Party Politics in the 1911 Elections," *Canadian Journal of Political Science* 23 (Dec. 1980): 711-29.

1288. Norris speech. No. 1275.

1289. Poindexter speech. No. 1276.

1290. Stanwood, Edward. "Trade Reciprocity with Canada," *Massachusetts History Society Proceedings* 47 (1912):141-78.

1291. Swartz, W.G. "The Proposed Canadian-American Reciprocity Agreement of 1911," *Journal of Economic and Business History* 3 (1930):118-47.

1292. Taussig, Frank W. "Reciprocity with Canada," *Journal of Political Economy* 19 (1911):542-49.

1293. Tiveton, D. Jerome. "Border Farmer and Canadian Reciprocity Issue, 1911-1912," *Agricultural History* 37 (1963): 235-59.

1294. U.S. President. "Address of President Taft at the Joint Session of the Forty-seventh General Assembly of Illinois at Springfield, Feb. 11, 1911, on the Canadian Reciprocity Agreement." U.S. Cong., *Cong. Rec.* 61st Cong., 3d Sess., 46 pt. 5, pp. 146-47.

1295. ———. "Reciprocity with Canada. Message to Congress, Jan. 26, 1911." U.S. Congress. *Cong. Rec.*, 61st Cong., 3d Sess., 46, pt. 2, pp. 1468-70. Sen. Doc. 787.

1296. ———. "Tariff Speech: Address . . . at Winona, Minn., Sept. 17, 1909." Washington: GPO, 1911.

1297. Taft, William H. "Reciprocity with Canada." No. 145.

22. Women's Suffrage

While fourteen states permitted women to vote by 1914, Taft was hostile to the women's suffrage movement, saying that most women were not interested in obtaining suffrage, and if they did, the ballot would be controlled by women of the "less desirable class."

1298. "President Taft on Woman Suffrage," *The Outlook* 94 (Apr. 23, 1910):860-1.

1299. [Editorial.] "President Taft and the Suffragettes," *The Independent* 68 (Apr. 21, 1910):879.

1300. "The President on Woman Suffrage," *Literary Digest* 41 (Apr. 30, 1910):830.

See also titles in 14 D.

J. Foreign Affairs

Bibliographic Guides

1301. Bemis, Samuel Flagg, and Grace Gardner Griffin, eds. *Guide to the Diplomatic History of the Untied States, 1775-1921.* Washington: GPO, 1935, 1963.

1302. Burns, Richard Dean, ed. *Guide to American Foreign Relations Since 1700.* Santa Barbara, Calif.: ABC-Clio, 1983. Reference aids and citations by topics are followed by titles dealing with various countries. Also includes international organization, economic issues, and the armed forces.

1303. Findling, John E. *Dictionary of American Diplomatic History.* Westport, Conn.: Greenwood Press, 1980. 1050 entries from William Jon Abbot to the Zimmermann Telegram, and useful appendixes. Taft, s.v.

1304. Fowler, Wilton B. *American Diplomatic History Since 1890.* Northbrook, Ill.: AHM, 1975. Some 3,000 annotated entries arranged by chronological periods, geographic regions, and topical themes.

1305. Haines, Gerald K., and Samuel J. Walker, eds. *American Foreign Relations: A Historiographical Review.* Westport, Conn.: Greenwood Press, 1981. See Chapter 6: Paolo E. Coletta, "The Diplomacy of Theodore Roosevelt and William Howard Taft."

1306. Plischke, Elmer, ed. *U.S. Foreign Relations: A Guide to Information Sources.* Detroit: Gale, 1980. The emphasis is on the foreign policy process rather than on diplomatic history.

1307. Trask, David F., Michael C. Meyer, and Roger R. Trask, eds. *A Bibliography of United States-Latin American Relations Since 1810.* Lincoln: University of Nebraska Press, 1968. With Supplement by Michael C. Meyer, ed. 1979.

1. General

Monographs

For each country with which the United States had diplomatic relations during Taft's terms, see the volumes for 1909-1913 in *Papers Relating to the Foreign Relations of the United States*, cited as *FRUS*.

1308. Barrileaux, Ryan J. *The President and Foreign Affairs: Evaluation, Performance, and Power.* New York: Praeger, 1985.

1309. Barnes, W., and John H. Morgan. *The Foreign Service of United States.* Washington: GPO, 1961.

1310. Bemis, Samuel Flagg. *The Latin American Policy of the United States.* New York: Harcourt, Brace, 1943.

1311. Collier, Ellen C. *The Power of the President in the Field of Foreign Policy.* Washington: Library of Congress, 1969.

1312. Corwin, Edward S. *The President's Control of Foreign Relations.* Princeton, N.J.: Princeton University Press, 1917.

1313. Griswold, A. Whitney. *The Far Eastern Policies of the United States.* New York: Harcourt Brace, 1938.

1314. Johnson, Loch K. *The Making of International Agreements: Congress Confronts the Executive.* New York: New York University Press, 1984.

1315. Osgood, Robert E. *Ideals and Self-Interest in America's Foreign Relations: The Transformation of the Twentieth Century.* Chicago: University of Chicago Press, 1953.

1316. Paolucci, Henry. *War, Peace, and the Presidency.* New York: McGraw-Hill, 1968.

1317. Perkins, Dexter. *The United States and the Caribbean*, rev. ed. Cambridge, Mass.: Harvard University Press, 1966.

1318. Pratt, Julius W. *Challenge and Rejection: The United States and World Leadership, 1900-1921.* New York: Macmillan, 1967. The chapter on the Taft administration is entitled "The Epigoni," i.e., second rate imitators.

1319. Schulzinger, Robert D. *The Making of the Diplomatic Man: Training, Outlook, and Style in United States Foreign Service Officers, 1908-1931.* Middletown, Conn.: Weslyan University Press, 1975.

Articles

1320. DeNovo, John. "The Enigmatic Alvey A. Adee and American Foreign Relations, 1870-1924," *Prologue* 7 (Summer 1975):69-80. A bachelor who slept at the State Department when necessary, Second Secretary Adee was a master of protocol and provided continuity in the office.

1321. Graebner, Norman A. "Presidential Power and Foreign Affairs." In *Future of the American Presidency.* Ed. by Charles W. Dunn. Morristown, N.J.: General Learning Press, 1975, pp. 179-203.

1322. Livermore, Seward W. "American Naval Base Policy in the Far East, 1850-1914," *Pacific Historical Review* 13 (June 1944):11-35.

2. Taft and Foreign Affairs

1323. Coletta, *Taft*, Chapter 10. No. 231.

1324. "Foreign Policy of the Presidents: Selections from Speeches of the American Presidents," *Current History* 7 (Oct. 1944):265-71, 367-73, 485-89; and (Mar. 1945):39-42, 122-26, 223-28. Taft, s.v.

1325. Mowry, George E. *The Era of Theodore Roosevelt, 1900-1912.* New York: Harper, 1958. The last three chapters.

1326. Pringle, *Taft*, 2:678-715. No. 248.

1327. Scholes, Walter V., and Marie V. Scholes. *The Foreign Policies of the Taft Administration.* Columbia: University of Missouri Press, 1970. Despite the title, this work covers only Latin America and the Far East.

3. The Monroe Doctrine

1328. Hart, Albert Bushnell. *The Monroe Doctrine: An Interpretation.* Boston: Little, Brown, 1916.

1329. LaFeber, Walter, "The Evolution of the Monroe Doctrine from Monroe to Reagan." In Lloyd C. Gardner, ed. *Redefining the Past: Essays in*

Diplomatic History in Honor of William A. Williams. Corvallis: Oregon State University Press, 1986. Exploration of the ways in which the doctrine has been interpreted to justify expanded definitions of "national security."

1330. "Resolution on Reported Purchase of Land at Magdalena Bay, Baja California, by Japanese Government or Company," *CIS*, 62-2. S. Report 996. 6128.

1331. U.S. Congress. Senate. *Memorandum on the Monroe Doctrine*. J. Reuben Clark. 71st Cong., 2d Sess. 1930. Sen. Doc. No. 144. Clark denied that the original doctrine implied that corollaries could be added to it.

1332. Van Alstyne, Richard W. "The Monroe Doctrine." In Alexander DeConde, ed. *Encyclopedia of American Foreign Policy*, 2 vols. New York: Charles Scribner's Sons, 1978. 2:584-96.

4. Dollar Diplomacy, General

1333. Munro, Dana G. *Intervention and Dollar Diplomacy in the Caribbean, 1900-1921*. Princeton, N.J.: Princeton University Press, 1964.

1334. Nearing, Scott, and J. Freeman. *Dollar Diplomacy*. 1925; rept. New York: Arno Press, 1970. A scathing denunciation.

1335. Sands, W.F. *Our Jungle Diplomacy*. Chapel Hill: University of North Carolina Press, 1944. Severe criticisms of Taft's policies.

5. Argentina

1336. Livermore, Seward W. "Battleship Diplomacy in South America," *Journal of Modern History* 16 (Mar. 1944):31-48.

1337. Peterson, Harold R. *Argentina and the United States, 1810-1960*. Albany: State University of New York, 1964.

1338. Whitaker, Arthur P. *The United States and Argentina*. Cambridge, Mass.: Harvard University Press, 1954.

6. Brazil

1339. Hill, Lawrence F. *Diplomatic Relations between the United States and Brazil*. Durham: Duke University Press, 1932.

7. Canada

1340. "Treaty between United States and Great Britain Concerning International Boundary, Passamaquoddy Bay." *CIS* 61-2. H. Doc. 924.

1341. "North Atlantic Fisheries Arbitration. Vol. 01; Final Report, Protocols. Award of Tribunal, and Dissenting Opinion, Case of the United States." *CIS* 61-3. S. Doc. 870. 2529.

1342. Callahan, James M. *American Foreign Policy in Canadian Relations.* New York: Macmillan, 1937.

1343. "The Fisheries Decision," *The Outlook* 96 (Sept. 17, 1910):93-94.

1344. Martin, Lawrence. *The Presidents and the Prime Ministers: Washington and Ottawa Face to Face: The Myth of Bilateral Bliss, 1867-1982.* New York: Doubleday, 1982.

1345. Perkins, Bradford. *The Great Rapprochement: England and the United States, 1895-1914.* No. 405.

1346. Tansill, Charles C. *Canadian-American Relations, 1875-1911.* New Haven: Yale University Press, 1943.

8. China

1347. Cameron, Meribeth. "American Recognition Policy toward the Republic of China, 1912-1913," *Pacific Historical Review* 2 (June 1933):214-30.

1348. Clubb, Oliver E. *Twentieth Century China*, 3d ed. New York: Columbia University Press, 1964.

1349. Clyde, Paul H. *International Rivalries in Manchuria, 1689-1922*, 2d ed. New York: Octagon books, 1928.

1350. Crane, Daniel M., and Thomas A. Breslin. *An Ordinary Relationship: American Opposition to Republican Revolution in China.* Miami: Florida International University Press, 1986. The economic and political relations surrounding the abortive overthrow of the Chinese dynastic pattern in 1911. The authors suggest that there was no great divide between the so-called "dollar" diplomacy of Taft's presidency and the "missionary" diplomacy of Woodrow Wilson.

1351. Fairbank, John K. *The United States and China*, 3d ed. Cambridge, Mass.: Harvard University Press, 1971.

1352. Field, Frederick V. *American Participation in the China Consortium.* Chicago: University of Chicago Press, 1931.

1353. Hart, Robert. *The Eccentric Tradition: American Diplomacy in the Far East*. New York: Charles Scribner's Sons, 1976. The chapter on Taft is entitled "Fools Rush In. . . ."

1354. MacMurray, John V.A., ed. *Treaties and Agreements With and Concerning China, 1894-1912*, 2 vols. New York: Oxford University Press, 1921.

1355. "Propping Up the Open Door in Manchuria," *Literary Digest* 40 (Jan. 22, 1910):131.

1356. Taft, *Present Day Problems*, pp. 45-48. No. 108.

1357. Varg, Paul A. *The Making of a Myth: The United States and China, 1897-1912*. 1968; rept. Westport, Conn.: Greenwood Press, 1979. U.S. sales to China remained small despite Taft's dollar diplomacy in the Far East.

1358. ———. "The Myth of the China Market, 1890-1914," *American Historical Review* 73 (Feb. 1968):742-58. Despite Taft's dollar diplomacy American trade with China did not expand appreciably.

1359. Vevier, Charles C. *The United States and China, 1906-1913*. New Brunswick, N.J.: Rutgers University Press, 1955. Taft had a "shopkeeper mentality."

9. Colombia

1360. Parks, E. Taylor. *Colombia and the United States, 1765-1934*. Durham: Duke University Press, 1935.

1361. Rippy, J. Fred. *The Capitalists and Colombia*. New York: Vanguard Press, 1931.

10. Cuba

1362. Fitzgibbon, Russell H. *Cuba and the United States 1900-1935*. Menasha, Wis.: George Banta Pub. Co., 1935. Taft mentioned *passim*.

1363. Reynolds, Bradley M. "Guantanamo Bay, Cuba: The History of an American Naval Base and Its Relationship to the Formulation of United States Foreign Policy and Military Strategy toward the Caribbean, 1895-1910." Ph.D diss., University of Southern California, 1982.

1364. Smith, Robert F. "Cuba: Laboratory for Dollar Diplomacy, 1898-1917," *Historian* 37 (1968):586-609. In the end, dollar diplomacy produced instability in Cuba.

11. Ecuador

1365. See *FRUS*.

12. Germany

1366. Schieber, Clara Eve. *The Transformation of American Sentiment toward Germany, 1870-1914*. Boston: Cornhill Publishing Co., 1923.

1367. Vagts, Alfred. "Hopes and Fears of an American-German War, 1870-1915," *Political Science Quarterly* 54 (Dec. 1939): 514-35, and 55 (Mar. 1940):53-76.

13. Great Britain

1368. Allen, Harry C. *Great Britain and the United States: A History of Anglo-American Relations*. New York: St. Martin's Press, 1955.

1369. Brinton, Crane. *The United States and Britain*. 1945; rept. Westport, Conn.: Greenwood Press, 1975.

1370. Perkins, Bradford. *The Great Rapprochement: England and the United States, 1895-1914*. No. 405.

14. Honduras

1371. See *FRUS*.

15. Japan

1372. Iriye, Akira. *Pacific Estrangement, 1897-1911*. Cambridge, Mass.: Harvard University Press, 1972.

1373. Neumann, William L. *America Encounters Japan: From Perry to MacArthur*. Baltimore: Johns Hopkins Press, 1963.

1374. Reischauer, Edwin O. *The United States and Japan*, rev. ed. Cambridge, Mass.: Harvard University Press, 1965.

1375. "The New Treaty with Japan," *Literary Digest* 42 (Mar. 1911):394-95.

1376. "Treaty with Japan," *Army and Navy Journal* 48 (Mar. 4, 1912):784.

16. Mexico

1377. Cline, H.F. *The United States and Mexico*, rev. ed. Cambridge, Mass.: Harvard University Press, 1963.

1378. Raat, William D. "The Diplomacy of Suppression: Los Revoltosos, Mexico, and the United States, 1906-1911," *American Historical Review* 56 (Nov. 1976):529-50.

1379. Rippy, J. Fred. *The United States and Mexico*, rev. ed. New York: Knopf, 1931.

17. Near (Middle) East

1380. DeNovo, John. *American Interests and Policies in the Middle East, 1900-1939*. Minneapolis: University of Minnesota Press, 1963.

1381. Bryson, James A. *American Diplomatic Relations with the Middle East, 1784-1975: A Survey*. Metuchen, N.J.: Scarecrow Press, 1977.

1382. ———. *Tars, Turks, and Tankers: The Role of the United States Navy in the Middle East, 1800-1979*. Metuchen, N.J.: Scarecrow Press, 1980.

1383. Speiser, Ephraim A. *The United States and the Near East*, rev. ed. Cambridge, Mass.: Harvard University Press, 1950.

18. Montenegro

1384. Stevenson, Francis Seymour. *A History of Montenegro*, 1913; rept. New York: Arno Press, 1971.

19. Morocco

1385. Collins, George W. "United States-Moroccan Relations, 1904-1912." Ph.D. diss., University of Colorado, 1965.

1386. Gallagher, Charles F. *The United States and North Africa: Morocco, Algeria and Tunisia.* Cambridge, Mass.: Harvard University Press, 1963.

1387. Turner, Edward Raymond. "The Moroccan Crisis of 1911," *South Atlantic Quarterly* 11 (Jan. 1912):22-32. England and Germany almost went to war, but Taft said it was not his problem.

20. Nicaragua

1388. Cox, Isaac J. *Nicaragua and the United States, 1900-1927.* Boston: World Peace Foundation, 1927.

1389. Powell, Anna I. "Relations between the United States and Nicaragua, 1896-1916," *Hispanic American Historical Review* 8 (Feb. 1928):49-52.

1390. U.S. Department of State. *The United States and Nicaragua: A Survey of their Relations from 1909 to 1932.* Latin American Series, No. 6. Washington: 1933.

21. Open Door

1391. Campbell, Charles S., Jr. *Special Business Interests and the Open Door Policy.* New Haven: Yale University Press, 1951.

1392. Croly, Herbert. *Willard Straight.* New York: Macmillan, 1928. As consul in Mukden, Manchuria, and then in charge of the Far Eastern Desk at the State Department, Straight could not entice American bankers to invest in China.

1393. Esthus, Raymond A. "The Changing Concept of the Open Door, 1899-1910," *Mississippi Valley Historical Review* 46 (Dec. 1959):435-54.

1394. Israel, Jerry. *Progressivism and the Open Door: America and China, 1905-1921.* Pittsburgh: University of Pittsburgh Press, 1971. Concludes that Taft, although looked upon as one who could reconcile the "competitors" with the "cooperators," widened rather than closed the rift between them.

1395. Kennan, George F. *American Diplomacy, 1900-1950.* Chicago: University of Chicago Press, 1952. See the chapter on the Open Door.

1396. Moore, John Allphin, Jr. "From Reaction to Multilateral Agreement: The Expansion of America's Open Door Policy in China, 1899-1922," *Prologue* 15 (Spring 1983):23-36.

1397. Munro, Dana G. *Intervention and Dollar Diplomacy in the Caribbean, 1900-1921.* Princeton, N.J.: Princeton University Press, 1964. Covers both Taft's interventions and dollar diplomacy.

1398. Ninkovitch, Frank. "Ideology, the Open Door, and Foreign Policy," The Society for Historians of American Foreign Relations *Newsletter* 8 (1977):2-16.

1399. Varg, Paul A. *Open Door Diplomat: The Life of W. W. Rockhill.* Urbana; University of Illinois Press, 1952. Rockhill passed his ideas about the open door to Secretary of State John Hay, who adopted them as his own.

22. Panama

1400. U.S. Congress. Senate. *Diplomatic History of the Panama Canal.* 63rd Cong., 2d Sess. Sen. Doc. 474. Washington: GPO, 1914.

1401. Goethals, George W., ed. *The Panama Canal: an Engineering Treatise*, 2 vols. New York: McGraw-Hill, 1916.

1402. Keller, Ulrich. *The Building of the Panama Canal in Historic Photographs.* New York: Dover, 1983.

1403. McCullough, David. *The Path Between the Seas: The Creation of the Panama Canal, 1870-1914.* No. 400.

1404. Mack, Gerstle. *The Land Divided.* New York: Alfred A. Knopf, 1944.

23. The Panama Tolls Question

1405. Coker, William S. "The Panama Tolls Controversy," *Journal of American History* 55 (Dec. 1969):555-64.

24. Pan Americanism

1406. Meacham, J.L. *The United States and Inter-American Security, 1889-1960*. Austin: University of Texas Press, 1961.

1407. Whitaker, Arthur P. *The Western Hemisphere Idea*. Ithaca, N.Y.: Cornell University Press, 1954.

25. The Philippines

1408. Bryan, William Jennings. "Ultimate Independence for Filipinos," *The Commoner* 12 (Oct. 1913):4.

1409. ———. "Their Faith Justified," *The Commoner*, 12 (Nov. 1913):2.

1410. Elliott, Charles Burke. *The Philippines to the End of the Military Regime*. Indianapolis: Bobbs-Merrill, 1916.

1411. Grunder, Garel A., and William E. Livezey. *The Philippines and the United States*. Norman: University of Oklahoma Press, 1951.

26. Puerto Rico

1412. Carr, Raymond. *Puerto Rico: A Colonial Experiment*. New York: New York University Press, 1984.

1413. Puerto Rico, Governor. *Annual Report*. Washington: GPO, 1901.

1414. Verrill, Alpheus H. *Puerto Rico Past and Present and San Domingo of Today*. New York: Dodd, Mead, 1914.

27. Russia

1415. Bailey, Thomas A. *America Faces Russia*. Ithaca, N.Y.: Cornell University Press, 1950.

1416. Cohen, Naomi W. "The Abrogation of the Russo-American Treaty of 1832," *Jewish Social Studies* 25 (1963):3-41.

1417. Zabriskie, Edward H. *American-Russian Rivalry in the Far East: A Study in Diplomacy and Power Politics, 1895-1914*. Philadelphia: University of Pennsylvania Press, 1946.

28. San Domingo

1418. Welles, Sumner. *Naboth's Vineyard: The Dominican Republic, 1844-1924*, 2 vols. 1928; rept. New York: Ayer, 1972.

29. Treaties

1419. Butler, Charles H. *The Treaty Making Power of the United States*, 2 vols. New York: The Banks Law Pub. Co., 1902.

1420. Fleming, Denna F. *The Treaty Veto of the American Senate*. New York: G.P. Putnam's Sons, 1910.

1421. Holt, W. Stull, *Treaties Defeated by the Senate*. Baltimore: Johns Hopkins Press, 1933.

1422. Moore, John Bassett. *International Adjudications.* . . . New York: Oxford University Press, 1929.

1423. *United States. Statutes at Large*, 1789. Vol. 8 contains treaties with foreign nations.

1424. *United States Treaties and Other International Agreements*. Washington: GPO. An annual since 1950.

1425. *Unperfected Treaties of the United States of America, 1776-1976*. Dobbs Ferry, N.Y.: Oceana Publications, 6 vols. 1976. Vol. 6 (1984) carries the series to 1925.

1426. Whiteman, Marjorie M. *Digest of International Law*, 11 vols. Washington: GPO, 1963-1969.

30. World Peace

Bibliographic Guide

1427. *Peace Archives: A Guide to the Library Collections of American Peace Organizations and of Leaders in the Public Effort for Peace*. New York: World Without War Council, 1986. Identifies substantial organizational archives in some 30 major repositories and lists over 70 individual collections.

1428. *Arbitration and the United States.* Boston: World Peace Foundation, 1926.

1429. Bacon, Senator Augustus O. "The Senate Amendments to the Arbitration Treaties," *North American Review* 195 (May 1912): 673-86.

1430. Bartlett, Ruhl J. *The League to Enforce Peace.* Chapel Hill: University of North Carolina Press, 1944. Covers Taft's service as president of the League.

1431. Campbell, J.B. "Taft, Roosevelt and the Arbitration Treaties of 1911," *Journal of American History* 53 (Sept. 1966):279-98. Before he became president, international peace was at best a perfunctory concern of Taft. However, while president he tried to make it his crowning success.

1432. Curti, Merle E. *Peace or War: The American Struggle, 1636-1936.* New York: W.W. Norton, 1936.

1433. "The General Arbitration Treaties," *The Outlook* 98 (Aug. 26, 1911):914.

1434. Hugins, Roland, "Armageddon and the Peace Advocates," *South Atlantic Quarterly* 14 (Apr. 1915):116-25. The war has set back the cause of peace; many American pacifists are abandoning neutrality and opting for the Allied side.

1435. Nurnberger, Ralph D. "America's Peace Movement, 1900-1986: 'Bridling the Passions,'" *Wilson Quarterly* 11 (New Year's 1987):96-107.

1436. Patterson, David S. *Toward a Warless World: The Travail of the American Peace Movement, 1887-1914.* Bloomington: University of Indiana Press, 1976.

1437. Pringle, *Taft*, 2:926-50. No. 248.

1438. "The Senators and the Arbitration Treaties," *The Outlook* 100 (Mar. 14, 1912):561-62.

1439. Taft, W.H. *Present Day Problems*, pp. 45-48. No. 108.

1440. ———. *The United States and Peace.* New York: Charles Scribner's Sons, 1914.

1441. ———. *World Peace: A Written Debate between William Howard Taft and William J. Bryan.* 1917; rept. Millwood, N.Y.: Kraus Reprint Co., 1970.

9
Administration Personnel

While President, Taft's relations with Congressmen and administration personnel, for better or worse, included the following:

A. Cabinet Members

BALLINGER, RICHARD A. Secretary of the Interior, 1909-1911.

1442. *DAB*, 1:556-57.

1443. Papers. University of Washington Libraries. Microfilm copy in Manuscript Division, Library of Congress.

1444. Mason, Alpheus Thomas. *Bureaucracy Convicts Itself: The Ballinger-Pinchot Controversy of 1910*. New York: Viking Press, 1941.

1445. Penick, James, Jr. *Progressive Politics and Conservation; The Ballinger-Pinchot Affair*. Chicago: University of Chicago Press, 1968.

1446. Richardson, Elmo R. *The Politics of Conservation: Crusades and Controversies, 1897-1913*. Berkeley: University of California Press, 1962.

DICKINSON, JACOB McGAVOCK. Secretary of War.

1447. *DAB*, 3:198-99.

1448. Papers. Tennessee Archives and Library, Nashville.

1449. Baldwin, E.F. "New Secretary of War," *The Outlook* 92 (May 22, 1909):167-70.

1450. Blewett, Lee. "Jacob McGavock Dickinson, 1851-1928," *Journal of the American Bar Association*, February 1929, pp. 69-71.

1451. Dickinson, Jacob McGavock, "Southerner At Gettysburg," *The Century Magazine* 78 (Aug. 1909):635-36.

1452. Obituary, Jacob McGavock Dickinson, *New York Times*, Dec. 14, 1928, p. 29.

FISHER, WALTER L. Secretary of the Interior, 1913.

1453. Papers. Manuscript Division, Library of Congress.

1454. Gould, Alan Brant. "Secretary of the Interior Walter L. Fisher and the Return to Constructive Conservation: Problems and Policies of the Conservation Movement, 1909-1913." Ph.D. diss., West Virginia University, 1969. Ann Arbor, Mich.: University Microfilms International, 1970.

1455. "New Secretary of the Interior," *The Outlook* 97 (Mar. 18, 1911):567-68.

1456. Sikes, G.C. "New Secretary of the Interior," *The Outlook* 97 (Mar. 25, 1911):633-35.

HITCHCOCK, FRANK HARRIS. Postmaster General.

1457. Papers. Manuscript Division, Library of Congress. There is also some Hitchcock correspondence in the Charles Dewey Hilles Papers, Manuscript and Archives, Yale University.

1458. Smith, S. "Chairman Hitchcock," *Review of Reviews* 38 (Oct. 1908):435-42.

KNOX, PHILANDER CHASE. Secretary of State.

1459. Papers. Manuscript Division, Library of Congress.

1460. Cox, Isaac J. *Nicaragua and the United States, 1907-1927.* Boston: World Peace Foundation, 1927.

1461. Croly, Herbert. *Willard Straight.* No. 1392.

1462. Esthus, Raymond A. "The Changing Concept of the Open Door." No. 1393.

1463. Nearing, Scott, and J. Freeman. *Dollar Diplomacy.* No. 1334.

1464. Sands, W.F. *Our Jungle Diplomacy.* No. 1335.

1465. Scholes, Walter V., and Marie V. Scholes. *The Foreign Policies of the Taft Administration.* No. 1327.

1466. Scholes, Walter V. "Philander C. Knox (1909-1913)." In Norman A. Graebner, ed. *An Uncertain Tradition: American Secretaries of State in the Twentieth Century.* New York: McGraw-Hill, 1961, pp. 59-78.

1467. Wright, Herbert F. "Philander C. Knox." In Bemis, Samuel Flagg, ed. *The American Secretaries of State and Their Diplomacy,* 10 vols. 1928; rept. New York: Pageant Book Co., 1958.

McVEAGH, FRANKLIN. Secretary of the Treasury.

1468. Papers. Manuscript Division, Library of Congress.

1469. Portraits: *Review of Reviews* 49 (Apr. 1909):338 and (July 1909):40; *Current Literature* 46 (Apr. 1909):341; *Harper's Weekly* 53 (Mar. 6, 1909):10; *The Independent* 66 (Mar. 11, 1909):510; *The World's Work* 17 (Apr. 1909):11396.

MEYER, GEORGE VON LENGERKE. Secretary of the Navy.

1470. *DAB*, 6:587-88.

1471. Papers. Manuscript Division, Library of Congress.

1472. "American Navy," *Scientific American* 71 (Feb. 18, 1911):1067.

1473. Coletta, Paolo E. "George von Lengerke Meyer, 6 March 1909-4 March 1913." In Paolo E. Coletta, Robert G. Albion, and K. Jack Bauer, eds. *American Secretaries of the Navy.* No. 811.

1474. DeWolfe, Mark A. *George von Lengerke Meyer: His Life and Public Services.* New York: Dodd, Mead, 1920.

1475. Wiegand, Wayne A. "Patrician in the Progressive Era: A Biography of George von Lengerke Meyer." Ph.D. diss., Southern Illinois University, 1974.

NAGEL, CHARLES. Secretary of Commerce and Labor.

1476. Papers. Yale University Library.

1477. Portraits: *Review of Reviews* 39 (Mar. 1909):272, and 40 (Sept. 1909):267; *Current Literature* 46 (Apr. 1909):344; *Harper's Weekly,* 53

(Mar. 6, 1909):10; *The Independent* 66 (Mar. 11, 1909):511; *The Outlook* 91 (Mar. 27, 1909):70.

STIMSON, HENRY L. Secretary of War.

1478. Papers. Yale University Library.

1479. Morison, Elting, E. *Turmoil and Tradition: A Study of the Life and Times of Henry L. Stimson.* Boston: Houghton Mifflin, 1960.

1480. Stimson, Henry L., and McGeorge Bundy. *On Active Service in Peace and War.* New York: Harper, 1947.

WICKERSHAM, GEORGE W. Attorney General.

1481. Papers. In hands of the estate.

1482. "Address on Interpretation of Sherman Act, by George W. Wickersham." *CIS.* 62-1. S. Doc. 83. 6107.

1483. "Wickersham and His New Job." *Current Literature* 47 (June 1909):615-16.

1484. "Wickersham's Work," *Harper's Weekly* 26 (Mar. 1912):39597.

1485. Portraits: *Review of Reviews* 39 (Mar. 1909):272, and 40 (Apr. 1909):137; *Collier's* 44 (Nov. 13, 1909):17; *Current Literature* 46 (Apr. 1909):339; *Harper's Weekly* 53 (Mar. 6, 1909):10; *The Independent* 66 (Mar. 11, 1909):510; *The Outlook* 91 (Apr. 1909):11399.

WILSON, JAMES. Secretary of Agriculture.

1486. Papers. Some correspondence is in the papers of James R. Mann, William McKinley, Elihu Root, and W.H. Taft. No. 92.

1487. "James Wilson's Sixteen Years of Service," *The Outlook* 102 (Dec. 21, 1912):831-33.

1488. Wilson, James. "Cabinet Record Without Precedent." *The World's Work* 17 (Feb. 1909):11189-90.

1489. Willis, H.P. "Secretary Wilson's Record," *Collier's* 49 (Mar. 23, 1912):10-11, (Mar. 30, 1912):15-16, and (Apr. 6, 1912):10-11.

B. Vice Presidents and Cabinet Members

1490. Healy, Diana Dixon. *America's Vice-Presidents: Our First Forty-three Vice-Presidents and How They Got to Be Number Two*. New York: Atheneum, 1984.

1491. Vexler, Robert. *The Vice Presidents and Cabinet Members: Biographies Arranged Chronologically by Administration*, 2 vols. Dobbs Ferry, N.Y.: Oceana Publications, 1975. James S. Sherman, 2:452-56.

C. Congressmen

ALDRICH, SEN. NELSON W. Rhode Island.

1492. Papers. In custody of Winthrop Aldrich, New York City. A conservative upon whom Taft relied heavily, and who was anathema to the Insurgents. No. 46.

1493. "Address by Nelson W. Aldrich on Work of the National Monetary Commission." *CIS*. 61-2. S. Doc. 406. 5611.

1494. Stephenson, Nathaniel. *Nelson W. Aldrich*, 1930; rept. Port Washington, N.Y.: Kennikat Press, 1971.

BEVERIDGE, SEN. ALBERT J. Indiana.

1495. Papers. Manuscript Division, Library of Congress. No. 750.

1496. Bowers, Claude G. *Beveridge and the Progressive Era*. Boston: Houghton Mifflin, 1932, tells how Beveridge opposed Taft in most instances but supported his quest for a Tariff Commission.

BORAH, SEN. WILLIAM E. Idaho.

1497. Papers. Manuscript Division, Library of Congress. No. 49.

1498. Johnson, Claudius I. *Borah of Idaho*. 1936; rept. Seattle: University of Washington Press, 1967.

1499. McKenna, Mariane C. *Borah*. Ann Arbor: University of Michigan Press, 1961.

1500. Maddox, Robert James. *William E. Borah and American Foreign Policy*. Baton Rouge: Louisiana University Press, 1969. Member of the Republican National Committee 1908-1912; delegate to the Republican National Convention at Chicago in 1912 that nominated Taft; elected to the U.S. Senate in 1903 and to four other terms.

1501. Stoddard, *As I Knew Them*, pp. 524-27. No. 253.

BRISTOW, SEN. JOSEPH. Kansas.

Insurgent opponent of Taft. Instrumental in drafting the charter of the National Republican League.

1502. Papers. Kansas Historical Society. No. 51.

1503. *Biographical Dictionary of the American Congress, 1774-1949*. Washington: GPO, 1950, p. 891.

BURTON, SEN. THEODORE ELIJAH. Ohio.

Served in the House of Representatives from 1891 to 1893 and from 1895 to 1909, when he entered the Senate. Delegate to the Republican National Conventions of 1904, 1908, and 1912. Member of the National Monetary Commission, 1908-1912. A Taft supporter. Some of his correspondence is in the papers of Philippine Bunau-Varilla, Theodore Roosevelt, Henry Cabot Lodge, and John Hay.

1504. Crissey, Forrest. *Theodore E. Burton: American Statesman*. Cleveland: World, 1956.

CANNON, REP. JOSEPH GURNEY. Illinois.

Saved by Taft as Speaker of the House of Representatives until 1910, when his powers were clipped by the Insurgents.

1505. Papers. Illinois State Historical Society. No. 53.

1506. "Tariff Speech of J.G. Cannon, Speaker of the House, Delivered at Kansas City, Mo., November 26, 1909." *CIS*. 61-2. S. Doc. 163. 5657.

1507. Bolles, Blair. *Tyrant from Illinois: Uncle Joe Cannon's Experiment with Personal Power*. New York: W.W. Norton, 1951.

1508. Busbey L. White. *Uncle Joe Cannon: The Story of a Pioneer American*. New York: Henry Holt, 1927.

1509. Stoddard, *As I Knew Them*, pp. 329-31, 357-61. No. 253.

CAPPER, SEN. ARTHUR. Kansas.

Newspaper reporter and then owner of a string of newspapers and magazines that countered Taft's domestic policies because they endangered America's farmers. Delegate to the Republican National Convention of 1908.

1510. Papers. Kansas State Historical Society.

1511. Socolofsky, Homer E. *Arthur Capper: Publisher, Politician, and Philanthropist*. Lawrence: University of Kansas Press, 1962.

CLAPP, SEN. MOSES E. Minnesota.

In office from 1901 to 1917, Clapp was an Insurgent who opposed Taft's domestic policies.

1512. Papers. Minnesota Historical Society. No. 55.

1513. *Biographical Dictionary of the American Congress, 1774-1949*. Washington: GPO, 1950, pp. 978-79.

CLARK, REP. CHAMP (JAMES BEAUCHAMP). Missouri.

Served in the House of Representatives from 1893 to 1895 and again from 1897 until his death in 1921. As Speaker of the House during Taft's last two years he stoutly opposed Taft's domestic reforms. Though named as a Democratic presidential candidate in 1912, in great part because of W.J. Bryan he lost out to Woodrow Wilson.

1514. Papers. In the hands of the estate.

1515. Clark, Champ. *My Quarter Century of American Politics*, 2 vols. New York: Harper, 1921.

1516. Kennon, Donald R., ed. *The Speakers of the House of Representatives: A Bibliography, 1789-1984*. Baltimore: Johns Hopkins University Press., 1986. Forty-six chapters cover every Speaker of the House to date.

CRANE, SEN. WINTHROP MURRAY. Massachusetts.

Member of the Republican National Committee, 1892-1908. Senator 1904-1913. Conservative Taft supporter.

1517. Papers. Boston Public Library; many privately owned.

1518. Johnson, Carolyn W. *Winthrop Murray Crane: A Study in Republican Leadership 1892-1920*. Northampton, Mass.: Smith College, 1967. Taft relied heavily upon Crane's judgment.

1519. Stoddard, *As I Knew Them*, pp. 32, 240, 307, 435, 450, 455. No. 253.

CULLOM, SEN. SHELBY MOORE, Illinois

Served in the Senate from 1883 to 1913. A conservative in outlook, he was the Chairman of the Foreign Relations Committee from 1901 to 1913.

1520. Papers. Chicago Historical Society; Illinois State Historical Society.

CUMMINS, SEN. ALBERT B. Iowa.

An anti-Taft Insurgent. Served from 1908 until his death in 1925.

1521. Papers. Historical and Art Department of Iowa, at Des Moines.

1522. "Address on Payne Tariff Bill by Albert B. Cummins." *CIS*, 61-2. S. Doc. 204. 5657.

DICK, SEN. CHARLES W.F. Ohio.

Served from 1901 to 1911. A Taft supporter.

DOLLIVER, SEN. JONATHAN P. Iowa.

Served from 1901 until his death in 1910. An anti-Taft Insurgent.

1523. Papers. Historical and Art Department of Iowa, at Des Moines. No. 58.

1524. Ross, Thomas Richard. *Jonathan Prentiss Dolliver: A Study in Political Integrity and Independence.* Iowa City: State Historical Society of Iowa, 1958.

1525. Stoddard, *As I Knew Them*, pp. 32, 59, 248, 369. No. 253.

ELKINS, SEN. STEPHEN BENTON, West Virginia.

Served from 1895 until his death in 1911. Important for his part in Taft's railroad regulation battles.

1526. Papers. West Virginia University Library.

1527. Stoddard, *As I Knew Them*, pp. 33, 126, 138, 157, 158, 160, 172, 180. No. 253.

FORAKER, SEN. JOSEPH BENSON. Ohio.

Early Taft supporter and later opponent.

1528. Papers. Historical and Philosophical Society of Ohio, Cincinnnati. No. 60.

1529. Foraker, Joseph B. *Notes of a Busy Life*, 2 vols. Cincinnati: Stewart & Kidd, 1916.

1530. Stoddard, *As I Knew Them*, pp. 32, 154, 264, 329, 330.

1531. Walters, Everett. *Joseph Foraker Benson: An Uncompromising Republican.* Columbus: Ohio History Press, 1948.

FRY, SEN. WILLIAM PIERCE. Maine.

Served as president pro tempore from 1881 until his death in 1911.

1532. Papers. Maine Historical Society, Portland.

GORE, SEN. THOMAS P. Oklahoma.

Though blind, served from 1909 to 1921. Democratic opponent of Taft.

1533. Papers. University of Oklahoma.

1534. Billington, Monroe Lee. "Thomas P. Gore: Oklahoma's Blind Senator." Ph. D. diss., University of Kentucky, 1955.

HALE, SEN. EUGENE. Maine.

Served from 1887 to 1911. Opposed to America's acquisition of empire in 1898 though a Republican, and thereafter opposed any increase in the Navy. A member of Aldrich's National Monetary Commission and a conservative Taft adviser.

1535. Papers. Maine Historical Society, Portland.

1536. Coletta, *Fiske*, No. 789.

1537. Morison, *Sims*. No. 1479.

1538. Meadows, Martin. "Eugene Hale and the American Navy," *American Neptune* 22 (July 1922):187-93.

JOHNSON, SEN. HIRAM. California.

An anti-Taft Insurgent who was one of the founders of the Progressive Republican party and was Theodore Roosevelt's running mate in 1912. Served as Governor of California from 1910 to 1917.

1539. Papers. Bancroft Library, University of California, Berkeley. No. 63.

1540. Fitzpatrick, John James III. "Senator Hiram W. Johnson: A Life History, 1868-1945." Ph.D. diss., University of California, Berkeley, 1975. Ann Arbor, Mich.: University Microfilms International, 1976.

KITCHIN, REP. CLAUDE C. North Carolina.

Served from 1901 until his death in 1923. Spoke especially for the Southern farmer in opposing Taft's tariff and income tax policies.

1541. A microfilm version of his papers at the Southern Historical Collection, University of North Carolina, Chapel Hill, is in the Manuscript Divison, Library of Congress.

1542. Arnett, Alex Mathew. *Claude Kitchin and the Wilson War Policies*. Boston: Little, Brown, 1937.

LA FOLLETTE, SEN. ROBERT MARION. Wisconsin.

As a Representative, served in the Forty-ninth, Fiftieth, and Fifty-first Congresses; delegate at large to the Republican National convention of 1912; reform governor of his State 1900-1906, when elected to the Senate, in which he served until his death in 1925. Helped form the National Republican League and Progressive Republican Party, but lost the presidential nomination of the latter to Theodore Roosevelt in 1912. An anti-Taft Insurgent.

1543. Papers. Manuscript Division, Library of Congress. No. 65.

1544. La Follette, Belle Case, and others. *Belle: The Biography of Belle Case La Follette*. New York: Beaufort Books, 1986. Has much on her father, Sen. Robert M. La Follette. Taft, pp. 90-1, 104, 106-7, 109-10, 112, 116, 118-22, 148.

1545. La Follette, Belle Case, and Fola La Follette. *Robert M. La Follette*, 2 vols. New York: Macmillan, 1953.

1546. La Follette, Robert M. *La Follette's Autobiography: A Personal Narrative of Political Experience*. Madison, Wis.: La Follette Publishing Co., 1913.

1547. Bliven, Bruce. "Robert M. La Follette's Place in Our History," *Current History* 22 (Aug. 1925):716-22.

1548. Cooper, John Milton, Jr. "Robert M. La Follette: Political Prophet," *Wisconsin Magazine of History* 69 (Winter 1985-1986):91-105.

1549. "The Senator for the Ultimate Consumer: How Robert M. La Follette Contended for an Honest Tariff," *Harper's Weekly* 53 (July 24, 1908):7-8.

1550. Stoddard, *As I Knew Them*, pp. 548-51. No. 253.

LODGE, SEN. HENRY CABOT, Massachusetts.

Theodore Roosevelt's Harvard classmate. Served as a Representative in the Forty-ninth, Fiftieth, and Fifty-first Congresses and in the Senate from 1893 until his death in 1924. Delegate to the Republican National Conventions from 1884 to 1924, serving as chairman in 1908. Anti-Taft not only in domestic matters but on general arbitration treaties.

1551. Papers. Massachusetts Historical Society. No. 67.

1552. "Speech on Arbitration Treaties with Great Britain and France by Henry C. Lodge," *CIS*, 62-2. S. Doc. 353. 6175.

1553. Garraty, John A. *Henry Cabot Lodge: A Biography*. New York: Knopf, 1953.

1554. Lodge, Henry Cabot. *Selections from the Correspondence of Theodore Roosevelt and Henry Cabot Lodge, 1885-1918*, 2 vols. Henry C. Lodge, ed. New York: Charles Scribner's Sons, 1925.

1555. Widenor, William C. *Henry Cabot Lodge and the Search for an American Foreign Policy*. Berkeley: University of California Press, 1983.

LONGWORTH, REP. NICHOLAS. Ohio.

Born in Cincinnati and practiced law there before being elected to the State House of Representatives and then to the national House from 1903 to 1913. He was often embarrassed because, while he supported many of Taft's undertakings, his wife was Alice Roosevelt, Theodore's daughter.

1556. Papers, Manuscript Division, Library of Congress.

1557. Chambrun, Clara L. de. *The Making of Nicholas Longworth*. New York: Long and Smith, 1933. TR's son-in-law; supported Taft and was defeated for reelection to Congress in 1912.

1558. Felsenthal, Carol. *Alice Longworth Roosevelt*. New York: G.P. Putnam's Sons, 1988. Much on the hard-drinking, gambling, and girl-chasing Ohioan who married Alice Roosevelt. He eventually matured and became Speaker of the House of Representatives.

1559. Longworth, Alice Roosevelt. *Crowded Hours*. New York: Charles Scribner's Sons, A poorly-written autobiography. Alice's strength was in her sharp tongue, not her pen.

NEWLANDS, SEN. FRANCIS G. Nevada.

A Democrat who served in the House of Representatives from 1893 to 1903 and in the Senate from 1903 until his death in 1917. A spokesman for Western conservationists.

1560. Papers. Yale University Library.

1561. Newlands, Francis G. "Development of the West." Articles by Francis G. Newlands on Irrigation and Dry Farming. *CIS*, 63-2. S. Doc. 588. 6596.

1562. Darling, Arthur Burr, ed. *The Papers of Francis G. Newlands*, 2 vols. Boston: Houghton Mifflin, 1932.

NORRIS, SEN. GEORGE W. Nebraska.

Served in the House of Representatives from 1891 to 1913; elected to the Senate in 1912 and served until 1943. An anti-Taft insurgent.

1563. Papers. Manuscript Division, Library of Congress. No. 75.

1564. Lief, Alfred. *Democracy's Norris: The Biography of Lonely Crusader*. New York: Stackpole, 1939.

1565. Lowitt, Richard. *George W. Norris: The Making of a Progressive, 1861-1912*. Syracuse, N.Y.: Syracuse University Press, 1963.

1566. ———. *George W. Norris: The Persistence of a Progressive, 1913-1933*. Urbana: University of Illinois Press, 1971.

1567. Neuberger, Richard L., and Stephen Kahn. *Integrity: The Life Story of George W. Norris*. New York: Vanguard Press, 1937.

1568. Norris, George W. *Fighting Liberal: The Autobiography of George W. Norris*. New York: Macmillan, 1945.

OWEN, SEN. ROBERT LATHAM. Oklahoma.

Owen was a key figure in currency and banking reform during the Progressive Era.

1569. Papers. Manuscript Division, Library of Congress.

1570. *DAB*, s.v.

1571. Keso, Edward E. "The Senatorial Career of Robert Latham Owen." Ph.D. diss., Georgetown University, 1937.

1572. Owen, Robert L. *The Federal Reserve Act*. New York: The Century Co., 1919.

POINDEXTER, SEN MILES. Washington.

Served as a Representative from 1909 to 1911 and then as a Senator until 1923. An anti-Taft Insurgent.

1573. Papers. University of Washington Libraries; microfilm copy in Manuscript Division, Library of Congress.

1574. Allen, Howard Wilson. "Miles Poindexter: A Political Biography." Ph.D. diss., University of Washington, 1959.

1575. ———. *Poindexter of Washington: A Study in Political Politics.* Carbondale: Southern Illinois University Press, 1981. Poindexter bedeviled Taft while he was in the White House but became a reactionary after 1917.

ROOT, ELIHU. New York.

Served in the Senate from 1909 to 1915. Chairman of the National Republican conventions of 1904 and of 1912, in the latter of which he supported Roosevelt against Taft. Counsel for the North Atlantic Fisheries Arbitration at The Hague, 1910, and member of the Permanent Court of Arbitration at The Hague, 1910. Also president of the Carnegie Endowment for International Peace, 1910-1925.

1576. Papers. Manuscript Division, Library of Congress.

1577. Jessup, Philip. *Elihu Root*, 2 vols. New York: Dodd, Mead, 1938.

1578. Leopold, Richard. *Elihu Root and the Conservative Tradition.* Boston: Little, Brown, 1954.

SHERMAN, JAMES SCHOOLCRAFT. New York.

Served in the House of Representatives from 1887 to 1891 and again from 1893 to 1909, when he became Taft's vice president.

1579. Papers. New York Public Library. No. 80.

1580. *Biographical Dictionary of the American Congress, 1774-1949.* Washington: GPO, 1950, p. 1806.

1581. Vexler, Robert. *The Vice Presidents and Cabinet Members.* . . . 2:452-56. No. 739.

SPOONER, SEN. JOHN COIT. Wisconsin.

Served in the Senate from 1881 to 1907. Declined Taft's offer to be his Secretary of State, and Taft lost a staunch supporter when he retired from the Senate.

1582. Papers. Manuscript Division, Library of Congress. No. 84.

1583. *Biographical Dictionary of the American Congress, 1774-1949.* Washington: GPO, 1950, p. 1849.

UNDERWOOD, SEN. OSCAR WILDER. Alabama.

Elected as a Democrat to the House of Representatives, he served in 1895-1896 and again from 1897 to 1915. As the Democratic floor leader of the House from 1911 to 1915 he staunchly opposed Taft especially on tariff reform. Elected to the Senate in 1914.

1584. Papers. Alabama Department of Archives and History, Montgomery, Alabama.

1585. Underwood, Oscar. *The Drifting Sands of American Party Politics.* New York: The Century Co., 1928.

WARREN, SEN. FRANCIS E. Wyoming.

Elected to the U.S. Senate in 1894, Warren had a close friendship with Taft and opposed Bryan, Theodore Roosevelt, and Woodrow Wilson.

1586. Papers. University of Wyoming, Laramie, Wyoming State Archives, Cheyenne.

1587. Schlup, Leonard. "A Taft Republican: Sen. Francis E. Warren and National Politics," *Annals of Wyoming* 54 (Nov. 1982):62-66.

WATSON, REP. JAMES E. Indiana.

Watson was elected to the House of Representatives in 1895, again from 1899 to 1909, and served in the Senate from 1916 to 1933. A delegate at large to nine Republican national conventions.

1588. *Biographical Dictionary of the American Congress, 1774-1949.* Washington: GPO, 1950, p. 1983.

1589. Owens, John W. "Watson of Indiana," *American Mercury* 2 (May 1924):35-38. Once a trusty lieutenant to Uncle Joe Cannon, in the Senate Watson worked hand in glove with Republican leader Boies Penrose.

Additional information on the careers and papers of federal representatives may be found in the following:

1590. Goehlert, Robert U., and John R. Sayre, comps. *The United States Congress: A Bibliography.* New York: Free Press, 1982.

1591. Jacob, Kathyrn Allamong, and Elizabeth Ann Hernak. *Guide to Research Collections of Former United States Senators, 1789-1982.* Washington: Historical Office, United States Senate, 1983.

1592. Holt, James. *Congressional Insurgents and the Party System, 1909-1916.* Cambridge, Mass.: Harvard University Press, 1967. Holt analyzes the Congressional Republicans opposed to Taft and concludes that the Insurgents were alienated alike by Taft's conservatism and Roosevelt's third-party strategy.

1593. Wilensky, Norman M. *Conservatives in the Progressive Era: The Taft Republicans of 1912.* Gainesville: University of Florida Press, 1965. Largely deals with this breed in the Republican national convention of 1912.

1594. Of special note, because it contains an analysis that has done much to restore Theodore Roosevelt's historical reputation, is John Morton Blum, *The Republican Roosevelt.* Cambridge, Mass.: Harvard University Press, 1954.

D. Military Leaders

AINSWORTH, FRED CLAYTON, Adjutant General of the Army.

Starting as an Assistant Surgeon the Army in 1874, in 1886 Ainsworth began an administrative and bureaucratic career that lasted over a quarter of a century. Among other things he saw to the completion of the 128-volume *Official Records of the War of the Rebellion.* As the Adjutant General of the Army after 1907, occasionally Acting Secretary, and a major general, he expected to become the Chief of Staff. However, that billet went to another physician, Leonard Wood. Differences with Wood would have led to a court martial had Taft not permitted Ainsworth to retire.

Administration Personnel 161

1595. Deutrich, Mabel E. *Struggle for Supremacy: The Career of General Fred C. Ainsworth.* Washington: Public Affairs Press, 1962.

1596. Ranson, Edward. "Ainsworth, Fred Clayton." In Roger J. Spiller, Ed., and Joseph G. Dawson III, Assoc. ed., *Dictionary of American Military Biography*, 3 vols. Westport, Conn.: Greenwood Press, 1984, 1:8-12.

BUTT, ARCHIBALD WILLINGHAM, Military Aide to the presidents Roosevelt and Taft.

1597. Butt, Archibald Willingham. *Taft and Roosevelt: The Intimate Lletters of Archie Butt, Military Aide*, No. 230.

1598. "Portrait" [Archibald Butt.] *Harper's Weekly* 56 (Apr. 20, 1912):29, and *Literary Digest* 44 (Apr. 27, 1912):966. These articles were inspired by Butt's tragic death in the sinking of the *Titanic*.

WOOD, MAJ. GEN LEONARD, Chief of Staff of the Army.

1599. Papers. Manuscript Division, Library of Congress. No. 93.

1600. Hagedorn, Hermann. *Leonard Wood: A Biography*, 2 vols. New York: Harper, 1931.

1601. Lane, Jack C. *Armed Progressive: Leonard Wood.* San Rafael, Calif.: Presidio Press, 1978.

1602. ———. "Leonard Wood." In Roger Spiller, Ed., and Joseph G. Dawson III, Assoc. ed. *Dictionary of American Military Biography.* 3 vols. Westport, Conn.: Greenwood Press, 1984, 3:1209-12.

1603. Nelson, Maj. Gen. Otto L., Jr. *National Security and the General Staff.* Washington: Infantry Journal Press, 1915.

E. Naval Officers

DEWEY, GEORGE. Admiral.

A graduate of the Academy Class of 1858, Dewey served as the executive officer of a steam frigate under David G. Farragut during the Civil War, including operations against New Orleans and Fort Fisher. From 1866 to 1872 he served under Admiral David D. Porter, Superintendent of the Naval

Academy. Bureaucratic billets ensued until at the prodding of Assistant Secretary of the Navy Theodore Roosevelt he obtained the Asiatic command. Most of his renown followed his victory over the Spanish Fleet in the Battle of Manila Bay, May 1, 1898. Beginning in 1900, he served as President of the General Board of the Navy, responsible for advising the Secretary of the Navy and other administration officials about naval matters. Although not a reformer, he insured that only the brightest officers served in the General Board.

1604. Dewey, George. *The Autobiography of George Dewey, Admiral of the Navy*. New York: Charles Scribner's Sons. 1916. Mostly ghost-written by the journalist Frederick Palmer.

1605. Spector, Ronald. *Admiral of the New Navy: The Life and Career of George Dewey*. Baton Rouge: Louisiana State University Press, 1974.

1606. Braisted, William R. "Dewey, George." In Roger J. Spiller, Ed., and Joseph W. Dawson III, Assoc. Ed. *Dictionary of American Military Biography*, 3 vols. Westport, Conn.: Greenwood Press, 1984, 1:260-03.

FISKE, BRADLEY A., Rear Admiral.

A graduate of the Academy Class of 1874, Fiske was the greatest naval inventor of his generation. He also commanded cruisers, monitors, and battleship divisions. In addition he was one of the insurgents who demanded reforms not only in gunnery and in optical and electrical instruments but also in naval general staff and national administrative policy for the Navy. He served with the General Board, 1910-1911, wherein he brought war plans up to date. He was also the first rear admiral to fly in an aircraft, in 1912. After serving as Aide for Inspections to Secretary of the Navy Meyer, he became his Aide for Operations, the prime professional post in the Navy. He got nowhere in requesting that ships of the Asiatic squadron concentrate in the Philippines during a war scare with Japan in 1911 and that the battleships on gunboat duty off Mexico's coasts be returned home because they were physically deteriorating in warm water, and the morale of their personnel was decreasing. He was instrumental in the creation of the Office of Chief of Naval Operations.

1607. Coletta, Paolo E. *Admiral Bradley A. Fiske and the American Navy*. Lawrence: University of Kansas Press, 1979.

1608. ———. "Bradley Allen Fiske." In Roger J. Spiller, Ed., and Joseph J. Dawon, Assoc. ed. *Dictionary of American Military Biography*, 3 vols. Westport, Conn.: Greenwood Press, 1984, 1:322-25.

1609. Fiske, Bradley A. *From Midshipman to Rear Admiral.* New York: The Century Co., 1919.

LUCE, STEPHEN B. Admiral.

Appointed by President Martin Van Buren as a midshipman in 1841, Luce saw service at sea before entering the Naval Academy, from which he graduated in 1849. Ship commands and a tour at the Naval Academy followed until the Civil War began and he saw action with the Southern Blockading Squadron. Moreover, he dreamed of a naval war college that would enable officers to obtain a graduate program in national policy and international affairs. His dream came true in 1884, and he served as its first president. Thereafter he wrote extensively on naval education and on the need of reorganizing the Navy Department in order to make it more efficient. Especially in the latter field he greatly influenced such rising officers as Fiske, Mahan, and Sims.

1610. Gleaves, Albert. *Life and Letters of Stephen B. Luce: Rear Admiral, U.S.N., Founder of the Naval War College.* New York: G.P. Putnam's Sons, 1925.

1611. Spector, Ronald. *Professors of War: The Naval War College and the Development of the Naval Profession.* Newport, R. I.: Naval War College Press, 1977.

1612. Hattendorf, John B., "Luce, Stephen Bleeker." In Roger J. Spiller, Ed., and Joseph J. Dawson III, Assoc. ed., *Dictionary of American Military Biography.* 3 vols. Westport, Conn.: Greenwood Press, 1984, 2:668-70.

1613. ———., and John D. Hayes, eds. *The Writings of Stephen B. Luce.* Newport, R.I.: Naval War College Press, 1975.

SIMS, WILLIAM SOWDEN. Admiral.

Of the Academy Class of 1880, Sims served at sea until 1888, when he was authorized to spend a year learning French in Paris. He served well as an intelligence officer and ship commander in the Far East for several years. By nature critical and willing to beard his superiors in order to improve the Navy, he risked his career by writing directly to President Roosevelt about deficiencies in the newest battleships. Roosevelt upheld him, with the result that follow-on construction improved. With Fiske, William F. Fullam, Albert L. Key, Homer Poundstone, and others, he led an insurgent group in demanding improvements not only in construction but in fire control equipment and naval organization. While commanding a battleship in 1910, at London's Guildhall he made a speech in which he promised Britain support if she went to war with Germany. The result was a letter of reprimand from President Taft. During the last days of Taft's terms Sims determined doctrine for the operations of the Atlantic destroyer flotilla.

1614. Papers. Manuscript Division, Library of Congress. No. 82.

1615. Dorwart, Jeffery M. *The Office of Naval Intelligence: The Birth of America's First Intelligence Agency, 1865-1918*. Annapolis, Md.: Naval Institute Press, 1979.

1616. ———. "Sims, William Sowden." In Spiller, Roger J., Ed., and Joseph G. Dawson III, Assoc. Ed., *Dictionary of American Military Biography*, 3 vols. Westport, Conn.: Greenwood Press, 1984, 3:1003-06.

1617. Morison, Elting E. *Admiral Sims and the Modern American Navy*. Boston: Houghton Mifflin, 1942.

F. State Department and Foreign Service

Leading Personnel

BACON, ROBERT.

Bacon had been the Assistant Secretary of State, member of the firm of J.P. Morgan, and Overseer at Harvard University.

1618. "The New Ambassador to France," *The Outlook* 17 (Aug. 1909):1861.

1619. Scott, James Brown. *Robert Bacon: Life and Labor*. 1923, rept. N.Y. Arno Press, 1975. After operating in Wall Street's security markets, Bacon moved to Washington and helped Taft particularly with Cuban affairs.

CRANE, CHARLES R.

1620. Johnson, Charles. "A New Guardian for the Open Door," *Harper's Weekly* 53 (Aug. 14, 1909):15. Taft's Minister to China.

DAWSON, THOMAS C.

1621. Minister to Panama and Taft's special envoy to settle the Honduran debt question and the Nicaraguan civil war.

HERRICK, MYRON T.

1622. Mott, Thomas Bentley. *Myron T. Herrick, the Friend of France: An Autobiographical Biography.* Garden City, N.Y.: Doubleday, Doran, 1930. Material on Herrick's terms as governor of Ohio, 1904-1906, and his ambassadorship to France.

1623. Shriver, Phillip R., ed. "William Howard Taft and Myron T. Herrick: Selected Letters, 1912-1919," *Bulletin Historical and Philosophical Society of Ohio* 14 (Oct. 1956):221-22. Herrick was a former governor of Ohio and supporter of Taft whom Taft named as Ambassador to France.

KNOX, PHILANDER C.

1624. *DAB*, s.v.

1625. Papers. Manuscript Division, Library of Congress.

1626. Baldwin, E.F. "Public Career," *The Outlook* 91 (Mar. 27, 1909):691-93.

1627. Clark, Walter. "How Mr. Knox Became Secretary of State," *The World's Work* 17 (Apr. 1909):11433-35. Because of his services to the Roosevelt administration, his personality, and Taft's personal choice.

1628. "Coming Secretary of State," *Current Literature* 46 (Feb. 1909):146-47.

1629. Hale, W.M. "With the Knox Mission to Central America," *The World's Work* 24 (June 1912):179-93, and (July 1912):323-36.

1630. Lowry, E.G. "Able Citizen," *Putnam's Magazine* 6 (Aug. 1909):526-38.

1631. Phillips, David Graham. "Creature of Almighty Aldrich," *Cosmopolitan Magazine* 41 (Aug. 1906):374-77.

REINSCH, PAUL S. Minister to China.

1632. Pugach, Noel H. *Paul S. Reinsch: Open Door Diplomat in Action.* Millwood, N.Y.: KTO Press, 1977.

WILSON, FRANCIS M. HUNTINGTON. First Assistant Secretary of State.

In his post, Wilson aided Secretary Knox to reorganize the department along "desk" lines, heartily supported Dollar Diplomacy in Latin America and China, but displeased Taft by urging him to intervene in Mexico's civil war.

1633. Papers. Ursinus College, Collegeville, Pa.

1634. Wilson, Francis M. Huntington. *Memoirs of an Ex-Diplomat.* Boston: B. Humphries, 1945.

WEITZEL, GEORGE. Minister to Nicaragua.

Weitzel drafted the Weitzel-Chamorro Treaty which contained protectorate features. Taft submitted the treaty to the Senate on Feb. 24, 1913, but it was not approved before he left office.

Some Foreign Representatives

BERNSTORFF, COUNT JOHANN VON. German Ambassador.

1635. Bernstorff, Count Johann von. *My Three Years in America.* New York: Charles Scribner's Sons, 1920.

1636. Tinneman, Sister Ethel Mary. S.N.J.M. "Count Johann von Bernstorff and German-American Relations, 1908-1917." Ph.D. diss., University of California, Berkeley, 1960.

1637. "The Arrival of the New German Ambassador," *Harper's Weekly* 53 (Jan. 9, 1909):21.

RICE, SIR CECIL SPRING. British Ambassador.

1638. *The Letters and Friendships of Sir Cecil Spring Rice*, 2 vols. Stephen Gwynn, ed. London: Constable, 1929.

VILALOBAR, MARQUIS DE. Spanish Minister.

1639. "Our New Minister from Spain: Marquis de Vilalobar," *Harper's Weekly* 53 (Aug. 21, 1090):31.

Monographs

1640. Barnes, William, and John Heath Morgan. *The Foreign Service of the United States: Origins, Development, and Functions.* Washington: Department of State, 1961. Includes the establishment of the State Department "desks" during Taft's presidential term.

1641. Challener, Richard D. *Admirals, Generals, and American Foreign Policy 1898-1914.* Princeton, N.J.: Princeton University Press, 1973. Shows that in most cases high military personnel had little effect in influencing the making of foreign policy.

1642. Cox, Isaac Joslin. *Nicaragua and the United States, 1909-1927.* Boston: World Peace Foundation, 1927. Includes Taft's use of the Marine Corps in Nicaragua.

1643. Grew, Joseph C. *Turbulent Era: A Diplomatic Record of Forty Years, 1904-1945*, 2 vols. Walter Johnson, ed. Boston: Houghton Mifflin, 1952.

1644. Langley, Lester D. *The Banana Wars: An Inner History of the American Empire, 1900-1934.* Lexington: University Press of Kentucky, 1983. Much on Taft's use of the Marine Corps and Navy in dealing with Caribbean and Central American nations.

1645. Munro, Dana Gardner. *Intervention and Dollar Diplomacy in the Caribbean, 1900-1921.* No. 367. A classic account.

1646. United States. Department of State. *Papers Relating to the Foreign Relations of the United States.* Washington: Department of State, 1909-1913.

1647. Vevier, Charles. *The United States and China, 1906-1913.* New Brunswick, N.J.: Rutgers University Press, 1955. In pushing dollar diplomacy in China, Taft revealed a "shopkeeper" mentality.

Articles

1648. Hyde, Henry M. "Dollar Diplomacy: Uncle Sam, Wall Street and Co., Open a Spanish-American Branch," *Everybody's Magazine* 25 (Dec. 1911):756-65. Under Knox, the State Department has started out on the road as an international bond salesman.

1649. "Propping Up the Open Door in China," *Literary Digest* 40 (Jan. 22, 1910):131.

G. Supreme Court Justices

BRANDEIS, LOUIS DENBITZ

1650. Papers. University of Louisville. No. 50.

1651. McGraw, Thomas K. "Louis D. Brandeis," *American Scholar* 54 (Autumn 1985):525-36. In a reevaluation, Brandeis seems to have misunderstood the forces underlying the rights of big business and advocated economic policies that reduced consumer welfare.

1652. Murphy, Bruce Allen. *The Brandeis-Frankfurter Connection: The Secret Political Activities of Two Supreme Court Justices.* New York: Oxford University Press, 1982.

FRANKFURTER, FELIX

1653. Papers. Manuscript Division, Library of Congress.

1654. *DAB*, s.v.

1655. Hirsch. H.N., *The Enigma of Felix Frankfurter.* New York: Basic Books, 1981. A psychological analysis of one of the most influential jurists of the twentieth century.

1656. Stevens. Richard G. *Frankfurter and Due Process.* Lanham, Md.: University Press of America, 1987. An examination of the relation betwen the due process clause of the fourteenth Amendment and the Bill of Rights. Frankfurter held the application within narrow bounds.

FULLER, MELVILLE WESTON.

A strong Democrat, Fuller was appointed to the Supreme Court by President Cleveland and served from 1888 until his death in 1910.

1657. *DAB*, s.v.

1658. Papers. Manuscript Division, Library of Congress.

1659. King, Willard Leroy. *Melville Weston Fuller, Chief Justice of the United States, 1888-1910.* New York: Macmillan, 1950.

HARLAN, JOHN MARSHALL.

1660. *DAB*, s.v.

1661. Papers. Manuscript Division, Library of Congress; University of Louisville.

1662. Lewin, Nathan. "Justice Harlan: The Full Measure of the Man," *American Bar Association Journal* 58 (June 1972): 579-83.

HOLMES, OLIVER WENDELL.

1663. *DAB*, s.v.

1664. Papers, Manuscript Division, Library of Congress; Supreme Court.

1665. Auchinloss, Louis. "Mr. Justice Holmes: His Long Life and Broad Mind," *American Heritage* 29 (June 1978):68-77.

1666. Bowen, Catherine E. *Yankee from Olympus: Mr. Justice Holmes and the Supreme Court.* Boston: Little, Brown, 1944.

1667. Garraty, John A., "Holmes's Appointment to the United States Supreme Court," *New England Quarterly* 22 (Sept. 1949):292-94.

1668. Konefsky, Samuel Joseph. *The Legacy of Holmes and Brandeis: A Study in the Influence of Ideas.* New York: Macmillan, 1956.

1669. Lerner, Max. *The Mind and Faith of Justice Holmes.* Boston: Little, Brown, 1943.

HUGHES, CHARLES EVANS.

1670. *DAB*, s.v

1671. Papers, Manuscript Division, Library of Congress. No. 62.

1672. Pusey, Merle J. *Charles Evans Hughes*, 2 vols. New York: Macmillan, 1951. A full-scale biography written with literary flair.

1673. Gossett, William T. "The Human Side of Chief Justice Hughes," *American Bar Association Journal* 59 (Dec. 1973):1413-19.

1674. Hyde, Charles Cheney. "Charles Evans Hughes as a Judge of the Permanent Court [of International Justice]," *American Journal of International Law* 22 (Oct. 1928):822-23.

1675. Stoddard, *As I Knew Them*. No. 253.

LAMAR, JOSEPH RUCKER.

1676. *DAB*, s.v.

1677. Papers. Manuscript Division, Library of Congress.

1678. Dinnerstein, Leonard. "Joseph Rucker Lamar." In Friedman and Israel eds. *The Justices of the United States Supreme Court*, 3:1873-2000. No. 1962.

1679. Lamar, Clarinda Pendleton. *The Life of Jos. Rucker Lamar*. New York: G.P. Putnam's Sons, 1926.

LURTON, HORACE HARMON.

1680. *DAB*, s.v.

1681. Papers. Manuscript Division, Library of Congress.

1682. Tucker, David M. "Justice Horace H. Lurton," *American Journal of Legal History*, July 1969, pp. 226-30.

1683. Watts, James F., Jr. "Horace Harmon Lurton." In Friedman and Israel, eds. *The Justices of the United States Supreme Court*, 3:1973-2001. No. 1962.

PECKHAM, RUFUS WHEELER.

1684. *DAB*, s.v.

1685. Papers. None.

1686. "Proceedings on the Death of Mr. Justice Peckham" 219 *U.S. Reports*, v-xiii.

1687. Skolnik, Richard. "Rufus Peckham." In Friedman and Israel, eds. *The Justices of the United States Supreme Court*, 3:1685-1818. No. 1962.

PITNEY, MAHLON.

1688. *DAB*, s.v.

1689. Papers, Destroyed.

1690. Israel, Fred. "Mahlon Pitney." In Friedman and Israel, eds. *The Justices of the United States Supreme Court*, 2:2001-22. No. 1962.

1691. Walker, E.R. "In Memoriam: Mahlon Pitney," *American Bar Association Journal* 11 (May 1925):322.

VAN DEVANTER, WILLIS.

Van Devanter graduated from the Cincinnati Law School in 1881; was Chief Justice of the Supreme Court of Wyoming, 1889-1890; chairman of the Republican National Committee, 1896-1900; U.S. Circuit Judge, 8th Judicial District, 1903-1910; and then served on the Supreme Court from 1910 until his death in 1937.

1692. *DAB*, s.v.

1693. Papers. Manuscript Division, Library of Congress.

1694. Burner, David. "Willis Van Devanter." In Friedman and Israel, eds. *The Justices of the United States Supreme Court*, 3:1945-72. No. 1962.

1695. *Who Was Who in America*. Chicago: Marquis Who's Who, 1943, 1:122-69.

WHITE, EDWARD DOUGLASS.

1696. *DAB*, s.v.

1697. Papers. Destroyed by his own instructions.

1698. Forman, William H., Jr. "Chief Justice Edward Douglass White," *American Bar Association Journal* 56 (Mar. 1970):260-62.

1699. Klinkhamer, Marie C. *Edward Douglass White: Chief Justice of the United States*. Washington: Catholic University of America Press, 1943.

1700. Watts, James F., Jr. "Edward Douglass White." In Friedman and Israel, eds. *The Justices of the United States Supreme Court*, 3:1633-84. No. 1962.

10
Elections of 1910

Congressional Insurgents opposed Taft because of his working with conservative Sen. Nelson A. Aldrich and House Speaker Joseph B. Cannon, his denial of patronage to them, his approval of the Payne-Aldrich tariff, and his deviation from Roosevelt's policies in general. If Roosevelt kept quiet about Taft's performance upon his return from a year abroad, after a year of Taft in the White House he and the Insurgents declared open war. Believing that Taft's bungling leadership had split their party and forecast Democratic victories in the elections of 1910, Roosevelt sought to mend the rift. After failing to do so, he offered his radical and progressive New Nationalism program. Taft thereupon decided to fight not only him but the Insurgents as well in the primary battles of the spring of 1910. He lost the fight then and in the fall elections as well.

Monographs

1701. Allen, Howard W. *Poindexter of Washington*. No. 864.

1702. Baker, Ray S., ed. *Woodrow Wilson: Life and Letters*, 8 vols. Garden City, N.Y.: Doubleday, Page, and Doubleday, Doran, 1927-1939. Vol. 3.

1703. Blum, John M. *The Republican Roosevelt*. No. 1594.

1704. Butt, Archibald Willingham. *Taft and Roosevelt: The Intimate Letters of Archie Butt, Military Aide*. No. 95.

1705. Clark, Champ. *My Quarter Century of American Politics*. No. 1515.

1706. Coletta, Paolo E. *William Jennings Bryan: Progressive Politician and Moral Statesman, 1909-1915*. Lincoln: University of Nebraska Press, 1969.

1707. ———. *Taft*, Chapter 5. No. 231.

1708. Ewing, Cortez, A.M. *Congressional Elections, 1896-1944: The Sectional Basis of Political Democracy in the House of Representatives*. Norman: University of Oklahoma Press, 1947. Sectional basis of political democracy.

1709. Ginger, Ray. *The Bending Cross: A Biography of Eugene Victor Debs.* New Brunswick, N.J.: Rutgers University Press, 1949.

1710. Harbaugh, *Roosevelt.* No. 443.

1711. Hechler, Kenneth. *Insurgency: Personalities and Politics of the Taft Era.* New York: Columbia University Press, 1940. Provides excellent insights into Insurgent personalities and policies.

1712. La Follette, Belle Case, and Fola La Follette. *Robert M. La Follette.* No. 1545.

1713. La Follette, Robert M. *La Follette's Autobiography.* No. 1546.

1714. Lief, Alfred. *Democracy's Norris: The Biography of a Lonely Crusader.* New York: Stackpole, 1939.

1715. Link, Arthur S. *Woodrow Wilson: The Road to the White House.* Princeton, N.J.: Princeton University Press, 1947.

1716. ———. *Woodrow Wilson and the Progressive Era, 1910-1917.* New York: Harper, 1954.

1717. Lodge, Henry Cabot, ed. *Selections from the Correspondence of Theodore Roosevelt and Henry Cabot Lodge.* No. 98.

1718. Lowitt, Richard. *George Norris: The Making of a Progressive.* No. 1565.

1719. Mowry, George. *Theodore Roosevelt and the Progressive Movement.* Madison: University of Wisconsin Press, 1946.

1720. ———. *The Era of Theodore Roosevelt, 1900-1912.* New York: Harper and Brothers, 1958. See especially chapters 12-14.

1721. Neuberger, Richard L., and Stephen B. Kahn. *Integrity: The Life of George Norris.* New York: Vanguard Press, 1937.

1722. Nye, Russel B. *Midwestern Progressive Politics: A Historical Study of its Origins and Development, 1870-1950.* East Lansing: Michigan State University Press, 1959.

1723. Pringle, *Taft*, 2:557-81. No. 248.

1724. Roosevelt, Theodore. *New Nationalism*. 1910; rept. Gloucester, Mass.: P. Smith, 1971.

1725. Ross, Thomas Richard. *Jonathan Prentiss Dolliver: A Study in Political Integrity and Independence*. Iowa City: State Historical Society of Iowa, 1958. Life of a prominent Insurgent.

1726. White, William Allen. *The Autobiography of William Allen White*. New York: Macmillan, 1946.

1727. ———. *Selected Letters of William Allen White*. Walter Johnson, ed. New York: Henry Holt, 1947.

Articles

1728. "Advance of the Insurgents," *Literary Digest* 41 (Oct. 15, 1910):629-30. Washington, Oregon, Maine, and Vermont preferred Insurgents or Democrats to Taft men.

1729. Anderson, Elaine S. "The Ohio Election of 1910: Harding and the Republicans." *Northwest Ohio Quarterly* 38 (1966):15-32. Harding's career before 1910 and the political situation in Ohio during the first decade of the 20th century.

1730. "An Itinerant President," *The World's Work* 18 (June 1909):11635. Taft pleases the public but is criticized for electioneering and spending government funds.

1731 "Are the Insurgents Traitors?" *Literary Digest* 41 (Apr. 23, 1910):792-93. If he could not find good Republicans to fill offices, Taft would fill them with Democrats.

1732. Coulter, E. M. "The Attempts of William Howard Taft to Break the Solid South," *Georgia Historical Review* 19 (1935):134-44.

1733. "Dolliver's Defense of Insurgency," *Literary Digest* 41 (June 25, 1910):1248. Taft had asked for the support of all Republicans. Dolliver wondered why he should exile those who sought the same objectives.

1734. Hale, William Bayard. "The Speaker [Cannon] or the People?" *The World's Work* 19 (Apr. 1910):12805-12.

1735. ———. "President at Work," *The World's Work* 20 (June 1910):13005-18.

1736. "How the People Regard the President," *The World's Work* 17 (April 1909):12662-64. The failure of Congress to support the President.

1737. "Insurgent Victories in the West," *The Independent* 69 (Aug. 11, 1910):272-74. Indiana, Michigan, Wisconsin, Iowa, and Kansas supported Insurgents rather than Taft men.

1738. Leupp, Francis E. "Taft and Roosevelt: A Composite Study," *Atlantic Monthly* 106 (Nov. 1910):648-53. Gives a favorable of view of Taft.

1739. ———. "President Taft's Own View: An Authorized Interview by Francis E. Leupp," *The Outlook* 99 (Dec. 2, 1911): 811-18. A fairly favorable view.

1740. "Little Journeys to Oyster Bay," *Literary Digest* 41 (July 23, 1910):117-19. Taft will not fight Roosevelt for the presidential nomination in 1912 unless he absolutely has to do so.

1741. MacAdam, Hastings. "The Insurgents," *Everybody's Magazine* 26 (June 1912):770-81. Taft's failure to unhorse Cannon and his closeness to Aldrich brought opposition from at least Beveridge, Bourne, Clapp, Cummins, Dolliver, Gronna, La Follette, Murdock, Knute Nelson, and Works.

1742. "Meaning of the Republican Waterloo," *Literary Digest* 41 (Nov. 19, 1910):915-17. The election might make the Democrats more conservative and the Republicans more progressive. But how would Taft get along with a more progressive party?

1743. Mowry, George E. "Theodore Roosevelt and the Election of 1910," *Mississippi Valley Historical Review* 25 (Mar. 1939):523-34. An excellent summary of the Insurgent-conservative battle.

1744. "The President and the People," *The World's Work* 19 (Mar. 1910):12648-51. Public opinion has withdrawn its approval from the administration since the summer of 1909.

1745. "President Taft and His Quiet Courage," *The World's Work* 17 (Mar. 1909):11299. Taft will move as effectively as Roosevelt did, but with less noise.

1746. "President's View of the Patronage," *The Outlook* 96 (Sept. 24, 1910):133-34. Taft promised not to use the patronage club against Insurgents. (He later did!)

1747. "Republican Disaffection," *Literary Digest* 40 (Apr. 1, 1910):627-30. As revealed in early state primaries.

1748. "The Return from Elba," *Literary Digest* 40 (Mar. 5, 1910):427-28. Speculation as to what Roosevelt would do after his return from a year abroad.

1749. "The Revolt of the Middle West," *The World's Work* 18 (Sept. 1909):11970. Midwestern Republican Insurgents voted against Taft's brand of tariff reform.

1750. "Mr. Roosevelt at Osawatomie," *The Independent* 69 (Sept. 8, 1910):505-6. Roosevelt launched his New Nationalism, in essence his liberal platform for 1912.

1751. "Mr. Roosevelt's Position," *The Outlook* 96 (Nov. 19, 1910):607. "The fight for progressive government has merely begun."

1752. Needham, Henry Beach. "The Insurgents vs. Aldrich, Cannon, et al: The Case of the Insurgents." *Everybody's Magazine* 22 (Jan. 1910):102-9.

1753. Rosenthal, Herbert H. "The Cruise of the Tarpon," *New York History* 39 (Oct. 1958):303-20. Taft's refusal following the New York state convention prevented an alliance of Roosevelt's supporters with the Old Guard.

1754. "Secretary North's Letter," *The Outlook* 96 (Sept. 22, 1910):658-59. Taft will not use the patronage club against Insurgents.

1755. "Six Months of President Taft," *The World's Work* 95 (Sept. 1909):11983-87. Taft has not always used his strength constructively.

1756. Solvick, Stanley D. "William Howard Taft and Cannonism," *Wisconsin Magazine of History* 48 (Aug. 1964):48-58. Taft's gains and losses by fraternizing with Cannon.

1757. "Taft Among the Snags," *Literary Digest* 40 (Feb. 26, 1910):381-82. Taft's deviation from Roosevelt's policies and its possible results for him.

1758. "Mr. Taft on the Party's Crisis," *Literary Digest* 40 (Feb. 26, 1910):375-79. Taft stands by his record.

1759. Welliver, Judson. "The Collapse of the Taft Administration," *Hampton's Magazine* 25 (Oct. 1910):419-31. Predictable Republican losses in the midterm elections.

1760. "Western Republican Opinion on the Winona Speech," *Harper's Weekly* 53 (Oct. 2, 1909):5-6. Opposition thereto.

1761. "What Congress Did," *Literary Digest* 41 (July 1910): 1-3. Because of reforms passed by Congress, Taft thought that his party would stand a good chance in the elections of 1910.

1762. Zanjani, Sally Springmeyer. "Losing Battles: The Revolt of the Nevada Progressives, 1910-1914," *Nevada History Society Quarterly* 24 (Spring 1981):17-38.

11
Elections of 1912

Although Taft had achieved more progressive reforms in four years than Roosevelt had in seven, Roosevelt's entrance into the presidential race split the Republican party and insured a Democratic victory.

Monographs

1763. Anderson, Judith Icke. *William Howard Taft*, Chapters 15-17. No. 226.

1764. Brengle, Fred E. "The Progressive Party and Its Part in the Campaign of 1912." Ph.D. diss., Indiana University, 1929. How Roosevelt "stole" the leadership of the party from La Follette, lost to Taft in the Republican national convention, and was then defeated in the fall elections.

1765. Bryan, William Jennings. *A Tale of Two Conventions.* . . . New York: Funk & Wagnalls, 1912. As a newspaper reporter, the thrice-defeated Democratic presidential candidate reported on both major national conventions.

1766. Campbell, Philip Pitt. *Roosevelt on Taft. Remarks of Hon. P.O. Campbell, of Kansas in the House of Representatives, Monday, June 24, 1912.* Washington: GPO, 1912.

1767. Coletta, Paolo E. *Bryan*, vol. 2, Chapters 2 and 3, for Bryan's influence in the nomination of Woodrow Wilson. No. 352.

1768. Ginger, Ray. *The Bending Cross*. No. 1709. Debs won more votes in 1912 than he had in his previous races.

1769. Goss, Hilton R. "The Pre-Convention Presidential Campaign of 1912." Ph.D. diss., University of California, Berkeley, 1943. The Roosevelt-Taft fight, with Taft sure to win because he controlled the Southern delegates.

1770. Kelly, Frank. *Fight for the White House: The Story of 1912*. New York: Thomas Y. Crowell, 1961. A month-by-month account.

1771. Kohlsaat, Herman Henry. *From McKinley to Harding: Personal Recollections of Our Presidents*. New York: Charles Scribner's Sons, 1923. Includes Taft's view of his break with Roosevelt.

1772. Link, Arthur S. *Woodrow Wilson: The Road to the White House.* Princeton, N.J.: Princeton University Press, 1947. How Wilson, disregarding advice offered by his most important campaign managers, nevertheless won the Democratic presidential nomination. No. 1715.

1773. Manners, William. *TR and Will: A Friendship That Split the Republican Party.* New York: Harcourt, Brace & World, 1969. A popularly written account. No. 243.

1774. Mowry, George E. *The Era of Theodore Roosevelt.* Chapters 11-14. No. 317.

1775. *Official Report of the Proceedings of the Fifteenth Republican National Convention, Held in Chicago, Illinois, June 18, 19, 20, 21, and 22, 1912.* New York: Tenny Press, 1912.

1776. Pinchot, Amos R. E. *History of the Progressive Party, 1912-1916.* 1958; rept. Westport, Conn.: Greenwood Press, 1977. The Chicago convention of 1912, which renominated Taft, the birth of the Progressive Republican Party, and its decline after Roosevelt refused to be its candidate in 1916.

1777. Porter, Kirk H., and Donald B. Johnson. *National Party Platforms, 1840-1956.* No. 463.

1778. Pringle, Henry F. *Taft*, 2:756-842. No. 248.

1779. *Report of the Committee on Political Reform in Support of the Platform of the Republican Party, Adopted at Chicago in June 1912, and Resolutions Ratifying the Nominations of William H. Taft and James S. Sherman.* New York: Union League Club, 1912.

1780. Rosewater, Victor. *Backstage in 1912: The Inside Story of the Split Republican Convention.* Philadelphia: Dorrance, 1932. With Taft's organization in control, Roosevelt bolted and formed his own party.

1781. Russell, Thomas H., ed. *The Political Battle of 1912. . . .* n.l.: L.H. Walter, 1912.

1782. Sponholtz, Lloyd Luther. "Progressivism in Microcosm: An Analysis of the Political Forces that Worked in the Ohio Constitutional Convention of 1912." Ph.D. diss., University of Pittsburgh, 1969. Despite the opposition of former Governor Foraker, Taft supporters won the state's endorsement for Taft.

1783. Wilensky, Norman M. *Conservatives in the Progressive Era: The Taft Republicans of 1912*. Gainesville: University of Florida Press, 1965.

Articles

1784. "Acceptance Speech by President William Howard Taft, Washington, August 2, 1912." In Arthur M. Schlesinger, Jr., and Fred Israel, eds. *History of American Presidential Elections 1788-1968*, 4 vols. New York: Chelsea House, 1971, 3:2204-19. No. 427.

1785. Bliven, Bruce. "Robert La Follette's Place in Our History," *Current History* 22 (Aug. 1925):716-22. Speaks of a devoted public servant whose ego was somewhat inflated.

1786. By the Editor [George Harvey]. "Roosevelt or the Republic!" *North American Review* 196 (Oct. 1912):433-35. Taft's had proved himself a failure, "not because he is a man of straw, but because he is not a man of iron."

1787. Carleton, William G. "Six Year Term for the Presidency?" *South Atlantic Quarterly* 71 (Spring 1972):165-76. Notes that Taft so favored.

1788. "Changing the Presidential Term to Six Years," *Current Opinion* 54 (Mar. 1913):178-80

1789. Clayton, Bruce L. "An Intellectual in Politics: William Garrot Brown and the Ideal of a Two-Party South," *North Carolina History Review* 42 (1965):319-44. An ardent advocate of the two-party system in the South, Brown found that Taft subordinated reform to his need for Southern votes in the 1912 nominating convention.

1790. Felt, Thomas E. "Organizing a National Convention: A Lesson from Senator [Charles W.F.] Dick," *Ohio History Quarterly* 67 (Jan. 1958):50-62. A veteran of state and national party conventions since 1892, Dick wrote a confidential 16-page outline of his ideas for the convention for the benefit of his colleagues. Tried to help Taft against Roosevelt.

1791. Garfield, James R. "How President Taft Pledged Himself to Follow the Roosevelt Policies—and Failed," *The Outlook* 101 (May 18, 1912):116-22. Garfield served in Roosevelt's cabinet but was dumped by Taft.

1792. Gatewood, Willard B., ed. "The President and the 'Deacon' in the Campaign of 1912: The Correspondence of William Howard Taft and James Calvin Hemphill, 1911-1912," *Ohio History Quarterly* 74 (Winter 1965):35-54. Taft and the Democratic Senator were drawn together because of their alienation from the more liberal majority leadership of their respective parties. They corresponded about the prospect of their defeat in the elections of 1912.

1793. Gould, Lewis L. "Theodore Roosevelt, William Howard Taft, and the Disputed Delegates in 1912: Texas as a Test Case," *Southwestern History Quarterly* 80 (1976):33-56. Taft leaders claimed most of the 40 Texas delegates, who were split between Roosevelt and Taft. The national convention rejected Roosevelt's challenge and gave Taft 31 of the 40 votes. A fairer distribution would have given 21 to Roosevelt and 19 to Taft.

1794. Hale, William Bayard. "Woodrow Wilson: Possible President." *The World's Work* 22 (May 1911):14339-52. Wilson would win if the Republicans split—which they did.

1795. Hammond, John Hays. "Why I Am for Taft," *North American Review* 196 (Oct. 1912):449-59. Because Taft recognized the limitations fixed by the Constitution and was a conscientious administrator.

1796. Hunter, George S. "The Bull Moose Movement in Arizona," *Arizona and the West* 19 (1968):343-62. Taft hurt his party when in a speech in 1910 in Phoenix he belittled the initiative, referendum, and recalls reforms the territory of Arizona hoped to incorporate into its constitution. In 1911 he vetoed that constitution, and popular support thereafter turned to the Democrats rather than to Roosevelt's Progressive Party.

1797. Johnson, David E. "Three Hats in the Ring," *American History Illustrated* 19 (Nov. 1984):12-17, 49. Roosevelt, Taft, and Wilson.

1798. Krukones, Michael G. "Predicting Presidential Performance through Political Campaigns [1912-1972]," *Presidential Studies Quarterly* 10 (Fall 1980):527-43. A difficult thing to do.

1799. Leupp, Francis E. "Dark Horse Convention," *The Outlook* 101 (June 8, 1912):297-302. With Republicans split between Taft and Roosevelt, a dark horse might appear.

1800. Low, A. Maurice. "William Howard Taft," *Yale Review* n.s. 1 (Apr. 1912):349-63. A favorable account of a Yale alumnus.

1801. ———. "The Greatest of All Issues: The Third Term Candidacy Is the Most Momentous Problem Which the American People Have to Solve," *Harper's Weekly* 56 (Sept. 14, 1912):20.

1802. MacVeagh, Franklin. "How President Taft is Following the Roosevelt Policies—and Improving upon Them," *The Outlook* 101 (May 18, 1912):110. By Taft's secretary of the Treasury.

1803. Manners, William. "There Was a Storm Outside and a Bit of Frost Inside," *American Heritage* 21 (Jan.-Feb. 1969):24-25, 75-80. Excerpted from Manners' book, *TR and Will*.

1804. "A Measure of the Candidates," *The World's Work* 24 (May 1912):9-10. Views on Taft, Roosevelt, and Wilson.

1805. Moody, Eric N. "Nevada's Bull Moose Progressives: The Formation and Function of a State Political Party in 1912," *Nevada History Society Quarterly* 16 (1973):59-79. Nevada Republicans split between Roosevelt and Taft in 1912. After Bull Moose Nevada Republicans made a very poor showing, most of them became regulars again.

1806. Mowry, George E. "The South and the Progressive Lily White Party of 1912," *Journal of Southern History* 6 (May 1940):237-47. Taft did worse than Roosevelt in eight of the twelve states of the South, receiving only 15.7 percent of the votes cast in the region.

1807. Pinci, A.V. "Mr. Taft on the Issues," *Harper's Weekly* 56 (Oct. 26, 1912):9-10. Whether he won or lost the election, Taft would be grateful to the people for having bestowed their greatest honor upon him.

1808. "President Taft on the Recall of Judges," *The Outlook* 100 (Mar. 23, 1912):604. Recall of judges would deprive the judiciary of that independence without which it could not dispense liberty.

1809. "President Taft's Attitude," *The Outlook* 101 (June 29, 1912):445. Taft felt that the conservatism shown by Republicans during the campaign augured well for the nation even if his party lost the election.

1810. "President Taft's Denunciation of Mr. Roosevelt," *Literary Digest* 44 (May 4, 1912):922-23. In Boston, Taft had severely lambasted TR.

1811. "The Presidential Campaign: Third Term Fears: Third Term Realities." *The Outlook* 100 (Feb. 17, 1912):337-38.

1812. "Principles and Personalities," *The Outlook* 101 (May 4, 1912):11-12. The choice was between the records of Taft and Roosevelt and between the tendency toward progressivism and the tendency toward conservatism.

1813. Pringle, Henry F. "Bull Moose Fiasco," *The Outlook* 159 (Dec. 23, 1931):529-31+. Roosevelt's failure to win the nomination and election in 1912.

1814. "The Republican Feud," *Literary Digest* 44 (Feb. 24, 1912):357-58. The campaign of 1912.

1815. Richardson, Elmo R. "Conservation as a Political Issue: The Western Progressives' Dilemma, 1909-1912," *Pacific Northwest Quarterly* 49 (Apr. 1958):49-54. To follow Roosevelt's or Taft's conservation policies?

1816. Robinson, Edgar E. "Distribution of the Presidential Vote of 1912," *American Journal of Sociology* 20 (July 1914):18-30. Wilson got fewer votes than either Taft or Roosevelt but won the presidency.

1817. "Mr. Roosevelt and the Presidential Nomination," *The Outlook* 100 (Mar. 2, 1912):475. In answer to a query from seven progressive governors, Roosevelt said he would run if asked to do so.

1818. Roosevelt, Theodore. "A Charter of Democracy: Address before the Ohio Constitutional Convention," *The Outlook* 100 (Feb. 24, 1912):390-402. In his speech Roosevelt foreshadowed the Progressive Party platform of 1912.

1819. ———. "A Charter of Democracy," *The Outlook* 100 (Mar. 2, 1912):476-77. Before the Ohio Constitutional convention, Roosevelt placed human rights above all others.

1820. ———. "Mr. Taft's Majority: An Analysis," *The Outlook* 101 (July 6, 1912):520-1. How Taft had "stolen" the disputed delegations in the Republican national convention.

1821. ———. "Thou Shalt Not Steal," *The Outlook* 101 (July 13, 1912):571-76. As above.

1822. ———. "Two Phases of the Chicago Convention," *The Outlook* 101 (July 20, 1912):620-30. As above.

1823. Rorvig, Paul. "Clash of Giants: The 1912 Presidential Election," *American History Illustrated* 14 (Nov. 1979):1315, 42-45. The competition among Roosevelt, Taft, and Wilson.

1824. "Senator La Follette as a Candidate: A Poll of the Press," *The Outlook* 100 (Jan. 20, 1912):120-22. La Follette held that "the President's course has been vacillating and without definite policy."

1825. Stevenson, Frederick Boyd. "The Presidential Skirmish Line: Roosevelt-Taft-Hughes. Part I," *Harper's Weekly* 52 (May 9, 1908):10-13. Taft had promised to follow Roosevelt's policies.

1826. ———. "The Presidential Skirmish Line: Bryan, Johnson, Wilson, Hearst," *Harper's Weekly* 52 (May 23, 1908):10-13. All were possible Democratic presidential candidates for 1912.

1827. Stockbridge, Frank Parker, "Champ Clark, of Pike County," *The World's Work* 24 (May 1912):26-36. Clark was a leading presidential candidate in the Democratic party.

1828. Strange, C.D. "Making a President, 1912: The Northern Negroes' View," *Negro History Bulletin* 31 (Nov. 1968):1424.

1829. "Taft Fires on His Opponents," *Review of Reviews* 45 (Mar. 1912):271. In a Lincoln Day Speech in New York City, Taft attacked both the Progressive Republicans and the Democrats.

1830. "Mr. Taft's Boston Speech," *The Outlook* 100 (Mar. 30, 1912):706-7. Taft's bill of particulars against Roosevelt.

1831. Taft, W. H. "What I am Trying to Do." No. 157.

1832. "To Be Accurate," *Harper's Weekly* 56 (Apr. 10, 1912): 4. On Roosevelt's announcing that his hat was in the ring.

1833. Turner, George K., and A. W. Dunn. "Forces behind Taft," *McClure's Magazine* 39 (May 1912):1-14. Mostly conservative.

12
Post-Presidential Career, 1913-1930

Far from going into eclipse following his defeat for re-election in November 1912, Taft battled it out with the third and final session of the Sixty-second Congress (December 1912-March 1913). He sang his swan song in one of the best speeches he ever made, to the Lotus Club of New York, on November 16, 1912. In it he revealed that a great burden had been lifted from his shoulders and that his sense of humor had returned. He also offered some suggestions about the limits on presidential power, adopting a single six-year term, granting cabinet members nonvoting seats in both houses of Congress, and relieving the president of much red tape by putting postmasters and consular officials under civil service. His chief regret as president was the failure of the Senate to agree to his general arbitration treaties with France and Great Britain, for these might have been steps toward general world peace.

Taft served as Kent Professor of Constitutional Law at Yale University for eight years (1913-1921), with a leave of absence to work on the National War Labor Board at Washington (1917-1918); and then presided as Chief Justice of the Supreme Court, 1921 to 1930. Along the way he had much to say about the Supreme Court and its justices, the Great War, world peace, politics, education, and the rights of women. He also wrote widely on his concept of the correct position of the president in a system of checks and balances.

1834. *Address of President Taft at the Banquet of the Lotus Club, New York City, November 16, 1912.* Washington: GPO, 1912.

To place Taft in the times of the 1920s, see:

Bibliographic Guides

1835. Carroll, Benerice A., Clinton F. Fink, and Jane E. Mohraz. *Peace and War: A Guide to Bibliographies.* Santa Barbara, Calif.: ABC-Clio, 1983.

1836. Coleman, Patrick K., and Charles R. Lamb, comps. *The Nonpartisan League, 1915-1922: An Annotated Bibliography.* St. Paul: Minnesota Historical Society Press, 1985. See comment under Viviani, No. 1862.

1837. Howlett, Charles F., and Glen Zeitler. *The American Peace Movement: History and Historiography.* Washington: American Historical

Association, 1985. Three centuries of the peace movement.

1838. Painter, Estella E., comp. *Selected Articles on the Six Year Presidential Term.* Minneapolis: H.W. Wilson, 1913.

Monographs

1839. Clark, James C. *Faded Glory: Presidents Out of Power.* New York: Praeger, 1985.

1840. Gable, John Allen. *The Bull Moose Years: Theodore Roosevelt and the Progressive Party.* Port Washington, N.Y.: Kennikat Press, 1978. History of the party from 1912 to 1916. Ohio progressives did not contribute in a major way to the party.

1841. Hecht, Marie. *Beyond the Presidency: The Residues of Power.* New York: Macmillan, 1976. The post-presidential careers of American presidents. Taft, s.v.

1842. Hicks, John D. *Republican Ascendancy, 1921-1933.* New York: Harper, 1960. Taft mentioned, p. 26.

1843. Hoover, Herbert. *Memoirs: The Cabinet and the Presidency, 1920-1933.* New York: Macmillan, 1952.

1844. Jernigan, Jay E. *William Allen White.* Boston: Twayne, 1983. White was a moralist in the Emersonian Christian tradition and a publicist for midwestern liberal Republican values. In addition to publishing the *Emporia Gazette*, he authored eight volumes of fiction, social history, and biography and served as an unofficial adviser to the Republican presidents from McKinley to Hoover.

1845. Kennedy, Jean L. "William Allen White: A Study of the Interrelationship of Press, Power, and Party Politics." Ph.D. diss., University of Kansas, 1981.

1846. Lovell, S.D. *The Presidential Election of 1916.* Carbondale: Southern Illinois University Press, 1980. Wilson probably won because of his stand on social legislation and world peace.

1847. McCoy, Donald R. *Calvin Coolidge: The Quiet President.* New York: Macmillan, 1967.

1848. ———. *Coming of Age: The United States during the 1920s and 1930s.* Baltimore: Penguin Books, 1973.

1849. Morgan, Howard Wayne. *Eugene V. Debs: Socialist for President.* Syracuse, N.Y.: Syracuse University Press, 1962.

1850. Morlan, Robert L. *Political Prairie Fire: The Nonpartisan League, 1915-22.* St. Paul: Minnesota Historical Society Press, 1955, 1985. See comment under Vivinai, No. 1862.

1851. Moum, Kathleen D. "Harvest of Discontent: The Social Origins of the Nonpartisan League, 1880-1922." Ph.D. diss., University of California, Irvine, 1986.

1852. Pinchot, Amos. *History of the Progressive Party.* No. 1776.

1853. Quint, Howard H. *The Forging of American Socialism.* Indianapolis: Bobbs-Merrill, 1953, 1964.

1854. *Republican Campaign Textbook, 1924.* New York: Republican National Committee, 1924. Taft managed to pack the Resolutions Committee with friends of the World Court. After brother Henry Taft addressed the delegates, an endorsement of a Permanent Court of International Justice was added to the platform.

1855. Richardson, John. *Our Ex-Presidents From Washington to Hoover: Their Lives after Leaving Office.* New Hope, Pa.: n.p., 1968. Taft, pp. 38-40.

1856. Salvatore, Nick. *Eugene V. Debs: Citizen and Socialist.* Urbana: University of Illinois Press, 1982.

1857. Schriftgiesser, Karl. *This Was Normalcy: An Account of Party Politics during Twelve Republican Years, 1920-1932.* Boston: Little, Brown, 1948.

1858. Shannon, David A. *Between the Wars: America 1919-1941*, 2d ed. Boston: Houghton Mifflin, 1979.

1859. ———. *Progressivism and Postwar Disillusionment, 1898-1928.* New York: McGraw-Hill, 1966.

1860. Sinclair, Andrew. *The Available Man: The Life Behind the Masks of Warren Gamaliel Harding.* New York: Macmillan, 1965.

1861. White, William Allen. *A Puritan in Babylon: The Story of Calvin Coolidge*. New York: Macmillan, 1938.

Article

1862. Viviani, James F. " 'Not a Patriotic American Party': William Howard Taft's Campaign Against the Nonpartisan League, 1920-1921," *North Dakota History* 50 (1983):4-10. While lecturing in North Dakota, Taft denounced the Nonpartisan League as socialistic, anti-American, and despotic. With the election of Harding he helped his party lessen the influence of the league.

A. Professor of Law

1863. Hicks, Frederic C. *Yale Law School: The Founders and the Founder's Collection*. Yale Law Library Publication, No. 1. New Haven: Yale University Press, 1936.

1864. ———. *William Howard Taft: Yale Professor of Law & New Haven Citizen*. New Haven Yale University Press, 1945.

1865. Martin, Asa Earl. *After the White House*. State College, Pa.: Penns Valley Publications, 1951. What happened to 24 former presidents after they retired from the White House. Ends with Herbert Hoover. Taft, s.v.

Among Taft's associates at Yale were the President, Arthur T. Hadley; Frederick S. Jones, Dean of the College; and some six other professors and part-time lecturers in the Law Department. While at Yale, Taft became formally reconciled with Theodore Roosevelt; strongly supported the Y.M.C.A. at meetings held in 1915, 1918, and 1921; in 1917 was elected Honorary President of the Unitarian General Conference held in Baltimore; represented Yale at meetings of the Association of American Universities; and spoke at fund-raising events for the Yale Medical School. He took leaves of absence to serve on the National War Labor Board and in 1920-1921 served as an arbitrator to appraise the Grand Trunk Railway system as a preliminary to its transfer to the Canadian government. He was still heavy. The author's stepmother, a teenager in the 1920s, recalls riding to her high school in New Haven in the same street car with him. When he left it, the car swung heavily to its other side and its springs lifted it up considerably. His major books and speeches during this period were:

1866. Taft. W.H. *Popular Government*. No. 38.

1867. ———. "Justice and Freedom for Industry: Address before the National Association of Manufacturers, May 16, 1915," in which he charged that the Clayton Act was passed for political purposes, to satisfy the demands of the leaders of the American Federation of Labor.

1868. ———. "Is a National Standard of Education Practical?" No. 174.

1869. ———. *The Presidency: Its Duties, Its Powers, Its Opportunities and Its Limitations.* No. 39.

1870. ———. *Our Chief Magistrate and His Powers.* No. 40.

1871. ———. *Liberty Under Law.* No. 41.

1872. ———. "Yale Contribution to the Spanish American War." In Nettleton, G.H. ed., *Book of the Yale Pageant.* New Haven: Yale University Press, 1916.

Other speeches and works are listed in the various categories that follow:

1873. *Our Chief Magistrate and His Powers,* a collection of lectures Taft delivered under the auspices of the George Blumethal Foundation in 1915, was resissued in paperback by the Columbia University Press in 1924 under the title of *The President and His Powers.* It contains a philosophical rather than personal account of Taft's conception of the distribution of governmental powers, the veto power, various minor powers, the power of appointment and of pardon, how a president executes the laws, and how he serves as commander-in-chief; and chief of foreign relations. In the last chapter, he noted that the manner in which a president uses his powers is determined by Congress, which sets limits beyond which he cannot go, and often gives quasi-legislative or quasi-judicial powers to officers he himself does not control. However, Congress cannot prevent his employment of means given him by the Constitution nor force him to disclose confidential information acquired in order to perform his duties. Very touchy subjects included how far a president could differ from a decision by the Supreme Court and if he could refuse to execute a decision with which he disagreed. His ideal for good government was one in which the three branches cooperated rather than sought to compel the other branches to undertake affirmative action, or to hinder their operations. Unlike Theodore Roosevelt, who sought constitutional support for some questionable action he had already taken, Taft held that "The true view of the Executive function is, as I conceive it, that the President can exercise no power which cannot be fairly and reasonably traced to some specific grant of power or justly implied and included within such express grant as proper and necessary to its exercise. Such specific grant must be either in the Federal Constitution or in an act of Congress passed in pursuance thereof. There is no undefined residuum of power which he can exercise because it seems to him to be in the public interest. . . . His jurisdiction must be justified and vindicated by affirmative constitutional or statutory provision, or it does not exist." (pp. 139-40)

1874. Much of the same material is found in *The Presidency*, a collection of three lectures he gave under the auspices of the Barbour-Page Foundation of the University of Virginia, and reissued by the Johnson Reprint Corporation in 1972.

1875. In *Liberty Under Law*, No. 184, Taft noted that while the Constitution created a governmental organization and the agencies to carry it on, it also imposed limitations upon them. The federal system provided for a representative government, but its checks and balances prevented changes according to the temporary whims of popular passion. The Constitution was designed to secure individual liberty, the right of personal and religious freedom, of property, and the pursuit of happiness, none of which could be denied except by due process of law. It also provided for its own amendment. And with the disappearance of property and religious requirements for voting, the nation had become increasingly democratic. While those in the minority must obey laws passed by the majority even though they are distasteful to them, he saw such methods of direct democracy as the initiative and referendum as "a disease of excessive legislation." As he defined the pursuit of happiness, it rested upon the right of property including the right of contract and the right of labor. "Our primary conception of a free man is one who can enjoy what he earns, who can spend it for his comfort or pleasure if he would, who can save it and keep it for his future use and benefit if he has the foresight and self-restraint to do so. Upon this right rests the motive of the individual which makes the world materially to progress. Destroy it and material progress ceases." (p. 25) This being so, and agreed that liberty must be ordered liberty, and that social legislation that attempted to "reform people by wholesale" would fail unless human nature changed.

1876. In *Four Aspects of Civic Duty*, No. 107, Taft defined the duties of citizenship when viewed from four viewpoints: those of a recent university graduate, a judge on the bench, a colonial administrator, and a national executive. College students may criticize the government but will learn better from subsequent experience as they engage in practical politics. A judge on the bench learns much about law, which should be dispensed in an impartial fashion.

The colonial administrator, illustrated from his experience in the Philippines, should cultivate the good will of its citizens, who, as Filipino citizens, owe their loyalty to the American government. Despite criticism from the press and opposition from Congress, the president should enforce the laws, demand support from the public for his conduct of foreign affairs, and be the leader in legislation and in party matters.

B. On World War I

A noninterventionist, Taft originally praised Woodrow Wilson's adopting a policy of neutrality toward the Great War. The taking of American and other neutral lives by German U-boats, however, gradually caused him to support the Allied side and American intervention. Greatly interested in the kind of peace settlement that would be made, he worked hard as president of the League to Enforce Peace to have adopted a world organization with teeth in it. Wilson disagreed. While he accepted an invitation from Taft to address his league, he declined a second invitation and also refused to name him as a delegate to the Versailles peace conference.

1877. Taft, William Howard. "It Is a Retrograde Step in Christian Civilization." Statement by W.H. Taft. *Addresses*, 34:327-41.

1878. ———. "Why We Entered the Great War," *Current History* 6 (Aug. 1917): pt. 2, pp. 317-20.

1879. ———., ed. *Service with Fighting Men: An Account of the American Young Mens' Christian Association in the World War*, 2 vols. New York: Associated Press, 1922.

1880. Herron, Harriet Collins. "William Howard Taft and the Great War," *Cincinnati Historical Society Bulletin* 34 (Spring 1976):6-23. Seven letters about the war Taft wrote in 1917-1918 to his mother-in-law.

C. Member of the National War Labor Board

In May 1918 Taft took up residence in Washington to serve as co-chairman of the National War Labor Board, whose mission was to solve problems between capital and labor in vital war industries. The board's decisions were published by the Bureau of Labor Statistics.

1881. Conner, Valerie Jean. *The National Labor Board: Stability, Justice, and the Voluntary State in World War I*. Chapel Hill: University of North

Carolina Press, 1985. "The conservative W.H. Taft confounded friends and enemies alike by his responsiveness to labor's claims."

1882. Cuff, Robert D. "The Politics of Labor Administration during World War I," *Labor History* 21 (Fall 1980):546-69.

D. On World Peace

1883. Four of Taft's lectures before the New York Peace Society were published in *The Independent* and then in book form as *The United States and Peace*. No. 173.

Taft was an active member of the World Court League and also President of the League to Enforce Peace from its origin on June 17, 1915, until 1921, when he went to the Supreme Court. Although disappointed that President Wilson did not appoint him as a member of the Versailles Conference, he fully supported the creation of the League of Nations. Other contemporary peace leaders were William Jennings Bryan, Theodore E. Burton, Andrew Carnegie, David Starr Jordan, Robert M. La Follette, Louis P. Lochner, Oswald Garrison Villard, and Lillian Wald. The contrtibutions of these and of many others may be followed in:

1884. Josephson, Harold, Editor-in-Chief. *Biographical Dictionary of Modern Peace Leaders*. Westport, Conn.: Greenwood Press, 1985. Taft mentioned, p. 890.

1885. Accinelli, Robert D. "Was There a 'New' Harding? Warren G. Harding and the World Court Issue, 1920-1921," *Ohio History* 84 (Autumn 1975):168-81.

1886. Bailey, Thomas A. *Woodrow Wilson and the Lost Peace*. New York: Macmillan, 1944.

1887. Bartlett, Ruhl J. *The League to Enforce Peace*. Chapel Hill: University of North Carolina Press, 1944. Contains much on Taft.

1888. Boothe, Leon. "Lord Grey, the United States, and the Political Effort for a League of Nations, 1914-1920," *Maryland Historical Review* 65 (Spring 1970):36-54. Woodrow Wilson's opposition to Taft's League to Enforce Peace.

1889. Bourne, Randolph S., ed. and comp. *Towards an Enduring Peace: A Symposium of Peace Proposals and Programs, 1914-1916.* New York: American Association for International Conciliation, 1916.

1890. Bryan, William Jennings. *The Forces that Make for Peace.* Address at Mohonk Conference on International Arbitration, 1910 and 1911. New York: 1911.

1891. Chatfield, Charles. *For Peace and Justice: Pacifism in America, 1914-1941.* Knoxville, Tenn.: University of Tennessee Press, 1971.

1892. Claude, Inis L., Jr. *Swords into Plowshares: The Problems and Progress of International Organization,* 2d rev. ed. New York: Random House, 1959.

1893. DeBenedetti, Charles. *Origins of the Modern American Peace Movement, 1915-1929.* Millwood, N.Y.: KTO Press, 1978.

1894. *Doves and Diplomats: Foreign Officers and Peace Movements in Eurore and America in the Twentieth Century.* Solomon Wank, ed. Westport, Conn.: Greenwood Press, 1978.

1895. Fleming, Denna F. *The Treaty Veto and the American Senate.* New York: G.P. Putnam's Sons, 1930. Fleming objected to vetoes by isolationists and nationalists of measures looking toward peace.

1896. House, Edward M. "America in World Affairs: A Democratic View," *Foreign Affairs* 2 (1922) (Special Supplement, No. 3):540-51. "The League of Nations . . . is common humanity's last hope. Its name was suggested, and its creation largely brought about, by men in the Republican Party like Taft, Lodge, Lowell, and their colleagues. The World Court, its very necessary adjunct, was mainly the work of Elihu Root."

1897. Jennings, David H. "President Harding and International Organization," *Ohio History* 75 (Spring-Summer 1966): 149-65.

1898. Kosberg, Roberta L. "Executive-Legislative Rhetoric Regarding American Participation in an Associaton of Nations, 1916-1920." Ph.D. diss., Pennsylvania State University, 1982.

1899. League to Enforce Peace. *Enforced Peace: Proceedings of the First Annual National Assemblage of the League to Enforce Peace, Washington, May 26, 27, 1916.* New York: League to Enforce Peace, 1916.

1900. Lodge, Henry Cabot. *The United States Senate and the League of Nations.* New York: Charles Scribner's Sons, 1925. Why he and like-minded men refused to approve the League.

1901. Lowell, A. Lawrence. "The League to Enforce Peace," *North American Review* 205 (Jan. 1917):25-30.

1902. Maddox, Robert James. "William E. Borah and the Crusade to Outlaw War," *Historian* 29 (Feb. 1967):200-20.

1903. Marchand, C. Roland. *The American Peace Movement and Social Reform 1898-1918.* Princeton, N.J.: Princeton University Press, 1973.

1904. Margulies, Herbert F. "The Senate and the World Court," *Capitol Studies* 4 (1976):147-50.

1905. Nelson, John K. *The Peace Prophets: American Pacifist Thought, 1919-1941.* Chapel Hill: University of North Carolina Press, 1967.

1906. Nurnberger, Ralph D. "America's Peace Movement, 1900-1986: 'Bridling the Passions,'" *Wilson Quarterly* 11 (New Year's 1987):96-107.

1907. Root, Elihu. *Men and Policies: Addresses by Elihu Root.* Collected and ed. by Robert Bacon and James Brown Scott. Cambridge, Mass.: Harvard University Press, 1925. Taft mentioned *passim.*

1908. Sprout, Harold and Margaret. *Toward a New Order of Sea Power: American Naval Policy and the World Scene, 19181-922.* 1940; rept. Westport, Conn.: Greenwood Press, 1969. In 1912, Taft advocated creating an international court as a preliminary step toward a universal reduction of armaments. The authors doubt that the Washington Naval Disarmament Conference of 1921-1922 portended world peace.

1909. Taft, William Howard. *The United States and Peace.* No. 173.

1910. ———., and Bryan, William Jennings. *World Peace. . . .* No. 176.

1911. ———. *America Can't Quit.* . . . No. 177.

1912. ———. *The Paris Covenant for a League of Nations.* No. 178.

1913. ———. *Ratify the Covenant.* New York: League to Enforce Peace, 1919.

1914. ———. *Taft Papers on the League of Nations.* Theodore Marburg and Horace C. Flack, eds., 1920; rept. Millwood, N.Y.: Kraus Reprint Co., 1971.

1915. Thernstrom, Stephan A. "Oswald Garrison Villard and the Politics of Pacifism," *Harvard Library Bulletin* 14 (Winter 1960):126-53.

1916. Wormuth, Francis D., and Edwin Firmage with Francis P. Butler. *To Chain the Dogs of War: The War Power of Congress in History and Law.* Dallas: Southern Methodist University Press, 1986. Leaves no doubt that the framers of the Constitution assigned "the power to initiate war solely to Congress."

1917. "Mr. Wilson and the Campaign," *Yale Review* 10 (Oct. 1920):1-25. Taft asserted that the elections of 1920 would be a referendum on Wilson's policies. He added that no domestic issue exceeded in importance "the maintenance of the Supreme Court as the bulwark to enforce the guaranty that no man shall be deprived of his property without due process of law." Taft was disappointed that the new President, Warren G. Harding, who objected to entering the League of Nations, failed to secure what he called a substitute "association of nations." He was happy when Harding actively campaigned for U.S. membership in the World Court.

1918. Accinelli, Robert D. "Was There a 'New' Harding?" No. 1885.

1919. DeBenedetti, Charles. *Origins of the Modern American Peace Movement, 1915-1929.* No. 1893.

1920. Jennings, David H. "President Harding and International Organization." No. 1897.

1921. Kosberg, Roberta L. "Executive-Legislative Rhetoric Regarding American Participation in an Association of Nations, 1916-1920." No. 1898.

E. On Women

Taft was rather hostile to the idea of women's suffrage, saying on one instance that most women were not interested in obtaining the ballot and if they did it would be controlled by women of the "less desirable class." Although while president he appointed a woman, Julia C. Lathrop, to head a Children's Bureau, the decisions of his Supreme Court did little to help women.

1922. Baer, Judith A. *The Chains of Protection: The Judicial Response to Women's Labor Legislation.* Westport, Conn.: Greenwood Press, 1978.

1923. Flexner, Eleanor. *Century of Struggle: The Woman's Rights Movement in the United States.* Cambridge, Mass.: Harvard University Press, 1959.

1924. Kraditor, Aileen. *The Ideas of the Woman Suffrage Movement, 1890-1920.* New York: Columbia University Press, 1965.

1925. Scott, Anne Firor, and Andrew MacKay Scott. *One Half the People: The Fight for Woman Suffrage.* 1975; rept. Urbana: University of Illinois Press, 1982.

1926. Taft, William H. "As I See the Future of Women," *Ladies' Home Journal* 36 (Mar. 1919):27, 113. During the Great War, women served in industry, in the Red Cross, and in other ways. They now will engage in some fields earlier monpolized by men.

F. On Prohibition

Taft had opposed prohibition because he did not believe it could be enforced. However, when cases arose under the Edwin Y. Webb law of 1913, which prohibited the shipment in interstate traffic of liquor intended for sale in dry states, and under the enforcement act of the Eighteenth Amendment, the Volstead Law, his Supreme Court upheld the laws.

1927. Blocker, Jack S., Jr., *Retreat from Reform: The Prohibition Movement in the United States, 1890-1913.* Westport, Conn.: Greenwood Press, 1976.

1928. Cherrington, Ernest H. *The Evolution of Prohibition in the United States of America.* Westerville, Ohio: The American Issues Press, 1920. The march from local option to state control and on to the Eighteenth Amendment.

1929. Coletta, Paolo E. *William Jennings Bryan: Progressive Politician and Moral Statesman, 1909-1915.* No. 1706.

1930. ———. *William Jennings Bryan: Political Puritan, 1915-1925.* Lincoln: University of Nebraska Press, 1969. Both of these volumes on Bryan contain much on his prohibition campaign and his success in winning the Eighteenth Amendment to the Constitution.

1931. Colvin, D. Leigh, *Prohibition in the United States: A History of the Prohibition Party and of the Prohibition Movement.* New York: Doran, 1926.

1932. Dabney, Virginius. *Dry Messiah: The Life of Bishop James Cannon, Jr.* New York: A.A. Knopf, 1949. Cannon's fight against alcohol reflected the opposition to it of the evangelical churches particularly of the South.

1933. Fish, Stuyvesant. "Prohibition's Results," *Current History* 16 (June 1922):377-95. Stimulates the violation of the law without curing the evil.

1934. Fisher, Irving. *Prohibition At Its Worst.* New York: Alcohol Information Committee, 1927.

1935. Fosdick, Harry E. *A Sermon: The Prohibition Question.* New York: New York Avenue Baptist Church, 1928. A modernist in religious matters, Fosdick saw evil in the use of alcohol.

1936. Furnas, Joseph C. *The Life and Times of Demon Rum.* New York: G.P. Putnam's Sons, 1965.

1937. Levine, Lawrence W. *Defender of the Faith: William Jennings Bryan, The Last Decade, 1915-1925.* New York: Oxford University Press, 1965. Includes the prohibition campaign.

1938. McAdoo, William Gibbs. *The Challenge: Liquor and Lawlessness versus Constitutional Government.* New York: The Century Co., 1928. The consumption of liquor stimulated crime, debased its user, and was illegal.

1939. Merz, Charles. *The Dry Decade.* 1931; rept. Seattle: University of Washington Press, 1969.

1940. Odegard, Peter H. *Pressure Politics: The Story of the Anti-Saloon League.* 1928. rept. New York: Octagon Books, 1966. An excellent story of how groups opposed to alcohol got together to pressure their representatives for prohibitive laws.

1941. Sinclair, Andrew. *The Era of Excess*. New York: Harper & Row, 1964. First published as *Prohibition: The Age of Excess*.

1942. Taft, William H. "Is Prohibition a Blow at Personal Liberty?" *Ladies' Home Journal* 35 (May 1919):31. He did not think so at the time.

1943. Timberlake, James H. *Prohibition and the Progressive Movement, 1900-1920*. Cambridge, Mass.: Harvard University Press, 1963.

13
Chief Justice of the Supreme Court, 1921-1930

A. The Supreme Court: General

As the Chief Justice, Taft strove to obtain unanimity for his court's decisions. He carefully assessed the capabilities of his associate members and those of prospective members. He also headed drives that resulted in reforms that speeded up court procedures, brought Supreme Court justices into closer contact with lower federal court judges, and obtained a new building in which to house the Supreme Court. The Judicial Conference of the United States supervises and directs the Administrative Office of the United States Courts. Its reports are available from the Chief, Analysis and Statistical Division, Administrative Office of the United States Courts, Washington, D. C. 20544. Useful also is the *Journal of the Supreme Court of the United States*, published daily when the court is in session. For Taft, see the years 1908-1935, 28 v.

1944. Anderman, Nancy. *United States Supreme Court Decisions: An Index to Their Locations*. Metuchen, N.J.: Scarecrow Press, 1976.

1945. Blanford, Linda A., and Patricia Russell Evans. *The Supreme Court of the United States, 1789-1980: An Index to Opinions Arranged by Justice*, 2 vols. Millwood, N.Y.: Kraus International Publications, 1983.

1946. Chase, Harold, and others. *Biographical Dictionary of the Federal Judiciary*. Detroit: Gale Research Co., 1976.

1947. Kay, Richard S., and others. *A Reference Guide to the United States Supreme Court*. Stephen P. Elliott, General Editor. New York: Facts on File, 1986. Contains biographies of the justices, pp. 253-370; an alphabetical listing of the chief justices, pp. 363-65; an alphabetical list of the associate justices, pp. 365-68; a chronology of the chief justices, pp. 368-84; and a chronology of the associate justices, pp. 372-84.

1948. Klein, Fannie J. *The Administration of Justice in the Courts: A Selected Annotated Bibliography*, 2 vols. Dobbs Ferry, N.Y.: Oceana Publications, 1976.

1949. Nelson, William E., and John Phillip Reid. *The Literature of American Legal History*. New York: Oceana Publications, 1983. A collection that supplements articles surveying American legal history published since 1962 in the *Annual Survey of American Law*.

1950. Stephenson, D. Grier, Jr. *The Supreme Court and the American Republic: An Annotated Bibliography*. New York: Garland, 1981. Chapter 1 includes research aids, general references, bibliographies, guides to manuscripts and archives, and guides to periodical literature. Chapter 6 deals with biographical and autobiographical material. Taft, Nos. 1258-66.

1951. Tompkins, Dorothy Campbell. *Court Organization and Administration: A Bibliography*. Institute of Governmental Studies. Berkeley: University of California, 1973.

1952. Wigdor, Alexandra K. *The Personal Papers of Supreme Court Justices: A Descriptive Guide*. New York: Garland, 1986. The major listings are organized alphabetically by justice, and each depository of papers is treated under as many as five heads: location, provenance and status, limitation on access, and description of collection.

Monographs

1953. Abraham, Henry Julian. *Courts and Judges*. New York: Oxford University Press, 1959.

1954. ———. *Justices and Presidents: A Political History of Appointments to the Supreme Court*, 2d ed., New York: Oxford University Press, 1985. No. 1080.

1955. ———. *The Judicial Process*. New York: Oxford University Press, 1962.

1956. Asch, Sidney H. *The Supreme Court and Its Great Justices*. New York: Arco, 1971. Includes Brandeis, Harlan, Holmes, and Hughes. Taft, excluded, is often mentioned.

1957. Bickel, Alexander M., and Benno C. Schmidt, Jr. *The Oliver Wendell Holmes Devise History of the Supreme Court of the United States. Vol. IX: The Judiciary and Responsible Government, 1910-21*. New York: Macmillan, 1984. Taft's painstaking search for a replacement for John Harlan is described in great detail, as is the explosive confrontation with the Senate when President Wilson put forward Louis Brandeis's name. There is also much on the rule of reason of the Edward Douglass White court and on how business used legal practices to insulate its activities from regulation.

1958. Boudin, Louis B. *Government by Judiciary*, 2 vols. 1932; rept. New York: Russell and Russell, 1968.

1959. Burch, Philip H., Jr. *Elites in American History: The Civil War to the New Deal*, 3 vols. New York: Holmes and Meier, 1981, 2:174-81. Discusses Taft's appointment to the court and the court's actions while he headed it.

1960. Butler, Charles Henry. *A Century at the Bar of the Supreme Court of the United States*. New York: Putnam, 1942.

1961. Dunne, Gerald T. *Monetary Decisions by the Supreme Court*. New Brunswick, N.J.: Rutgers University Press, 1960.

1962. Edwards, William H., Leon Friedman, and Fred L. Israel, eds. *The Justices of the United States Supreme Court, 1789-1978: Their Lives and Opinions*. 4 vols. Edgemont, Pa.: Chelsea House, 1987. Forty-six scholars examine the judicial approach, philosophy, and contributions of every justice who sat on the court during the period covered. Page references are given below for each judge of Taft's court. After Edwards died, the editors remained Friedman and Israel, and so will be noted.

1963. Ewing, Cortez A.M. *The Judges of the Supreme Court, 1789-1937: A Study of Their Qualifications*. Minneapolis: University of Minnesota Press, 1938.

1964. Frankfurter, Felix, and James M. Landis. *The Business of the Supreme Court*. New York: Macmillan, 1927. Good on the Judge's Act of 1925.

1965. Freund, Paul A. *On Understanding the Supreme Court*. 1949; rept. Westport, Conn.: Greenwood Press, 1977.

1966. Goldmark, Josephine. *Fatigue and Efficiency: A Study in Industry*, 2 vols. New York: Charities Publications Committee, Russell Sage Foundation, 1912. The injurious effect of uncontrolled hours of work in industry, and the work of Louis D. Brandeis and Miss Goldmark in submitting briefs on the subject to the U.S. Supreme Court and to the Supreme Courts of Illinois and Ohio.

1967. Hall, Kermit L. *The Supreme Court and Judicial Review in American History*. Washington: American Historical Association, 1985. Details the conflicts between the non-elected Supreme Court and the elected branches of government in shaping and applying the law.

1968. Harrell, Mary Ann. *Equal Justice Under the Law*, 4th ed. Washington: The Supreme Court Historical Society, 1982. Taft, pp. 80-3, 124, 151, 154.

1969. Hirsch, H.M. *The Enigma of Felix Frankfurter*. No. 1655.

1970. Holmes, Oliver Wendell. *Collected Legal Papers*. Harcourt, Brace and Howe, 1920.

1971. Hughes, Charles Evans. *The Supreme Court of the United States: Its Foundation, Methods and Achievements: An Interpretation*. 1928; rept. Garden City, N.Y.: Doubleday, 1936. The Chief Justice manages the docket, presents the cases in conference, and guides the discussion. When in the majority, he assigns the writing of opinions. Whatever influence he exerts in the exercise of these prerogatives rests less on formal authority than on elusive personal characteristics.

1972. Jackson, Robert H. *The Supreme Court in the American System of Government*. The Godkin Lectures. Cambridge, Mass.: Harvard University Press, 1955. The court as a unit of government, a law court, and a political institution.

1973. Kutler, Stanley I. *The Judicial Philosophy of Chief Justice Taft and Organized Labor, 1921-1930*. Ann Arbor, Mich.: University Microfilms, 1960.

1974. Mason, Alpheus Thomas. *The Supreme Court: Vehicle of Revealed Truth or Power Group, 1930-1937*. Boston: Boston University Press, 1953.

1975. ———. *The Supreme Court from Taft to Warren*, enl. ed. Baton Rouge: Louisiana State University Press, 1968. Chapter 2 is entitled "Taft: The Court as Supreme Legislature." Per Mason, "The Supreme Court could be counted on to save the businessman from the folly of legislatures, egged on by demagogues expounding human rights at the expense of property rights." (pp. 40-1)

1976. ———. *William Howard Taft: Chief Justice*. 1965; rept. Washington: University Press of America, 1983. The conventional picture of Taft is that of a stubborn defender of the status quo. In contrast, he revealed singleness of purpose, a fertile imagination, and extraordinary dynamism in seeking to make courts more efficient instruments of justice.

1977. Miller, Arthur Selwyn. *The Supreme Court: Myth and Reality*. Westport, Conn.: Greenwood Press, 1978.

1978. Murphy, Bruce Allen. *The Brandeis-Frankfurter Connection: The Secret Political Activities of Two Supreme Court Justices*. Paperback rept.: Garden City: Anchor, 1983. No. 1652.

1979. Murphy, Paul L. *The Constitution in the Twentieth Century*. Washington: American Historical Association, 1986. Investigates disputes over proper constitutional interpretation between World War I and the 1980s.

1980. Murphy, Walter F. *Congress and the Court*. Chicago: University of Chicago Press, 1962. Congress passes laws whose infractions the court may have to pass upon, approves nominations of federal judges, can set judges' salaries, and by the amendment process can change the jurisdiction of the court.

1981. ———., and C. Herman Pritchett, eds. *Courts, Judges, and Politics*. New York: Random House, 1961.

1982. Myers, Gustavus. *History of the Supreme Court of the United States*. Philadelphia: Burt Franklin, 1912.

1983. Pringle, *Taft*, 2:959-1049. No. 248.

1984. Ragan, Allen E. *Chief Justice Taft*. Columbus: Ohio State Archaelogical and Historical Society, 1938.

1985. Rodell, Fred. *Nine Men: A Political History of the Supreme Court from 1790 to 1955*. New York: Random House, 1955. Taft is mentioned *passim*.

1986. Ross, Ishbel. *An American Family*. Chapter 23. "Taft as Chief Justice." No. 275.

1987. Rubin, Eva R. *The Supreme Court and the American Family: Ideology and Issues*. Westport, Conn.: Greenwood Press, 1986.

1988. Scigliano, Robert G. *The Supreme Court and the Presidency*. New York: Free Press, 1971.

1989. Shapiro, Martin. *Law and Politics in the Supreme Court.* New York: Free Press, 1964.

1990. Smith, Herbert A. *The American Supreme Court as an International Tribunal.* New York: Oxford University Press, 1920. The Supreme Court is the only permanent court, as distinguished from occasional arbitration commissions, which has hitherto admitted in any degree the discussion of the functions of a truly international tribunal.

1991. Steamer, Robert J. *Chief Justices: Leadership and the Supreme Court.* Columbia: University of South Carolina Press, 1986. Examines the factors associated with effective leadership by each Chief Justice of the Supreme Court from Marshall to Burger. Argues that only Marshall, Hughes, and Warren deserve to be characterized as "great" chief justices.

1992. Stewart, David Michael. *The Supreme Court Appointments during the Harding and Coolidge Administrations: Influences, Critics, Voting.* Detroit: Wayne State University Press, 1974. Chapters 1-3 deal with the appointment of Taft. Chapter 8 is entitled "The Taft Court Characterized: The Record in Review."

1993. Strum, Philippa. *The Supreme Court and "Political Questions": A Study in Political Evasion.* Tuscaloosa: University of Alabama Press, 1974. Presumably, the court leaves political questions to other branches of government, yet charges have often been made that some of its decisions are politically motivated.

1994. ———. *The Anti-Trust Act and the Supreme Court.* No. 641.

1995. Umbreit, Kenneth Bernard. *Our Eleven Chief Justices: A History of the Supreme Court in Terms of Their Personalities,* 2 vols. 1938; rept. Port Washington, N.Y.: Kennikat Press, 1969. Fuller, pp. 329-58; White, pp. 359-92; Taft, pp. 393-450; Hughes, pp. 450-500.

1996. Wasby, Stephen L. *The Supreme Court in the Federal Judicial System.* New York: Holt, Rinehart and Winston, 1978. How the Court works. Taft, pp. 75, 98, 103-4, 112, 160-1, 193, 195.

1997. White, G. Edward. *The American Judicial Tradition: Profiles of Leading American Justices.* New York: Oxford University Press, 1976. Chapter 8 on "Holmes, Brandeis, and the Origins of Judicial Liberalism": Taft, pp. 180-90, 335.

1998. Witt, Elder, ed. *The Supreme Court and Its Work.* Washington: Congressional Quarterly 1981. An oversized and well illustrated history of the Supreme Court and its work. Taft, pp. 71-161, 204-5.

Articles

1999. Bickel, Alexander M. "Mr. Taft Rehabilitates the Court," *Yale Law Journal* 79 (Nov. 1969):1-45. How Taft strived to have only "safe" appointments made to his court, i.e., conservatives, but men with balance.

2000. Blaustein, Albert, and Roy Mersky. "The Twelve Great Justices of All Time," *Life* 57 (Oct. 15, 1971):52-59. Of the 96 Supreme Court Justices to date, 12 are rated as "great," 15 as "near great," 55 as "average," 6 as "below average," and 8 as "failures." Taft falls in the "near great" category.

2001. Caldera, Gregory A. "Neither the Purse nor the Sword: Dynamics of Public Confidence in the Supreme Court,"*American Political Science Review* 80 (Dec. 1986):1209-26.

2002. Carrott, M. Browning. "The Supreme Court and Minority Rights in the 1920s," *Northwest Ohio Quarterly* 41 (1969):144-56. The author argues that if the Supreme Court under Taft curbed the activities of labor and of radical political organizations it supported the personal liberties of ethnic, religious, and racial groups.

2003. ———. "The Supreme Court and Law and Order in the 1920s," *Maryland Historian* 16 (Fall/Winter 1985):12-26.

2004. Essary, J. Frederick, "The Human Side of the Supreme Court," *Scribner's Magazine* 86 (Nov. 1929):501-4.

2005. Frankfurter, Felix, "The United States Supreme Court: Molding the Constitution," *Current History* 19 (May 1930): 239-40.

2006. "Holmes of the Supreme Court," *American Bar Association Journal* 27 (May 1941):283-89.

2007. Lowndes, Charles L.B. "Federal Taxation and the Supreme Court," *Supreme Court Review* (1960):pp. 222-57.

2008. Kutler, Stanley I. "Chief Justice Taft, National Regulation, and the Commerce Power," *Journal of American History* 51 (Mar. 1965):651-58. High praise for Taft.

2009. Marcus, Maeva, and others. "The Documentary History of the Supreme Court of the United States," *Prologue* 18 (Fall 1986):181-88.

2010. Murphy, Walter F. "In His Image: Chief Justice Taft and Supreme Court Appointments," *The Supreme Court Review* (1961):159-63.

2011. "Taft and the Supreme Court," *The New Republic*, October 27, 1920, pp. 108-9.

2012. Taft, William Howard. "Adequate Machinery for Judicial Business." No. 179.

2013. ———. "Address." *American Bar Association Reports, Proceedings of the Judicial Section* 41 (Aug. 30, 1914): 731. On court reform.

2014. ———. "Address of the President," *American Bar Association Reports* 39 (1914):368. "We are in danger of excessive regulation which will really interfere with that freeedom of trade and unrestricted initiative which has helped so much the material progress of the country heretofore."

2015. ———. "The Attack on the Courts and Legal Procedure." No. 187.

2016. ———. "The Jurisdiction of the Supreme Court under the Act of February 13, 1925." No. 188.

2017. ———. "Procedure in Federal Court." No. 2119.

2018. ———. "The Social Importance of Proper Standards for Admission to the Bar," *American Bar Association Reports* 39 (1913):924-36. Knowledge of social needs will help judges to temper the demands of reformers and thus avoid "radical and impractical changes in law and government."

2019. ———. "The Supreme Court and the Public Welfare." No. 185.

2020. ———. "Statement before the Committee on the Judiciary, Oct. 5, 1921." No. 183.

2021. ———. "Statement." In *Hearings* before the Committee on the Judiciary, Dec. 18, 1924. No. 184.

2022. ———. "W.H. Taft to C.E. Hughes, April 27, 1926." No. 189.

2023. "Taft vs. Brandeis," *Harper's Weekly* 62 (Apr. 8, 1916): 359-60.

B. The Personnel of Taft's Court

Voting against confirming Taft as Chief Justice were Senators Beveridge, Borah, Burton, Clapp, Dolliver, Hiram Johnson, La Follette, Norris, and Watson. Oliver Wendell Holmes thought that Taft was "a first-rate second rate," then relented and said that his was the best nomination that could be made.

2024. *Holmes-Pollock Letters*, 2 vols. Mark A. De Wolfe Howe, ed. Cambridge, Mass.: Harvard University Press, 1941, 1:211, 2:797.

The dates following the names of the associate justices are those during which they served on the Supreme Court.

BRANDEIS, LOUIS DENBITZ, 1916-1939.

Taft harbored a grudge against Brandeis because of the latter's participation in the Ballinger case in 1910. He was horrified when Woodrow Wilson nominated him in 1916 because he opposed his sociological jurisprudence.

2025. Baker, Leonard. *Brandeis and Frankfurter: A Dual Biography*. New York: Harper & Row, 1984.

2026. Bickel, Alexander M., ed. *The Unpublished Opinions of Mr. Justice Brandeis*. Chicago: University of Chicago Press, 1967.

2027. Brandeis, Louis D. *Letters of Louis D. Brandeis. Vol. 1: Urban Reformer, 1870-1907*. Melvin I. Urofsky and David W. Levy, eds. Albany: State University of New York, 1971.

2028. *Encyclopedia of American Biography*, 3d ed. John A. Garraty, ed. New York: Charles Scribner's Sons, 1980, pp. 109-10.

2029. Gal, Allon. *Brandeis of Boston*. Cambridge, Mass.: Harvard University Press, 1980.

2030. Hirsch, H.N. *The Enigma of Felix Frankfurter*. No. 1655.

2031."Louis Denbitz Brandeis," *American Bar Association Journal* 27 (Nov. 1941):689.

2032. Mason, Alpheus Thomas. "Louis D. Brandeis." In *The Justices of the United States Supreme Court*. Friedman and Israel, eds. 3:2043-76. No. 1962.

2033. Murphy, Bruce Allen. *The Brandeis/Frankfurter Connection: The Secret Political Activities of Two Supreme Court Justices* [to effect social and political reforms from the Court's chambers]. No. 1652.

2034. Strum, Philippa. *Louis D. Brandeis: Justice for the People*. Cambridge, Mass.: Harvard University Press, 1984.

BUTLER, PIERCE, 1916-1939.

2035. Burner, David. "Pierce Butler." In Friedman and Israel, eds. *The Justices of the United States Supreme Court*, 3:2183-2202. No. 1962.

CLARKE, JOHN H., 1916-1922.

2036. Burner, David, "John H. Clarke." In Friedman and Israel, eds. *The Justices of the United States Supreme Court*, 3:2077-2102. No. 1962.

DAY, WILLIAM, 1903-1922.

2037. Watts, James F., Jr. "William R. Day." In Friedman and Israel, eds. *The Justices of the United States Supreme Court*, 3:1774-1800. No. 1962.

HOLMES, OLIVER WENDELL, 1902-1932.

2038. Bowen, Catherine D. *Yankee from Olympus: Mr. Justice Holmes and the Supreme Court*. No. 1666.

2039. *Encyclopedia of American Biography*, 3d ed. to 1960. John A. Garraty ed. New York: Charles Scribner's Sons, 1980, pp. 446-47. No. 2028.

2040. Fisch, M.H. "Justice Holmes, the Prediction Theory of Law and Pragmatism," *Journal of Philosophy* 39 (1942): 3-12.

2041. Freund, Paul A. "Oliver Wendell Holmes." In Friedman and Israel, eds. *The Justices of the United States Supreme Court*, 3:1755-71. No. 1962.

2042. Holmes, Oliver W. *Holmes-Laski Letters*, 2 vols. Cambridge, Mass.: Harvard University Press, 1953.

2043. Konefsky, Samuel J. "Holmes and Brandeis: Companions in Dissent," *Vanderbilt Law Review* 19 (1957):269-70.

2044. Lerner, Max. *The Mind and Faith of Justice Holmes*. Boston: Little, Brown, 1943.

2045. Richardson, Dorsey. *Constitutional Doctrines of Justice Oliver Wendell Holmes*. Baltimore: Johns Hopkins Press, 1924.

2046. Small, Miriam Rossiter. *Oliver Wendell Holmes*. New York: Twayne Publishers, 1963.

2047. Touster, Saul. "Holmes's *Common Law*: A Centennial View," *American Scholar* 51 (Aug. 1982):521-32.

HUGHES, CHARLES EVANS, 1910-1916.

2048. *Encyclopedia of American Biography*, 3d ed. to 1960. John A. Garraty, ed., pp. 548-51. No. 2028.

2049. Fish, Peter G. "William Howard Taft and Charles Evans Hughes: Conservative Politicians as Chief Judicial Reformers," *Supreme Court Review* (1976):123-46.

2050. Hendel, Samuel. "Charles Evans Hughes." In Friedman and Israel, eds. *The Justices of the United States Supreme Court*, 3:1893-1944. No. 1962.

2051. Jackson, Robert H. "The Judicial Career of Chief Justice Hughes," *American Bar Association Journal* 27 (July 1941):408-11.

2052. Perkins, Dexter. *Charles Evans Hughes and American Democratic Statesmanship*. Boston: Little, Brown, 1956. Hughes in New York politics, as Associate Justice of the Supreme Court, as Chief Justice, and more.

2053. Pusey, Merle J. *Charles Evans Hughes*. No. 1672.

McKENNA, JOSEPH, 1897-1925.

2054. Watts, James F., Jr. "Joseph McKenna." In Friedman and Israel, eds. *The Justices of the United States Supreme Court*, 3:1719-54. No. 1962.

McREYNOLDS, JAMES C., 1914-1921.

McReynolds was Attorney General under Theodore Roosevelt from 1903 to 1907; special counsel for the government in the American Tobacco Co. antitrust case; and Attorney General for Woodrow Wilson until he went to the Supreme Court in August 1914 to succeed Horace H. Lurton.

2055. Burner, David. "James C. McReynolds." In Friedman and Israel, eds. *The Justices of the United States Supreme Court*, 3:2023-42. No. 1962.

2056. *National Cyclopaedia of American Biography*, 33:1-2.

2057. Schimmel, Barbara B. "The Judicial Policy of Mr. Justice McReynolds." Ph.D. diss., Yale University, 1983.

SANFORD, EDWARD T., 1923-1930.

2058. Burner, David. "Edward T. Sanford." in Friedman and Israel, eds. *The Justices of the United States Supreme Court*, 3:2202-20. No. 1962.

STONE, HARLAN FISKE, 1925-1941.

2059. Bates, Henry M. "Chief Justice Harlan F. Stone," *American Bar Association Journal* 27 (Aug. 1941):469-74.

2060. "The Chief Justice," *American Bar Association Journal* 27 (July 1941):407-8.

2061. Frank, John R. "Harlan Fiske Stone: An Estimate," *Stanford Law Review* 9 (1957):629

2062. Mason, Alpheus Thomas. "Harlan Fiske Stone." In Friedman and Israel, eds. *The Justices of the United States Supreme Court*, 3:2221-22. No. 1962.

SUTHERLAND, GEORGE, 1922-1938.

2063. Burner, David. "George Sutherland." In Friedman and Israel, eds. *The Justices of the United States Supreme Court*, 3:3133-82. No. 1962.

VAN DEVANTER, WILLIS, 1910-1937.

2064. Burner, David. "Willis Van Devanter." In Friedman and Israel eds. *The Justices of the United States Supreme Court,* 3:1945-72. No. 1962.

2065. "Hon. Willis Van Devanter," *American Bar Association Journal* 27 (Mar. 1941):154.

2066. Nelson, Daniel A. "The Supreme Court Appointment of Willis Van Devanter," *Annals of Wyoming* 53 (1981):2-21. Taft's friend from Wyoming, Sen. Francis E. Warren, campaigned for Van Devanter, who was appointed by Taft following the resignation of William Moody. Van Devanter was one of the least productive members of the Supreme Court.

C. The Most Important Decisions of Taft's Court

2067. The cases noted below and all other cases decided by Taft's court are reported in *United States Reports: Cases Adjudged in the Supreme Court.* Washington: GPO, vols. 259-83.

2068. A handy summary of these cases is found in *United States Supreme Court Digest: Lawyers Edition.* Rochester, N.Y.: The Lawyers Co-operative Pub. Co., vol. 1, 1927.

2069. *Truax v. Corrigan.* 1921-1922. An Arizona statute barred state courts from issuing injunctions in labor cases except under special circumstances. The Supreme Court held that the law violated the Fourteenth Amendment.

2070. *United Mine Workers of America et al v. Coronado Coal Co. et al.* 1922. Labor unions, though unincorporated, could be sued in federal courts if in restraint of trade.

2071. *Stafford v. Wallace.* 1922. The Supreme Court upheld broad federal power under the Commerce clause to prohibit a packers' monopoly.

2072. *Board of Trade v. Olsen.* 1922. The Supreme Court forbade trading in grain futures except under the supervision of the Secretary of Agriculture.

2073. *Bailey v. Drexel Furniture Co.* 1922. Judicial nullification of Congressional efforts to regulate child labor for the second time in four years. Congress cannot use its tax power to destroy what it considers a noxious practice.

2074. *Adkins v. Children's Hospital.* 1923. The Supreme Court overturned the Minimum Wage Act of 1918 establishing standards for minimum wages for women in all occupations in the District of Columbia.

2075. *Wolff Packing Co. v Court of Industrial Relations of Kansas.* 1923. Taft raised the question of when a business became "clothed with a public interest."

2076. *Myers v. United States.* 1926. The Supreme Court upheld the President's authority to remove a postmaster without the consent of the Senate. However, he could not do so if an appointee had quasi-legislative or quasi-judicial powers.

2077. *Olmstead v. United States.* 1928. It is constitutional to tap the private telephone lines of suspected criminals.

Articles

2078. Abraham, Henry J., and Edward M. Goldberg. "A Note on the Appointment of Justices of the Supreme Court of the United States," *American Bar Association Journal* 46 (Feb. 1969):147-56.

2079. "American Law Institute Holds Fourth Meeting," *American Bar Association Journal* 12 (May 1926):300. Taft told the meeting that this association was central to his reform effort.

2080. "The Chief Justice: A Mistaken Appointment," *The Nation* 113 (July 13, 1921):32. The hour called for a Brandeis or Holmes, not for Taft.

2081. "Chief Justice Taft," *Literary Digest* 70 (July 16, 1921):13. Opposed to Taft's nomination were the *New Republic, Nation, Socialist Call, Herald*, and the Hearst papers. The *Call* characterized Taft as a tool of capitalism who "can be depended upon to stand for property rights whenever they come into conflict with human rights."

2082. "Mr. Chief Justice Taft," *The New Republic* 27 (July 27, 1921):230-1. The conservative in the White House was the same conservative on the Supreme Court.

2083. "Does Mr. Taft Want Direct Action? Supreme Court Decision in the Truax Case," *The Nation* 114 (Jan. 11, 1922):32-33. Against striking working restaurant workers.

2084. Edwards. William H. "The Supreme Court Justices: Their Lives and Opinions," *American Bar Association Journal* 57 (Sept. 1971):908-10.

2085. Freund, Paul A. "Storms over the Supreme Court," *American Bar Association Journal* 69 (Oct. 1983):1474-81. Photograph of Taft on p. 1478.

2086. Genovese, Michael A. "The Supreme Court as a Check on Presidential Power," *Presidential Studies Quarterly* 6 (Winter-Spring, 1976):40-4.

2087. Goldberg, Edward M. "The Right to Be Left Alone," *Rendezvous* 3 (1968):15-21. Taft supported the uses of such devices as wiretaps to prevent crime, specifically with respect to prohibition, but other justices held that the government's use of illegal means to secure evidence promoted lawbreaking by citizens.

2088. Harlan, John M. "The Bill of Rights and the Constitution," *American Bar Association Journal* 50 (Oct. 1964):918-21. By an Associate Justice.

2089. Hazard, Henry B. "The Supreme Court Holds Madam Schwimmer, Pacifist, Ineligible to Naturalization," *American Journal of International Law* 23 (July 1929):626-32. By a 6 to 3 decision on May 27, 1929, because she was not attached to the principles of the Constitution and could not swear the oath of allegiance without a mental reservation.

2090. Hughes, Charles Evans, Chief Justice. "Corner Stone of New Home of Supreme Court of the United States Is Laid," *American Bar Association Journal* 18 (Nov. 1932):723, 728. Hughes stated that for the new home of the Supreme Court "We are indebted to the late Chief Justice William Howard Taft more than anyone else."

2091. Keefe, Arthur John. "The Marble Palace at 50," *American Bar Association Journal* 68 (Oct. 1982):1224-29. Credits Taft for finding a new home for the Supreme Court. Taft obtained approval from the Court members, funds from Congress, chose Cass Gilbert as the architect, but was dead for two years before even the cornerstone was laid. Mrs. Taft was present when President Hoover laid the first bit of cement, then turned the proceedings over to Hughes.

2092. Kutler, Stanley I. :"Labor, the Clayton Act, and the Supreme Court," *Labor History* 3 (1962):19-38.

2093. ———. "Chief Justice Taft, National Regulation and the Commerce Power," *Journal of American History* 51 (Mar. 1965):56-68. The decisions of Taft's court decisively helped to increase national power.

2094. ———. "Chief Justice Taft, Judicial Unanimity, and Labor: The Coronado Case," *Historian* 24 (1961):68-83. The unanimous decision in the Coronado Co. cases in 1922 and 1925 proved to be stepping stones to a new national labor policy as expressed in the Wagner Act of 1937. Despite the UMW's opposition, the court decided that labor unions were corporations that could be sued.

2095. Lambeth, Harry J. "The Lawyers Who Became President," *American Bar Association Journal* 63 (Oct. 1977):1430-32. Among these were John Adams, Jefferson, Monroe, J.Q. Adams, Jackson, Tyler, Polk, Fillmore, Pierce, Buchanan, Hayes, Arthur, Cleveland, McKinley, Taft, and Wilson.

2096. Lawson, Steven F. "Progressives and the Supreme Court: A Case for Judicial Reform in the 1920s," *Historian* 42 (May 1980):419-36. How Taft defeated progressives by curbing freedom of speech, emasculating progressive economic legislation, and limiting efforts at labor unionization.

2097. Little, Herbert. "The Omnipotent Nine," *American Mercury* 15 (Sept. 1928):49. Chief Justice Taft insisted upon proper dress by his justices and by those who appeared before them.

2098. Mason, Alpheus T. "The Labor Decisions of Chief Justice Taft," *University of Pennsylvania Law Review* 78 (1930): 585-625. Taft's efforts to slow labor unionization.

2099. ———. "President by Chance, Chief Justice by Choice," *American Bar Association Journal* 55 (1969): 35-39. Taft failed to exercise the expansive powers of the presidency but capitalized on the limited powers of the chief justiceship.

2100. Morris, Jeffrey B. "What Heaven Must Be Like: William Howard Taft as Chief Justice, 1921-1930," Supreme Court Historical Society*Yearbook* 8 (1983):80-101. Taft was not the most respected of the chief justices, but his estimate of the duties of the chief justice set a precedent.

2101. Murphy, Walter F. "Chief Justice Taft and the Lower Court Bureaucracy: A Study in Judicial Administration," *Journal of Politics* 24 (1962):453-76. Taft created the Judicial Conference as a way to build a rapproachement between the Supreme Court and the lower Federal Courts. As president, Taft had appointed almost 30 percent of the Federal Judges, many of them still serving when he became the Chief Justice.

2102. Nagel, Stuart S. "Characteristics of Supreme Court Greatness," *American Bar Association Journal* 56 (Oct. 1970):956-63.

2103. "New Chief Justice," *The Outlook* 128 (July 13, 1921): 436-37.

2104. Paper, Lewis J. "The Not So Sinister Brandeis-Frankfurter Connection," *American Bar Association Journal* 69 (Sept. 1983):1860-64. These men had been friends since 1905, and Frankfurter had financially supported Brandeis.

2105. Pusey, Merle J. "The 'Judge's Bill' After Half a Century," Supreme Court Historical Society. *Yearbook* 1 (1976):73-81. Largely at Taft's prodding, the Judiciary Act of 1925 gave the court a large amount of control over its workload.

2106. ———. "The Court Copes with Disability," Supreme Court Historical Society. *Yearbook* 6 (1981):68-73.

2107. Rehnquist, Justice William H. "The Supreme Court: Past and Present," *American Bar Association Journal* 59 (Apr. 1973):361-64. Mentions the Judge's Act of 1891 and of 1925, each successfully enabling the Court to retain its place in our judicial system by changing its method of operation.

2108. Shaw, Albert. "Mr. Taft's Retirement from the Bench," *Review of Reviews* 81 (Mar. 1930):33-36. Kind words.

2109. Skefos, Catherine Hetos. "The Supreme Court Gets a Home," Supreme Court Historical Society. *Yearbook* 1 (1976):23-36. Largely at Taft's prodding, the Supreme Court obtained its first permanent meeting place.

2110. Slotnick, Elliott E. "The Quality Principle and Majority Opinion: Assignment on the United States Supreme Court," *Policy* 12 (1979):318-52. On how Taft and certain other chief justices tried to equalize the justices' work loads while reserving the writing of important opinions to themselves.

2111. Stagner, Stephen. "The Recall of Judicial Decisions and the Due Process Debate," *American Journal of Legal History* 24 (July 1980):257-72. Taft was heartily opposed to the recall of judicial decisions.

2112. "Supreme Court Decisions on Alien Land Law Cases," *American Journal of International Law* 18 (1924):125. On Nov. 11, 1923, Justice Butler spoke for the Court in upholding the right of states to exclude Japanese from leasing agricultural land.

2113. Swindler, William J. "Justices in Academe," Supreme Court Historical Society. *Yearbook* 4 (1979):31-37.

2114. Taft, William H. "Address of the President," *American Bar Association Reports* 39 (1914):369.

2115. ———. "Adequate Machinery for Judicial Business." Address Delivered at the Forty-fourth Meeting of the American Bar Association, at Cincinnati, Ohio, Aug. 30, 1921. *American Bar Association Journal* 7 (Sept. 1921): 453. Congress has failed to provide adequate judicial machinery. More judges should be added and an executive director should be provided to assign them their work and to schedule judicial conferences. Similar remarks are found in 2127.

2116. ———. "Three Needed Steps of Progress," *American Bar Association Journal* 8 (1922):24, and "Possible and Needed Reforms in the Administration of Justice." ibid., 8 (1922):601.

2117. ———. "Statement before the Committee of the Judiciary, U.S. Congress, Senate." 67th Cong., 1st Sess., p. 16, Oct. 5, 1921. On court reforms.

2118. ———. "The Supreme Court and the Public Welfare." *The Outlook* 130 (June 20, 1923):67-68. At the unveiling of a monument to Chief Justice Salmon Portland Chase, Taft responded to criticism of the Supreme Court judges as "actually Supreme Rulers."

2119. ———. "Procedure in Federal Courts," *Hearings, Subcommittee of the Judiciary Committee, U.S. Senate*. U.S. Congress, Senate, 68th Cong., 1st Sess., Feb. 2, 1914, on S. 2020 and S. 2061, p. 76. On Federal Uniform Procedure.

2120. ———. "Statement of Chief Justice William Howard Taft." *Hearings before the Committee on the Judiciary*. U.S. Congress, House. 68th Cong., 2d Sess., on HR. 8206. Dec. 18, 1924. On court reforms.

2121. ———. "The Attack on the Courts and Legal Procedure," *Kentucky Law Journal* 5 (1924):18. Taft's recommendation that by reducing the

Supreme Court's obligatory jurisdiction and extending discretionary review he hoped to reroute many cases on appeal to the Circuit Courts.

2122. ―――. "The Jurisdiction of the Supreme Court under the Act of February 13, 1925," *Yale Law Journal* 35 (Nov. 1925):1. Explains how the Court could be more selective in the cases it chose to hear under the law he had fought for.

2123. "W.H. Taft to C.E. Hughes, April 27, 1926," *American Bar Association Journal* 12 (May 1926):326. Taft blasted local bar associations as being social groups rather than attempting to secure self-discipline and "real reform measures of legal procedure."

2124. Teger, Stuart H., and Douglas Kosonski, "The Cue Theory of Supreme Court Certiorari Jurisdiction: A Reconsideration," *Journal of Politics* 42 (Aug. 1980):834-46. The theory need *not* always determine which cases will be heard.

14
Taft's Personal Life

A. Personal Characteristics

Some witticisms and peculiarities of Taft are found in the following.

Monographs

2125. Adler, Bill. *Presidential Wit from Washington to Johnson.* New York: Trident Press, 1966.

2126. Boller, Paul F., Jr. *Presidential Anecdotes.* New York: Oxford University Press, 1981.

2127. Harnsberger, Caroline, ed. *Treasury of Presidential Quotations.* Chicago: Follett Publishing Co., 1964.

2128. Smith, Don. *Peculiarities of the Presidents: Strange and Intimate Facts Not Found in History,* 4th rev. ed. Van Vert, Ohio: Wilkinson Printing Co., 1946.

Articles

2129. Abbot, Laurence. "Human Qualities of Taft," *The Outlook* 88 (Apr. 4, 1908):773-77.

2130. "Character of Taft," *The Independent* 66 (Mar. 4, 1909):492-94.

2131 Gleason, A.H. "Bill Taft of Yale," *Collier's* 42 (Mar. 6, 1909):19-20.

2132. "How the President Plays Golf," *Harper's Weekly* 53 (July 17, 1909):27. Includes a photograph showing Taft playing golf with his vice president, "Sunny Jim" Sherman, at a Chevy Chase, Md., course.

2133. "Our New Summer Capital," *Harper's Weekly* 53 (June 26, 1909):13. The Tafts rented the Stetton cottage on Woodbury's Point east of Beverly and about 19 miles from Boston.

2134. "Mr. Taft's Bed in the White House," *Harper's Weekly* 53 (Mar. 20, 1909):29. An extra large bed presented to Taft by some Filipinos.

2135. *Notable Names in American History: A Tabulated Register*, 3d ed. of *White's Conspectus of American Biography*. Clifton, N.J.: James T. White. Co., 1973. Taft, pp. 13, 17, 18, 30, 44, 270, 271, 564, 569, 575, 603.

2136. Ravis, W.J. "Golfing with the President," *Century Magazine* 80 (Sept. 1910):651-56.

2137. "Temperament and Character of Taft," *Living Age* 261 (Apr. 17, 1909):182-84.

2138. Thomas, A.E. "Golfing with the President," *Everybody's Magazine* 23 (July 1910):24-32. A self-made, conservative golfer, Taft played with the course cleared of all other persons.

2139. Tittle, W. "Glimpses of Interesting Americans," *Century Magazine* 110 (Sept. 1925):72. A kind of futility marked Taft's term as president.

2140. "With the President on His Vacation," *Harper's Weekly* 53 (Aug. 28, 1909):17. Includes a photograph showing Taft in his office in Beverly.

B. Health

Although corpulent, Taft was very light on his feet and was a good dancer. Until his last years he ate heavily and often would drop his head on his chest and take a fifteen minute nap before awakening. He rode horseback until his fifties, but his favorite sport was golf. He drank only sparingly of wine or beer, and never smoked. While Civil Governor of the Philippines he had to return to the United States because he had symptoms of amoebic dysentery and had an operation to remove gravel from his bladder. During the early 1920s he had digestive disturbances. Because he had high blood pressure and hardening of the arteries, during his last years he used an elevator to reach the upper floors of his home. He suffered his first heart attack in February 1924, the day after the funeral of Woodrow Wilson, and had a second one at the end of April. When he reached seventy years of age, his health noticeably began to fail, and he had a downturn in June 1929 after disregarding medical advice and attending the funeral of his brother Charles in Cincinnati. He returned to Washington so weak that he had to be hospitalized, and he subsequently declined into an all but helpless state from cardiovascular collapse. He lapsed into periods of unconsciousness in February and died in his seventy-third year on 8 March 1930.

Monographs

2141. The psychological implications of Taft's obesity are thoroughly covered in Anderson, Judith Icke. *William Howard Taft: An Intimate History.* New York: W.W. Norton, 1981.

2142. Baker, Charles E. Doctor of Physical Culture and Hygiene. *With President Taft in the White House: Memoirs of William Howard Taft.* Chicago: A. Kroch and Sons, 1947. Taft good-naturedly accepted jokes about his fatness and obesity. During the winter of 1906 he put himself in Dr. Baker's care and reduced his weight from 330 to 256 pounds—and got a $1,000 bill for suit alterations! While vacationing at Beverly after his presidency, he was in the care of a number of physicians and for several years was a member of Isador "Izzy" Winters' Health Farm.

2143. Marks, Rudolph, M.D. *The Health of Presidents.* New York: G.P Putnam's Sons, 1960. Contains a chapter on each president from George Washington to F.D. Roosevelt, excluding Hoover.

2144. Wold, Karl. *Mr. President: How Is Your Health?* St. Paul, Minn.: Bruce Publishing Co., 1948.

Articles

2145. Blazer, Alfred, M.D. "The Obese Character," *International Record of Medicine* 164 (1951):24-30.

2146. Lowry, E.G. "Keeping the President in Physical Trim," *Collier's* 47 (June 19, 1911):19. Taft's physical fitness program.

2147. Plesure, M. "The Health of the President." In Tugwell, Rexford G., and Thomas E. Cronin, eds. *The Presidency Reappraised.* New York: Praeger, 1974. A good brief review of the literature on presidential health.

2148. Rennie, Thomas, M.D. "Obesity as a Manifestation of Personality Disturbance," *Diseases of the Nervous System* 1 (1940):238-47.

C. Religion

Bibliographic Aid

2149. Menendez, Albert J. *Religion and the U.S. Presidency: A Bibliography.* New York: Garland, 1986. Taft, pp. 111-12.

Monographs

2150. Fuller, Edmund, and Green, David E. *God in the White House: The Faiths of American Presidents*. New York: Crown, 1968. Taft, pp. 169-73.

2151. Isely, Bliss. *The Presidents: Men of Faith*. Boston: W.A. Wilde Co., 1953. From Washington through Eisenhower.

Article

2152. "Taft and His Religion," *The Nation* 87 (Sept. 24, 1908):278-79.

D. Marriage

In 1886 Taft married the intelligent, charming, often critical, sometimes possessive if not dictatorial Helen "Nellie" Herron. Although he dealt expertly with figures involved in many court cases, he had no great affinity for amassing wealth and left the care of family finances pretty much to Mrs. Taft. He and she opposed women's suffrage, which their daughter supported. She died on 22 May 1943, one week before her eighty-second birthday, and is buried beside her husband in Arlington Cemetery.

2153. Anderson, *William Howard Taft*, Chapter 2. No. 224.

2154. Busbey, Katherine G. "Mrs. Taft's Home Making," *Good Housekeeping* 53 (Sept. 1911):290-98.

2155. Coletta, *The Presidency of William Howard Taft*, pp. 259-60. No. 231.

2156. Furman, Bess. *White House Profile: A Social History of the White House, Its Occupants and Festivities*. Indianapolis: Bobbs-Merrill, 1951.

2157. Hill, George. "Wife of the New President," *Ladies Home Journal* 26 (Mar. 1909):6.

2158. Hoover, Irwin Hood. *Forty-two Years in the White House*. Boston: Houghton Mifflin, 1934. Hoover, the Chief Usher at the White House, was displeased with some aspects of Mrs. Taft's management of the mansion, such as her putting footmen in livery.

2159. Jaffray, Elizabeth. *Secrets of the White House*. New York: Cosmopolitan Book Corp., 1926. Personal observations of the Tafts in the White House. Tafts, pp. 3-33.

2160. Jeffries, Ona Griffin. "Four Years of Strife: William Howard Taft and Helen Taft." In *In and Out of the White House.* New York: W. Funk, 1960. Tafts, pp. 285-96.

2161. Jensen, Amy (La Follette). Howard C. Jensen, Art Editor. *The White House and Its Thirty-five Families.* New York: McGraw-Hill, 1971. A smoothly written popular account with excellent illustrations. Taft, pp. 192-99.

2162. Kehl, James A. "White House or Animal House?" *South Atlantic Quarterly* 79 (Autumn 1980):343-54. Should the public pay for transporting White House pets?

2163. Kirk, Elise K. *Music in the White House: A History of the American Spirit.* Urbana: University of Illinois Press, 1986.

2164. Leish, Kenneth W., ed. *The White House.* New York: Newsweek, 1972. Taft, pp. 94, 95, 147, 149, 150, 153.

2165. Loots, Barbara Kunz. *Fascinating First Ladies: Memorable Moments in the Lives of Fifteen Presidents' Wives.* Kansas City, Mo.: Hallmark Cards, 1977. Nothing on Taft.

2166. Parks, Lillian Rogers. *My Thirty Years Backstairs at the White House.* New York: Fleet Publishing Corp. 1961. Personal recollections of the Tafts in the White House.

2167. ———. *It Was Fun Working at the White House.* New York: Fleet Publishing Corp. 1969. Reprint of No. 2166. Mrs. Taft, pp. 26-35.

2168. Pringle, *Taft,* 2:1071-82. No. 248.

2169. Reit, Seymour. *Growing Up in the White House.* New York: Crowell-Collier Press, 1968. Taft children, pp. 73-76.

2170. Selden, C.A. "Six White House Wives and Widows," *Ladies Home Journal* 44 (June 1927):18. Mrs. Taft, pp. 109-12.

2171. Seuling, Barbara. *The Last Cow on the White House Lawn, and Other Little Known Facts about the Presidency.* Garden City, N.Y.: Doubleday, 1978. Juvenile. Tafts, pp. 53-55.

2172. Smith, Marie D. *Entertaining in the White House*, rev. and updated ed. New York: Macfadden-Bartell, 1970.

2173. Taft, Mrs. William Howard. *Recollections of Full Years*. New York: Dodd, Mead, 1914. The book was serialized in *Delineator Magazine* between May and November 1914.

2174. ———. "Mrs. Taft's Plans for the White House," *Ladies Home Journal* 26 (Mar. 1909):26.

2175. ———. "Six Weeks I Spent on a Farm," *Ladies Home Journal* 35 (June 1918):28.

2176. ———. "Does America Need College Women?" *Collier's Magazine* 65 (Jan. 31, 1920):7. Yes.

2177. ———. "Women in Politics," *Woman's Home Companion* 47 (Apr. 1920):4.

E. Children

The Tafts had three children: Charles Phelps II, Robert A., and Helen (Mrs. Frederick Manning).

2178. Cavanaugh, Frances. *Children at the White House*. New York: Rand McNally, 1936.

2179. Lawson, Don. *Young People in the White House*, rev. ed. London and New York: Abelard-Schuman, 1970.

2180. Perling, Joseph Jerry. *Presidents' Sons: The Prestige of Name in a Democracy*. 1947; rept. Freeport, N.Y.: Books for Libraries, 1971. Charles: pp. 281-85, 290-91; Robert: 274-81, 286-89.

2181. Quinn, Sandra L., and Sanford Kanter. *America's Royalty: All the Presidents' Children*. Westport Conn.: Greenwood Press, 1983. Sketches of each child, if any.

2182. Sadler, Christine. *Children in the White House*. New York: Putnam, 1967.

2183. Sweetser, Kate D. *Famous Girls of the White House*, rev. ed. New York: Crowell, 1957. Mrs. W.H. Taft, s.v.

CHARLES PHELPS, 1897-1983

Of an outgoing and enthusiastic nature, Charles attended the Taft School, Watertown, Connecticut, where he prepared for attending Yale University. He spent a year overseas during World War I, married Eleanor Chase, became prosecuting attorney of Hamilton County Ohio, a longtime member of the Cincinnati City Council, and was the city's mayor from 1955 to 1957. He was an idealistic and active crusader in the 1940s on such issues as civic reform, slum clearance, labor relations, and welfare for the deprived and disabled.

2184. Bartlett, Robert Merrill. *They Work for Tomorrow*. 1943; rept. Freeport, N.Y.: Books for Libraries, 1970. Includes a chapter on Charles: "Man's More Honorable Calling," pp. 89-98.

2185. *Notable Names in American History*. Charles P. Taft, pp. 143, 152. No. 2135.

2186. Ross, Ishbel, *An American Family*, Chapter 26. No. 275.

2187. Taft, Charles P. *City Management: The Cincinnati Experiment*. New York: Farrar and Rinehart, 1933. Charles served as mayor of Cincinnati.

2188. Tucker, Robert Whitney. *The Descendants of the Presidents*. Charlotte, N.C.: Delmar Printing Co., 1975.

ROBERT A., ("Mr. Republican"), 1889-1953

Robert graduated from Harvard Law School and was a partner in the law firm of Taft, Stettinius, and Hollister. His wife was the politically ambitious Martha Bowers. He served in the Ohio House of Representatives, 1921-1926, and in the U.S. Senate from 1938 to his death in 1953. He made three unsuccessful attempts to obtain the Republican presidential nomination.

2189. Alexander, Holmes Moss. *The Famous Five*. New York: Bookmailer, 1958. Includes R.A. Taft.

2190. Armstrong, John P. "The Enigma of Senator Taft and Foreign Policy," *Review of Politics* 17 (1955):206-31.

2191. *Encyclopedia of American Biography*. John A. Garraty, ed. New York: Harper & Row, 1974, pp. 1073-74. No. 2028.

2192. Felsenthal, Carol. *Alice Roosevelt Longworth*. Robert Taft, pp. 181, 189-90, 201, 226, 228. Often mentioned *passim*. No. 1558.

2193. Manning, Helen Taft. "My Brother Bob Taft," *American Magazine* 153 (Jan. 1952):14.

2194. Matthews, Geoffrey. "Robert A. Taft, the Constitution, and American Foreign Policy, 1939-1953," *Journal of Contemporary History* 17 (July 1982).

2195. Obituary, "Robert A. Taft," *New York Times*, August 1, 1953, 1:8

2196. *Notable Names in American History*, pp. 211-34, *passim*. No. 2135.

2197. Perling, *President's Sons*, No. 2180.

2198. Radosh, Ronald. *Prophets on the Right: Profiles of Conservative Critics of American Globalism*. New York: Simon and Schuster, 1975, pp. 11, 113, 119-93, and *passim*.

2199. Ross, Ishbel. *An American Family*, Chapters 20, 25, 27. No. 275.

2200. Tucker, Robert Whitney. *The Descendants of the Presidents*. No. 2188.

HELEN (MRS. FREDERICK MANNING), 1891-1957

Helen obtained a B.A. degree from Bryn Mawr in 1915, a doctorate in history from Yale in 1924, and a law degree from George Washington University in 1936. She married a professor of political science at Yale, Frederick J. Manning, in 1920. Her publications include:

2201. Manning, Helen (Mrs. Frederick). *British Colonial Government After the American Revolution, 1782-1820*. New Haven: Yale University Press, London: Oxford University Press, 1934.

2202. ———. *The Revolt of French Canada 1800-1935*. New York: St. Martin's Press, 1962.

2203. Obituary, *New York Times*, August 9, 1957, 19:5.

2204. Ross, Ishbel. *An American Family*, Chap. 22. No. 275.

2205. Tucker, Robert Whitney. *The Descendants of the Presidents.* No. 2188.

F. Mrs. William Howard Taft

2206. Anderson, Mary. "The Costumes of the Mistresses of the White House," *Americana* 23 (Oct. 1929):427-50.

2207. Barzman, Sol. *The First Ladies.* New York: Cowles Book Co., 1970. Taft, pp. 236-46.

2208. Blumberg, Rhoda. *First Ladies*, rev. ed. New York: Franklin Watts, 1981.

2209. Boller, Paul F., Jr. *Presidential Wives: An Anecdotal History.* New York: Oxford University Press, 1988. Mrs. Taft, pp. 206-18.

2210. Brooks, Gertrude L. *The First Ladies of the White House.* Ed. by Jan Pitts. Chicago: Hallberg, 1967.

2211. Brown, Margaret W. *The Dresses of the First Ladies.* Washington: Smithsonian Institution, 1952. Photographs, paintings, and short biographies of the first ladies.

2212. Carosso, Vincent P. "Music and Musicians in the White House," *New York Historical Society Quarterly* 48 (Apr. 1964):101-29.

2213. Chaffin, Lillie D. *America's First Ladies.* Minneapolis, Minn.: Lerner, 1969.

2214. Furman, Bess. *White House Profile: A Social History of the White House, Its Occupants and Its Festivities.* Indianapolis: Bobbs-Merrill, 1951. Taft, pp. 274-75.

2215. Gerlach, Robert. *First Ladies.* New York: French, 1984.

2216. Gerlinger, Irene. *Mistresses of the White House; Narrator's Tale of a Pageant of First Ladies.* 1950; rept. Freeport, N.Y.: Books for Libraries, 1970, pp. 85-88.

2217. Holman, Hamilton. *White House Images and Realities.* Gainesville: University of Florida Press, 1958. Taft, pp. 2, 6, 25, 74, 80.

2218. Hurd, Charles. *The White House Story*. New York: Hawthorn Books, 1966.

2219. James, Edward T., Janet Wilson, and Paul S. Boyer, eds. *Notable American Women, 1607-1950: A Biographical Dictionary*, 3 vols. Cambridge, Mass.: Belknap Press of Harvard University, 1971. Mrs. Taft, 3:420-1.

2220. Jeffries, Ona Griffin, "Four Years of Strife: William Howard Taft and Helen Taft." No. 2160.

2221. Klapthor, Margaret Brown. *The First Ladies*. Washington: White House Historical Association, with the Cooperation of the National Geographic Society, 1975, pp. 60-1.

2222. Logan, Logna B. *Ladies of the White House*. New York: Vantage Press, 1962.

2223. Loots, Barbara Kunz. *Fascinating First Ladies*. No. 2165.

2224. McConnell, Jane and Burt. *Our First Ladies from Martha Washington to Pat Ryan Nixon*. New York: Thomas Y. Crowell, 1969, pp. 253-62.

2225. Means, Marianne. *The Woman in the White House*. New York: Random House, 1963.

2226. Prindville, Kathleen. *First Ladies*. 2d ed. New York: Macmillan, 1964. Taft, pp. 203-10.

2227. Rosebush, James S. *First Lady, Public Wife*. Lanham, Md.: Madison Books, 1987. Traces the evolution of the role of the president's wife from colonial days to the present. Mrs. Taft, pp. 8, 82.

2228. Slayden, Ellen M. *Washington Wife. . . .* New York: Harper and Row, 1962. Taft, pp. 121-26, 151, 156-57, and *passim*.

2229. An obituary notice about Mrs. Taft is in *New York Times*, May 23, 1943.

15
Historiographical Materials

A. Biographers and Others

Among biographers and others who place Taft in historical perspective are:

2230. Anderson, Donald F. *William Howard Taft: A Conservative Conception of the Presidency.* No. 224.

2231. Anderson, Judith Icke. *William Howard Taft: An Intimate History.* No. 226.

2232. Burton, David H. *William Howard Taft: In the Public Service.* No. 229.

2233. Butler, Nicholas Murray. *Across the Busy Years: Recollections and Reflections*, 2 vols. New York: Charles S. Scribner's Sons, 1939.

2234. Butt, Archibald Willingham. *Taft and Roosevelt: The Intimate Letters of Archie Butt, Military Aide.* No. 95.

2235. Coletta. *Presidency of William Howard Taft.* No. 231.

2236. ———. *William Jennings Bryan.* No. 352.

2237. Cotton, Edward. *William Howard Taft: A Character Study.* No. 233.

2238. Dunn, Robert Lee. *William Howard Taft: American.* Boston: Chapple Pub. Co., 1908. A campaign biography.

2239. Hammond, John Hays. *The Autobiography of John Hays Hammond.* No. 1795.

2240. Hargrove, Erwin C. *Presidential Leadership: Personality and Political Style.* No. 236.

2241. Hicks, Frederick C. *William Howard Taft: Yale Professor of Law and New Haven.* No. 239.

2242. La Follette, Belle Case and Fola La Follette. *Robert M. La Follette.* No. 1545.

2243. La Follette, Robert M. *Autobiography.* No. 1546.

2244. McHale, Francis. *President and Chief Justice: The Life and Services of William Howard Taft.* No. 242.

2245. Leopold, Richard. *Elihu Root and the Conservative Tradition.* No. 1578.

2246. Mason, Alpheus Thomas. *William Howard Taft: Chief Justice.* No. 245.

2247. Myers, Elisabeth P. *William Howard Taft.* No. 246.

2248. Patterson, Raymond Albert. *Taft's Training for the Presidency.* No. 247.

2249. Pinchot, Gifford. *Breaking New Ground.* No. 965.

2250. Pringle, Henry F. *The Life and Times of William Howard Taft.* No. 248.

2251. Ragan, Allen. *Chief Justice Taft.* No. 1984.

2252. Severn, Bill. *William Howard Taft: The President Who became Chief Justice.* No. 252.

2253. Taft, Horace Dutton. *Memories and Opinions.* No. 255.

2254. Taft, Mrs. William Howard. *Recollections of Full Years.* No. 256.

B. On Taft's Contributions to History

Evaluations of Taft, among others, are found in the following:

2255. Agar, Herbert. *The American Presidents: From Washington to Harding.* London: Eyre and Spottiswoode, 1933.

2256. Anderson, Donald F. "The Legacy of William Howard Taft," *Presidential Studies Quarterly* 12 (1982):26-33. Taft acted from his beliefs in constitutional democracy and the separation of powers.

2257. Adams, Henry. *The Selected Letters of Henry Adams.* Newton Arvin, ed. New York: Farrar, Straus and Young, 1951.

2258. Armbruster, Maxim E. *The Presidents of the United States and Their Administrations from Washington to Reagan,* rev. ed. New York: Horizon Press, 1982.

2259. Barber, James David. "Analyzing Presidents: From Passive-Positive Taft to Active-Positive Nixon," *Washington Monthly* 1 (Oct. 1969):33-54.

2260. Bonsal, Stephen. "The Man Who Served Us: Taft," *The World's Work* 59 (Apr. 1930):76-80. A biographical sketch by a journalist who had been Taft's friend for 20 years.

2261. Burns, James MacGregor. *Presidential Government: The Crucible of Leadership.* Boston: Houghton Mifflin, 1966. Neither a "great" president nor a "failure," Taft had been an "average" president.

2262. Adams, Henry. *Henry Adams and His Friends: A Collection of His Unpublished Letters.* Harold Carter, ed. Boston: Houghton Mifflin, 1947. Contains observations and impressions of Taft.

2263. Cole, Cyrenus. *I Remember, I Remember.* Iowa City: State Historical Society of Iowa, 1936.

2264. Colucci, Vito E. *Biographies of the Presidents,* 4th ed. Woodside, New York: The Author, 1966.

2265. Davis, Oscar King. *Released for Publication: Some Inside Political History of Theodore Roosevelt and His Times, 1898-1918.* Boston: Houghton Mifflin, 1925. A reporter whose reminiscences are critical of Taft.

2266. Depew, Chauncey M. *My Memories of 80 Years.* New York: Charles Scribner's Sons, 1922.

2267. Doane, Franklin C. *The Presidents of the United States: Biographies.* New York: Pickwick Publications, 1930.

2268. Dunn, Arthur W. *From Harrison to Harding: A Personal Narrative Covering a Third of a Century, 1888-1921,* 2 vols. New York: G.P. Putnam's Sons, 1922. A journalist whose reminiscences are critical of Taft.

2269. Filler, Louis, ed. *The Presidents in the Twentieth Century.* Englewood Cliffs, N.J.: Prentice-Hall, 1983.

2270. Frank, John O. *Marble Palace: The Supreme Court in American Life.* New York: Knopf, 1961. The author evaluates the 92 judges of the Supreme Court who served to date. He found 8 to be failures, 6 below average, 27 average, and Taft among the 15 "near greats."

2271. Frankfurter, Felix. "The Supreme Court in the Mirror of Justices," *Pennsylvania Law Review* 78 (1957):10-15. The author thought that 19 of the 92 justices who had served were preeminent—but not Taft.

2272. ———. "Chief Justices I Have Known," Supreme Court Historical Society. *Yearbook* 5 (1980):3-9.

2273. "Great Public Servant," *Saturday Evening Post* 202 (Apr. 12, 1930):34.

2274. Hansborough, Henry Clay. *The Wreck: A Historical and a Critical Study of the Administrations of Theodore Roosevelt and of William Howard Taft.* New York: The Neale Publishing Co., 1913.

2275. Hart, Albert Bushnell. "William Howard Taft: His Place in American History," *Current History* 32 (May 1930):2-5.

2276. Harvey, George. *Henry Clay Frick the Man.* New York: Charles H. Scribner's Sons, 1929.

2277. Hughes, Emmet John. "Our Presidents, Heroes or Nobodies? They All Had Their Own Style," *Smithsonian Magazine* 2 (Mar. 1972):28-37. Includes Taft.

2278. Kane, Joseph N. *Facts about the Presidency: A Compilation of Biographical and Historical Information*, 4th ed. New York: H.W. Wilson, 1981. Taft, s.v.

2279. Krock, Arthur. *Memoirs: Intimate Recollections of Twelve American Presidents from Theodore Roosevelt to Richard Nixon.* London: Cassell, 1970. Memories of a reporter who specialized in politics.

2280. Luke, James. *Our Glorious Heritage: The Presidents from Washington to Eisenhower.* New York: Vantage Press, 1961.

2281. Lynch, Frederick. "William Howard Taft's Labors for International Peace," *Current History* 32 (May 1930): 195-98. Taft was the first president to offer arbitration treaties covering all kinds of disputes, even those involving questions of "national honor and vital interests." He also contributed to the policy in the Covenant of the League of Nations.

2282. Mason, Alpheus Thomas. "President by Chance, Chief Justice by Choice," *American Bar Association Journal* 55 (Jan. 1969): 35-39. How successful was Taft, who failed to exercise the expansive power of the presidency, in capitalizing on the limited power of the chief justiceship? Rates Taft as one of the court's most effective administrators, along with Fuller and Hughes.

2283. "Mr. Taft's Place in All Hearts," *Literary Digest* 104 (Mar. 22, 1930):15. About Taft's good sportsmanship in defeat and his long public service.

2284. Moran, Thomas F. *American Presidents: Their Individualities and Their Contributions to American Progress.* 1917; new ed., rev. and enl. by Louis Martin Sears. New York: Crowell, 1933.

2285. Murphy, Arthur B. "Evaluating the Presidents of the United States," *Presidential Studies Quarterly* 14 (Winter 1984):117-27.

2286. Murray, Robert K., and Tim H. Blessing. "The Presidential Performance Study: A Progress Report," *Journal of American History* 70 (Dec. 1983):535-55.

2287. *Obituary Record of Graduates.* Yale University, Nos. 1-110. New Haven: Yale University Press, 1860-1952.

2288. Pringle, Henry F. *Theodore Roosevelt: A Biography.* No. 248. A prize-winning biography that says much about the Roosevelt-Taft relationship.

2289. "The Retiring President," *The Outlook* 103 (Mar. 8, 1913):520-2. Taft's greatest service was to support the cause of conservative constitutionalism and defend it against the assaults of direct democracy.

2290. Schultz, Louis Peter. "William Howard Taft: A Constitutionalist's View of the Presidency." Ph.D. diss. Illinois University, 1979.

2291. ———. "William Howard Taft: A Constitutionalist's View of the Presidency," *Presidential Studies Quarterly* 9, No. 4 (1979):402-14. While Taft failed to put much pressure on Congress, he stuck by his authority as president in the field of foreign affairs.

2292. Schlesinger, Arthur M., Jr. "Rating the Presidents." In his *Paths to the Present.* Boston: Houghton Mifflin, 1964, pp. 104-14.

2293. Schlesinger, Arthur M., Sr. "Historians Rate U.S. Presidents." *Life* 25 (Nov. 1948):65-66. 68, 73-74.

2294. ———. "Our Presidents: A Rating by 75 Historians," *New York Times Magazine* 29 (July 1962):12-13, 40-1, 43.

2295. "Sizing Up Mr. Taft's Record," *Literary Digest* 46 (Mar. 14, 1913):558. Contemporaries evaluated Taft as president as "far from the bottom, though not near the top."

2296. Stoddard, Henry L. *As I Knew Them: Presidents and Politics from Grant to Coolidge.* New York: Harper & Bros., 1927. An able reporter whose reminiscences were critical of Taft. No. 253.

2297. Thompson, Charles W. "Two Tafts," *American Mercury* 1 (Mar. 1924):315-19. A poor president but a good judge.

2298. ———. *Presidents I've Known and Two Near-Presidents.* Indianapolis: Bobbs-Merrill, 1929. By a journalist whose reminiscences are critical of Taft.

2299. Villard, Oswald Garrison. *Fighting Years: Memoirs of a Liberal Editor.* New York: Harcourt, Brace, 1939. Taft was honest, guileless, and lazy.

2300. ———. *Prophets True and False.* New York: Alfred A. Knopf, 1928. A journalist whose reminiscences are critical of Taft.

2301. Walker, Kenneth R. "Ohio's Three Chief Justices: Puritans on the Bench," *Northwest Ohio Quarterly* 38 (1966):6673. Salmon P. Chase, Morrison R. Waite, and Taft.

2302. ———. *The Days the Presidents Died.* Little Rock: Arkansas Press, 1966.

2303. Watson, James E. *As I Knew Them: Memoirs of James E. Watson, Former United States Senator from Indiana.* Indianapolis: Bobbs-Merrill, 1936. Contains some insights into Taft's politics.

2304. White, William Allen. "Should Old Acquaintances Be Forgot?" *American Magazine* (May 1912):13-18. Not as critical of Taft as White had been earlier.

2305. ———. "A Page of National History," *Saturday Review of Literature* 7 (Oct. 25, 1930):261-63. A book review essay on Duff's biography of Taft, publicist Norman Hapgood's autobiography, and writing about Archie Butt.

2306. Whitney, David C. *The American Presidents*, rev. ed. Garden City, N.Y.: Doubleday, 1982.

2307. "William Howard Taft," *Current History* 32 (Apr. 1930):140-1.

2308. Wolf, Simon. *The Presidents I Have Known from 1860 to 1918*. Washington: Byron S. Adams, 1918.

C. Bibliographies

Because there is no authoritative bibliography about Taft, recourse must be had to bibliographies contained in the works mentioned above.

D. Oral Histories

There are no transcripts of oral interviews in any Ohio repository nor in the Yale University Library. However, Taft is discussed in part in the following oral interviews conducted by the Columbia University Oral History Program:

2309. Curtis, James Freeman (1878-1952). Lawyer, Assistant Secretary of the Treasury, Customs Bureau, 1909-1913; Establishment of the Federal Reserve System, 1914-1919; impressions of Franklin MacVeagh and Taft.

2310. Du Bois, William Edward Burghardt (1868-1967). Comments on a lifetime spent in improving the quality of black life.

2311. Frankfurter, Felix. Impressions of judicial colleagues.

2312. Griscom, Lloyd Carpenter (1872-1959). Especially valuable for his comments on T. Roosevelt, Mark Hanna, and others; his diplomatic experiences from 1893 to 1909; and his engaging in New York City politics, 1910 and 1911.

2313. Hand, Learned, Judge (1972-1961). Impressions of Brandeis and Frankfurter.

2314. Johnson, Nelson Trusler (1887-1954). On the Battle of the Concessions; Open Door policy; Manchuria, 1909-1910; and Chinese Revolution of 1911.

2315. Taft, Robert A. (1889-1953) Project. Comments on brothers Charles P. and Horace D.

2316. Taft, William H. (1857-1930). Discussed in Sevelon Brown, Thomas Chamberlain, Candler Cobb, James F. Curtis, Goldthwaite Dorr, Roy Durstein, John P. Frey, and Frederick C. Tanner.

2317. Wadsworth, James Wolcott (1877-1954). About New York politics, 1910-1915; U.S. Senate, 1915-1927; Republican national convention of 1916; League of Nations and Senate debate; prohibition; and vignettes of political contemporaries.

2318. Wilkins, Roy. The NAACP and its journal, *The Crisis*.

E. In Memoriam

2319. "Appraisal," *The New Republic* 62 (Mar. 191, 1930): 111.

2320. "Appreciation," *The Nation*, 130 (Mar. 19, 1930):130.

2321. Bonsal, Stephen. "Man Who Served Us," *The World's Work* 59 (April 1930):76-79.

2322. *Cincinnati Commercial Tribune*, March 9, 1930, 1:8, 2:8; *Cincinnati Enquirer*, March 9, 1930, 27:1-8, 37:1-8.

2323. "Great Public Servant," *Saturday Evening Post* (April 12, 1930):34.

2324. Hart, A.B. "William Howard Taft. I. His Place in History," *Current History* 32 (April 1930):290-95. Taft was the only man to occupy the two highest public positions in the United States. He was no silver tongued orator; though versatile, he was not a literary soul. Roosevelt made him and in four years unmade him.

2325. *In Memory of William Howard Taft*. Cincinnati: Chamber of Commerce and Merchants Exchange. N.p., 1930.

2326. Lynch, Frederick. "William Howard Taft. II. Taft's Labor's for International Peace," *Current History* 32 (April 1930):295-98. Heavy on Taft's arbitration treaties and the League to Enforce Peace.

2327. Obituaries, *New York Times*, Mar. 9, 1930, 1:6-7; 26:1-8; 27:1-8; 28:1-3.

2328. *Proceedings of the Bar and Officers of the Supreme Court of the United States in Memory of William Howard Taft, December 13, 1930*. Washington: U.S. Supreme Court, 1931.

2329. Obituary, "William Howard Taft," *Times (London)*, March 10, 1930, 4:1-3.

2330. Obituaries, *Washington Post*, March 9, 1930, 1:7-8; 2:1-8; 3:1-8. 4:2-7.

2331. *William Howard Taft, in Memoriam: All Soul's Church, Washington, District of Columbia, 1930*. Washington: 1930.

Taft Homes

Taft's ancestral home, at 2038 Auburn Ave., Cincinnati, is a two-story brick building with an open veranda. Built by the father, Alphonso Taft, in 1853, it is a National Historic Site open to the public.

2332. Haas, Irvin. *Historical Homes of the American Presidents*. New York: David McKay Co., 1976. Presidents' homes that are still in existence and open to the public.

2333. Jones, Cranston. *Homes of the American Presidents*. New York: McGraw-Hill, 1962. The homes occupied by 34 presidents from Washington through Kennedy.

Taft Memorials

2334. Laird, Archibald. *Monuments Marking the Graves of the Presidents. . .* North Quincy, Mass.: Christopher Pub. House, 1971.

2335. Martin, Edgar S. *The Graves of Our Presidents. . . .* Philadelphia: Lefax, 1926.

William H. Taft School, on Southern Ave., Cincinnati, is a public grade school named after the former president, who attended it from 1862 to 1870.

The William H. Taft Road, dedicated in 1939 with son Robert Taft in attendance, is a major crosstown road that passes near Taft's birthplace.

2336. The Supreme Court Building on Capitol Hill, Washington D.C., is a permanent memorial to W. H. Taft. Plans for the building drafted by the architect, Gilbert Cass, are in keeping of the Curator of the Supreme Court. These are described in part in *Antiques*, October 1985, which includes the Taft-Cass relationship in its narration of the celebration of the fiftieth anniversary of the erection of the building. Also, a large number of newspaper clippings about the plans and construction of the building is maintained in the Office of the Curator of the Court. See also:

2337. Doumato, Lamia. *Cass Gilbert, 1859-1934*, Monticello, Ill.: Vance Bibliographies, 1980.

There is a monument to Taft at his gravesite in Arlington National Cemetery.

In 1985, a high school in San Antonio, Texas, was dedicated to Taft.

2338. U.S. National Park Service. *The President: Historical Places Commemorating the Chief Executive of the United States, Washington-Ford.* Washington: National Park Service/ GPO, 1976.

Taft in Ohio

Although the creation of some local institutions predated Taft's birth, their holdings or publications contain material valuable for his life.

Cincinnati Historical Society, Eden Park, contains genealogies, Hamilton County records, and vital statistics. A finding aid is available. It publishes the *Cincinnati Historical Society Bulletin*. The park itself contains a tree planted in Taft's honor in its Presidential Grove.

2339. Chace, Laura L., and Alice M. Vestal. *Guide to the Manuscripts at the Cincinnati Historical Society.* Librarians: Cincinnati Historical Society, 1972.

2340. *Ohio Cues for Ohio Youth* is published by the Historical Society of Northwestern Ohio, Toledo.

2341. The Ohio Historical Society is located in Columbus, Ohio. It publishes *Ohio History*. A finding aid is available.

2342. Biggert, Elizabeth C. *Guide to the Manuscript Collections in the Library of the Ohio State Archaeology and History Society*. Columbus: The Society, 1953.

Also helpful are:

2343. Coyle, William, ed. *Ohio Authors and Their Books: Biographical Data and Selective Bibliographies of Ohio Authors, Native and Resident*. Cleveland: World, 1962.

2344. Larson, David R. *Guide to Manuscript Collections and Institutional Records in Ohio*. N.p.: Society of Ohio Archivists, 1974.

2345. Lentz, Andrea D., ed., and Sara S. Fuller, Assistant ed. *A Guide to Manuscripts at the Ohio Historical Society*. Columbus: The Ohio Historical Society, 1972. Very briefly annotated.

2346. *Moore's Who Is Who in Ohio*. Los Angeles, Calif.: Moore's Who Is Who Publications, 1961.

2347. *Northwest Ohio Quarterly* is published by the Maumee Valley Historical Society.

The University of Cincinnati Central Library, among others, contains Hamilton County and municipal records.

2348. The University of Ohio, at Athens, publishes *Ohio Review: A Journal of the Humanities*, 1958, continued after 1980 as *Ohio University Review*.

William Howard Taft Memorial Association, Cincinnati, Ohio. Has memorabilia and some Taft Papers.

16
Iconography

Resources for the pictorial study of W.H. Taft are available in:

2349. Bassett, Margaret Byrd. *Profiles and Portraits of American Presidents.* New York: McKay, 1976.

2350. Blaisdell, Thomas C., Jr., and others. *The American Presidency in Political Cartoons, 1776-1976.* No. 504.

2351. Butterfield, Roger. "The Camera Comes to the White House," *American Heritage* 15 (August 1964):33-48. Taft photographs, pp. 35, 43.

2352. Cirker, Hayward and Blanche, eds. *The Dictionary of American Portraits.* New York: Dover Publications, 1968. See p. 607 for photographs of Charles Phelps Taft (brother, 1843-1929) and p. 608 for photographs of W. H. Taft and Mrs. W. H. Taft.

2353. Collins, Herbert Ridgeway. *Presidents on Wheels.* Washington: Acropolis Books, 1971. Presidential vehicles.

2354. Dietz, August. *Presidents of the United States of America: Portraits and Biographies*, 3d ed. Richmond: Dietz Press, 1953. Only 72 pages long.

2355. Durant, John, and Alice Durant. *Pictorial History of American Presidents*, 5th rev. ed. New York: A.S. Barnes, 1865, and New York: Castle Books, 1975.

2356. American Heritage Publishing Co. *The American Heritage Pictorial History of the Presidents of the United States*, 2 vols. Kenneth W. Leish, ed. New York: American Heritage Publishing Co., 1968.

2357. Editors of *News Front. Contest for Power: The Exciting Pictorial Story of the American Presidential Elections, the Personalities, the Issues, the Turning Points in U.S. Political History from 1778 to the Present.* New York: Year, 1968.

2358. Golterman, Guy. *The Book of the Presidents: A Gallery of Famous Portraits of the Presidents of the United States*, rev. ed. St. Louis: 1956, unpaged.

2359. Kennett, Teresa. *Thirty-Seven Personal Portraits of the Presidents of the United States of America*. Richmond, Calif.: Brombacher Books, 1975.

2360. Lane, William Coolidge, and Nina E. Browne, eds. *ALA Portrait Index: Index to Portraits Contained in Printed Books and Periodicals*, 3 vols. New York: Burt Franklin, 1906. See 3:1414 for photographs of Taft from *Harper's Weekly, Outlook, Review of Reviews*, and *World's Work*.

2361. Laird, Archibald. *Monuments Marking the Graves of Presidents*. No. 2334.

2362. Lee, Cuthbert. *Portrait Register*. Asheville, N.C.: Biltmore Press, 1968.

2363. Lorant, Stefan. *The Presidency: A Pictorial History*. New York: Macmillan, 1951.

2364. ———. *Glorious Burden: The American Presidency*. New York: Harper & Row, 1969. An updated version of the above. Contains a concise political history of the United States in terms of the presidents and presidential elections. Taft is covered on pp. 491-508, which contain many photographs of the Taft family and friends and cartoons.

2365. ———. *The Glorious Burden: The History of the Presidency and Presidential Elections from George Washington to James Earl Carter, Jr.* Lenox, Mass.: Authors Edition, 1976. A still further updated edition.

2366. Milhollen, Hirst Dillon, and Milton Kaplan. *Presidents on Parade*. New York: Macmillan, 1948. Photographs with brief commentary.

2367. Pach, Alfred. *Portraits of Our Presidents: The Pach Collection*. New York: Hastings House, 1943. Only 68 pages long.

2368. Pachter, Marc. *A Gallery of Presidents*. Washington: The Smithsonian Institution, 1968. Contains a portrait of each president from the National Portrait Gallery, with brief official histories of his tenure and background.

2369. Post, Robert C., ed. *Every Four Years*. Washington: Smithsonian Exposition Books, 1980. Illustrations and text.

2370. Purdy, Virginia G. *Presidential Portraits*. Washington, D.C. Published for the National Portrait Gallery by the Smithsonian Institution Press, 1968, 1986. Taft, pp. 54-55.

2371. Reinfeld, Don. *Picture Book of the Presidents*. New York: Sterling Publishing Co., 1961.

2372. Whitney, David C. *The Graphic Story of the American Presidents*. Ed. by Thomas C. Jones. Chicago: J.G. Ferguson Pub. Co., 1975. A new edition of *The American Presidents*, 1969.

2373. Wilson, Fred Taylor. *Pen Pictures of the Presidents*. Nashville, Tenn.: Southwestern Co., 1937. An extensive collection running to 574 pages.

2374. A photograph of Taft as he graduated from Yale University is available in Hicks, Frederick C., *William Howard Taft*, p. 18. No. 239.

2375. At an alumni luncheon on June 18, 1913, Taft's Yale classmates presented to the University an oil portrait of him painted by August Franzen. This same class presented to the Yale Law School still another portrait of Taft, this one painted in 1914 by Sergeant Kendall, the Dean of the Yale School of Fine Arts.

2376. An oil portrait of Taft by George B. Torrey, 1909, is in the Bridgeport Public Library [Connecticut].

2377. An oil portrait of Taft by Anders Zorn, 1911, is in the White House.

2378. Rutledge, Anna Wells. *Yale Portrait Index, 1701-1951*. New Haven: Yale University Press, 1701-1951, contains 1,108 portraits by 412 artists. Taft, s.v.

2379. Most generous with photographs of Taft during his presidency, both on its front covers and inside pages, was *Harper's Weekly*. See, for example, the front covers of the issues of January 30, March 6, March 13, March 27, and June 12, 1909.

2380. There is a large collection of Taft photographs in the Still Photographic Division of the Library of Congress. Still others in the National Archives. A few are in the Photographic Division of the Naval Historical Center, Washington, D.C.

Index to Authors

Note: numbers refer to items, not page numbers

Abbot, Lawrence, 2129
Abbott, Edith, 1074, 1075
Abel, Christopher A., 342
Abraham, Henry Julian, 1080, 1953, 1954; coau 2078
Abrams, Richard, 832, 833
Academic American Encyclopedia, 213
Accinelli, Robert D., 1885, 1918
Adams, Henry, 2257, 2262
Adler, Bill, 2125
Agar, Hebert, 2255
Agranoff, Robert, 604, 605
Alderson, William T., 897
Aldrich, Nelson, 46, 1492, 1493
Alexander, Herbert E., 616
Alexander, Holmes Moss, 2189
Alfonso, Oscar, M., 309
Alger, George W., 1105
Allen, Frederick Louis, 784
Allen, Harry C., 1368
Allen, Howard Wilson, 864, 1574, 1575, 1701
Aly, Bower, 616
American Heritage Publishing Company, 2356
Anderman, Nancy, 1944
Anderson, Chandler P., 47
Anderson, Donald, 224, 225, 2153, 2230, 2256
Anderson, Elaine, S., 1729
Anderson, Isabel (Perkins), 710
Anderson, Judith Icke, 226, 307, 310, 343, 407, 1763, 2141, 2231
Anderson, Mary, 2206
Anderson, Oscar Edward, 1185, 1186
Aptheker, Herbert, 1113

Armbruster, Maxim Ethan, 495, 503, 2258
Armstrong, John P., 2190
Arnett, Alexander Matthew, 1542
Arnold, Peri E., 1027, 1067
Arvin, Newton, 2257
Asbury, Eslie Asbury, 295
Asch, Sidney H., 1956
Auchinloss, Louis, 1665

Baack, Bennett D., coau 1061
Bach, Stanley, coau, 498
Bacon, Augustus Octavius, 1230, 1429
Bacon, Edwin M., 1201
Bacon, Robert, coau 1907
Baer, Judith A., 1922
Bailey, Harry A., Jr. 486
Bailey, Thomas A., 344, 345, 499, 500, 501, 1415, 1886
Bain, Richard C., coau, 617, 621
Baker, Charles E., 2142
Baker, H.L., 409
Baker, Leonard, 2025
Baker, Ray Stannard, 576, 1114, 1115, 1116, 1702
Baker, Richard C., 1209
Baldwin, E.F. 1449, 1626
Ballard, Rene N., 684
Ballinger, Richard A., 48, 974, 1443
Barber, James David, 410, 411, 619, 2259
Barclay, Barbara, 203
Barfield, Claude, E. 1231
Barger, Harold M., 502
Barilleaux, Ryan J., 577, 1640
Barker, Charles E., 227
Barnes, William, coau 1309, 1640
Bartlett, Robert Merrill, 2184

Bartlett, Ruhl J., 1430, 1887
Barzman, Sol, 740, 2207
Bassett, Margaret Boyd, 204, 2349
Bates, Henry, 2059
Bates, Leonard James, 809, 982
Baum, Lawrence, 1082
Bayne, Hugh A., 1035
Beale, Howard K., 311
Beard, Charles A., 214, 503, 1083
Beard, Mary R., 1097
Beaver, Daniel R., 475
Bell, Christopher, 735
Bell, Jack, 649
Bemis, Samuel Flagg, 1301; coau 1310
Bennett, A.L. 983
Berdahl, Clarence A., 650
Berman, Edward, 1098
Bernstorff, Johann von, 1635
Bernstein, Marner H., 1194
Bessette, Joseph M., coau 652
Beveridge, Albert J., 1285, 1495
Bickel, Alexander M., coau 1957, 1999, 2026
Biggert, Elizabeth C., 2342
Billington, Monroe Lee, 1534
Binkley, Wilfred E., 578, 653, 685, 765
Bishop, Joseph B., 412, 618
Black, Henry C., 1040
Blaisdell, T.C., Jr., 504, 2350
Blakey, Gladys C., coau 1041
Blakey, Roy B., coau 1041
Blanford, Linda A., coau 1945
Blaustein, Albert, coau 2000
Blazer, Alfred, 2145
Blessing, Tim H., coau 2286
Blewett, Lee, 1450
Bliven, Bruce, 1547, 1785
Blochman, Lawrence B., coau 743
Blocker, Jack S., Jr. 1927
Bloomfield, Davis, coau 1269

Blum, John Morton, 1594, 1703
Blumberg, Rhoda, 2208
Boller, Paul F., Jr. 413, 505, 579, 2126, 2209
Bolles, Blair, 1507
Bolt, Robert, 414
Bonnell, John Sutherland, 506
Bonsal, Stephen, 2260, 2321
Boothe, Leon, 1888
Borah, William E., 49, 1497
Boudin, Louis B., 1084, 1958
Bourne, Randolph S., 1889
Boutwell, George S., 1062
Bowen, Catherine D., 1666, 2038
Bowers, Claude G., 1496
Boyer, Paul S., coau 2219
Braisted, William R., 346, 347, 348, 788, 810, 1606
Brandeis, Louis D., 50, 930, 2027
Brengle, Fred E., 1764
Breslin, Thomas A., coau, 1350
Brigman, William E., 766
Bringhurst, Bruce, 875
Brinton, Crane, 1369
Bristow, Joseph L., 51, 1502
Broderick, Francis L., 1115
Brooks, Gertrude L., 2210
Brooks, Sydney, 415, 767
Brossard, Edgar Bernard, 1232
Brown, Margaret W., 2211
Brown, Stewart Gerry, 507
Brown, William B., 215, 606
Brown, William Garrott, 1157
Brown, William R., 614
Browne, Nina E., coau 2360
Brownlow, Louis, 508
Bryan, Mary Baird, coau 834
Bryan, Martin, 416
Bryan, William Jennings, 417, 418, 898, 1408, 1409, 1890, 1910; coau 834, 1441, 1765
Bryce, James, 1021

Bryson, James A., 1381, 1382
Buchanan, Bruce, 509
Bundy, McGeorge, coau 1480
Burch, Philip H., Jr. 487, 1959
Burner, David, 419, 1694, 2035, 2036, 2055, 2056, 2058, 2063, 2064
Burns, James McGregor, 2261; coau 1022
Burns, Richard Dean, 1302
Burt, Nathaniel, 228
Burton, Agnes Rose, 580
Burton, David H., 229, 2232
Burton, Theodore E., 420
Busbey, L. White, 1508
Busby, Katherine G., 2154
Butler, Charles H., 1419, 1960
Butler, Nicholas Murray, 52, 643, 2233
Butt, Archibald Willingham, 95, 230, 421, 1597, 1704, 2234
Butterfield, Roger, 2351

Caldera, Gergory A., 2001
Callahan, James M., 1342
Callcott, Wilfred H., 349
Cameron, Meribeth, 1347
Campbell, Alexander, E., 402, 403
Campbell, Charles S., 404, 1391
Cannon, Joseph Gurney, 53, 1210, 1505, 1506
Caplan, Lincoln, 305
Capper, Arthur, 1510
Carleton, William G., 581, 1787
Carnegie, Andrew, 54
Carosso, Vincent P., 2212
Carr, Raymond, 1412
Carroll, Berenice A., coau 1835
Carrott, M. Browning, 2002, 2003
Carson, Gerald, 1063
Carstensen, Vernon, 953
Carter, Harold, 2262

Casdorph, Paul D., 1116
Cavanaugh, Frances, 2178
Chace, Laura L., coau, 2339
Chako, Chirakaikaran J., 1270
Chaffin, Lillie D., 2213
Challener, Richard D., 1641
Chamberlain, Charles W.F., 582
Chamberlain, Lawrence H., 583
Chambers, Raymond I., 686
Chambrun, Clara L. de, 1557
Chase, Harold, 1946
Chatfield, Charles, 1891
Chay, Jongsuk, 350
Cherrington, Ernest H., 1928
Chessman, G. Wallace, 876
Child, Richard Washburn, 1234
Christensen, Bonniejean, 723
Christman, Kenneth W., 769
Cirker, Blanche, coau, 2352
Cirker, Hayward, coau 2352
Clapp, Moses, 55, 1512
Clark, Champ, 1514, 1515
Clark, J.C., 1839
Clark, James D., 877
Clark, Thomas D., coau 1117
Clark, Walter, 1627
Claude, Inis L., Jr. 1892
Clayton, Bruce L., 1789
Clift, Virgil A., coau 1110
Clinard, Outten J., 351
Cline, H.F., 1377
Clubb, Oliver E., 1348
Clyde, Paul H., 1349
Clymer, Ernest Fletcher, 741
Cohen, Naomi W., 1416
Cohn, Mark B., 687, 770
Coker, William S., 1405
Cole, Cyrenus, 2263
Coleman, Patrick K., coau 1836
Coletta, Paolo E., 23, 231, 232, 353, 585, 784, 785, 942, 1013, 1028, 1172, 1323, 1473, 1536,

1607, 1608; and *William Jennings Bryan*, 352, 426, 427, 428, 1706, 1767, 1929, 1930, 2236; and *The Presidency of William Howard Taft*, 1028, 1707, 2155, 2235
Collier, Ellen C., 1311
Collings, H.T., 1207
Collins, Charles Wallace, 1029
Collins, George W., 1385
Collins, Herbert Ridgeway, 2353
Colman, Edna, M. 711
Colucci, Vito E., 2264
Colvin, D. Leigh, 1931
Commager, Henry, 511
Commons, John R., 1099
Comstock, Alzada P., 1042
Congressional Information Service, 110
Congressionial Quarterly, 554, 609, 620
Congressional Quarterly Service, 584
Conner, Valerie Jean, 1881
Connolly, C.P., 986, 987
Cooke, Donald E., 205
Cooper, John Milton, Jr., 1548
Coppa and Avery Consultants, 607
Cornwell, Elmer E., 512, 513
Corwin, Edward S., 654, 754, 1312
Costello, Daniel J., 790
Cotton, Edward, 233, 2237
Coulter, E. Merton, 1158, 1732
Cox, Isaac, J., 1388, 1460, 1642
Coyle, David Cushman, 514
Coyle, William, 2343
Crane, Daniel M., coau 1350
Crane, Withrop Murray, 1517
Crissey, Forrest, 1502
Croly, Herbert, 835, 836, 1392, 1461
Cronin, Thomas E., 515
Crumpacker, E.D., 1235

Cuff, Robert E., 1882
Cullom, Shelby Moore, 1520
Culp, Maurice S., 771
Cummings, Damon, 791
Cummins, Albert B., 1521, 1522
Cunliffe, Marcus, 216, 516
Cunningham, William J., 1195
Curl, Donald W., 103, 296
Curti, Merle E., 1432
Curtis, James Freeman, 2309
Curtis, Richard, coau, 742
Cushman, Robert E., 1196
Cutright, Paul Russell, 955

Dabney, Virginius, 1932
Damon, Allan L., 688, 689, 690
Daniels, Josephus, 429
Dargin, Marion, 206
Darling, Arthur H., 99, 1562
Dauncey, E.C., 772
David, Paul T., coau 621
Davis, Oscar King, 234, 430, 2265
Davis, Richard C., 954
Davison, Kenneth, E., 488
Dawes, Charles Gates, 431
De Benedetti, Charles, 1893, 1919
De Clerico, Robert E., 517
De Gregorio, William A., 217, 518
De Marco, Joseph P., 1118
Dennett, Tyler, 354
De Novo, John, 1320, 1380
Dennis, Alfred L.P., 312
Depew, Chauncey M., 2266
Destler, I.M., 812
Deutrich, Mabel E., 1595
Dewey, Davis T., 1043, 1211
Dewey, George, 1604
DeWitt, Benjamin Parke, 837
DeWolfe, Mark A., 1474
Dick, Charles W. F., 1790
Dick, Reveror, J.O., 1236
Dickinson, Jacob McGavock, 57

Dietz, August, 2354
Dingilian, Arlene, 283
Dinnerstein, Leonard, 1678
Dinwiddie, W., 355
De Salle, Michael V., coau 743
Dix, George E., 899
Doane, Franklin C., 2267
Dolce, Philip C., 655
Dolliver, Jonathan, 58, 1237, 1238, 1523
Doris, A. Graber, 356
Dorwart, Jeffery M., 1615, 1616
Doumato, Lamia, 2337
Downes, Randolph C., 284
Driggs, Don W., 691
Dubofsky, Melvyn, 1101
Du Bois, W.E. Burghardt, 105, 1159, 2310
Dumond, Dwight L., 519
Dunn, Arthur Wallace, 434, 813, 1187, 2268; coau 1833
Dunn, Robnert Lee, 2238
Dunn, Samuel O., 1199
Dunne, Finley Peter, 1212
Dunne, Gerald T., 1961
Durant, Alice, coau 489, 2355
Durant, John, coau 489, 2355
Durbin, Louise, 712
DuVal, Miles P., 398

Eaton, Herbert A., 623
Eckes, Alfred E., coau 636
Editors of American Heritage, 216, 219, 220, 516
Editors of *News Front*, 2357
Edward, John Ray, coau, 1061
Edwards, George B., 520
Edwards, George C. III, 521, 522, 692, 693; coau 1962, 2084
Egger, Rowland Andrews, 523
Eleazar, D.J., 586
Elkins, Stephen Benton, 1526

Elliott, Charles Burke, 1410
Ellis, Elmer, 1064
Encyclopedia Americana, 221
Encyclopedia Britannica, 222, 223
Essary, J.F. 2004
Esthus, Raymond A., 357, 358, 359, 1393, 1462
Evans, Patricia Russell, coau 1945
Ewing, Cortez A.M. 435, 624, 1708, 1963

Faber, Doris, 269
Fahey, Charles, 306
Fairbank, John K., 1351
Faulkner, Harold U., 838, 1024
Featherton, Frank H., 814
Federal Writers' Program, 260
Federal Writers' Program, Ohio, 259
Felsenthal, Carol, 2192
Felt, Thomas E., 1790
Fersh, Seymour H., 713
Fichen, Robert E., 991
Field, Frederick V., 352
Filler, Louis, 524, 839, 2269
Findling, John E., 1303
Fink, Clinton, F., coau, 1835
Fink, Gary M., 1102
Fisch, M.H., 2040
Fisher, Robert A., 525
Fish, Peter G., 2049
Fish, Stuyvesant, 1933
Fishel, Jeff, 625
Fishel, Leslie H., Jr., coau 1119
Fisher, Irving, 1934
Fisher, Walter 59
Fisher, Walter Lourie, 992, 1453
Fiske, Bradley A., 792, 1609
Fitch, G., 436
Fitzgerald, Carol Bondhus, 29
Fitzgerald, Gerald F., coau 1269
Fitzgibbon, Russel H. 360
Fitzpatrick, John James III, 1540

Flack, Horace C., coau 42, 1914
Fleming, Denna F., 1420, 1895
Flexner, Eleanor, 1923
Foraker, Joseph Benson, 60, 285, 293, 297, 437, 1528, 1529
Foraker, Julia B., 298
Forcey, Charles, 840
Forman, William H., Jr. 1698
Fosdick, Harry E., 1935
Fowler, Wilton B., 1304
Frank, John O., 2270
Frank, John R., 2062
Frankfurter, Felix, 2005, 2272, 2272, 2311; coau 1103, 1964
Franklin, John Hope, coau 1120
Franzen, August, 2375
Fraser, Herbert F., 1241
Fredman, L.E. 587
Freidel, Frank, 526, 1073
Freitag, Ruth S., 709
Freund, Paul A., 1965, 2041, 2085
Friedman, Leon, coau 1962
Fry, William Pierce, 1532
Fuller, Edmund, coau 2150
Funderbunk, Charles, 658
Furman, Bess, 2156
Furnas, Joseph C., 1936

Gable, John Allen, 1840
Gal, Allon, 2029
Gallagher, Charles F., 1386
Ganoe, John T., 993
Garfield, James R., 1791
Garner, James W., 1160
Garraty, John A., 218, 1553, 1667, 2028, 2039, 2048, 2191
Gatewood, Willard B., 1161, 1792
Genovese, Michael A., 2036
Gerlach, Robert, 2215
Gerlinger, Irene, 2216
German, James C., Jr. 900, 901
Germino, Dante L., 714

Gillias, A., 439
Ginger, Ray, 440, 1709, 1768
Glass, Carter, 931
Glavis, Louis R., 994
Glazebrook, G.P. De T., 1272
Gleason, A.H., 2131
Gleaves, Albert, 1610
Goehlert, Robert U., coau 491, 1590
Goethals, George W., 1401
Goldberg, Edward M., 2087; coau, 2079
Goldman, Eric F., 694
Goldmark, Josephine, 1966
Goldsmith, William M., 659
Goldstein, Sidney M., 755
Gompers, Samuel, 1104
Gordon, David, 878
Gore, Thomas P., 1533
Goss, Charles Frederick, 261
Goss, Hilton R., 1769
Gossett, William T., 1673
Gould, Alan Brant, 971, 995, 1454
Gould, Lewis L., 1068, 1242, 1793
Graber, Doris A., 588
Graff, Henry F., 527
Graebner, Norman A., 1321
Grantham, Dewey W., Jr., 1121, 1122, 1162
Gray, C. Vernon, coau 646
Great Britain, 1271
Green, David E., coau 2150
Green, Nathan, coay 1103
Greenstein, Fred I., 490
Grenville, John A.S., 406, 793, 815
Grew, Joseph C., 1643
Griffin, Appleton P.C., 879, 1178, 1264
Griffin, Grace Gardner, coau 1301
Griscom, Lloyd Carpenter, 2312
Griswold, A. Whitney 1313
Grunder, Garel A., coau 1411
Gulick, Charles A., Jr., coau 884

Gunstein, Nathan D., 695
Gwynn, Stephen, 1638

Haas, Irvin, 2332
Haber, Samuel, 841, 956
Hagedorn, Hermann, 1600
Haig, Robert M., 1044
Haines, Gerald K., coau 1305
Hale, Eugene, 1535
Hale, W.M., 1629
Hale, William Bayard, 1734, 1735, 1794
Hall, Harry Orville, 235
Hall, Kermit L., 1967
Halsey, Edwin A., 589
Hamilton, Lee H., coau, 696
Hammond, John Hays, 1795, 2239
Hampton, William Judson, 270
Hand, Learned, 2323
Handlin, Oscar, 1036, 1073
Handsbrorough, Henry Clay, 2274
Haney, James E., 442
Harbaugh, William Henry, 443, 444, 452, 710,
Hargrove, Erwin, C., 236, 528, 660, 2240
Harlan, John M., 2088
Harlan, Louis R., 1123, 1124
Harnsberger, Caroline, 2126
Harrell, Mary Ann, 1968
Harper's Weekly, 2379
Harris, Irving D., 279
Harrison, Benjamin, 61
Hart, Albert Bushnell, 1328, 2275, 2324
Hart, James, 661, 773
Hart, Robert, 1353
Harvey, George B.M., 880, 1233, 1786, 2276
Harvey, Roland Hill, 445
Hassler, Warren W., 794
Hathaway, Esse Virginia, 529

Hattendorf, John B., 1612; coau 1613
Havemeyer, Loomis, 957
Hayes, John D., coau 1613
Hays, Samuel P., 842, 958
Hazard, Henry B., 2089
Healy, Diana Dixon, 1490
Heard, Alexander, 626
Hechler, Kenneth, 1711
Hecht, Marie, 1841
Heclo, Hugh, coau, 530
Heller, Francis H., 531
Helms, E. A., 590
Hemphill, J.C., 816
Hendel, Samuel, 2050
Henry, Reginald D., 271
Hernak, Elizabeth Ann, coau, 1591
Herron, Harriet, Collins, 1880
Heslop, David Alan, 532
Hess, Stephen, 237, 238, 272
Hibbard, Benjamin H., 959
Hicks, Frederick C., 239, 1863, 1864, 2241, 2374
Hicks, Granville, coau 863
Hicks, John D., 1842
Higham, John, 1078
Hill, George, 2157
Hill, John P., 948
Hill, Kim Q., coau 1030
Hill, Lawrence F. 1339
Hilles, Charles D., 26, 1106
Hinsdale, Mary L., 744
Hirsch, H.N., 1655, 1969, 2030
Hirschfield, Robert S., 662
Hitchcock, Frank Harris, 446, 1180, 1457
H.J.H., 447
Hockstra, Douglas J., 591
Hofstadter, Richard, 843
Holman, Hamilton, 2217
Holmes, Oliver Wendell, 1970, 2042
Holt, James, 1592

Holt, W. Stull, 1421
Hoppes, Roy, 538
Hoover, Herbert, 1843
Hornbeck, Stlanley Kuhl, 1273
Hornig, Edgar A., 446, 449, 490
House, Edward M., 1896
Hoxie, B. Gordon, 697, 751
Howe, Mark A. De Wolfe, 2024
Howlett, Charles F., coau 1837
Hughes, Charles Evans, 62, 1971, 2090
Hughes, Emmet John, 2277
Hugins, Roland, 1434
Huidekoper, Frederick, 797
Humbert, Willard, 663, 756
Hunter, George S., 1796
Hurd, Charles, 534, 2218
Hurja, Emil E., 715
Hutchins, John G.B., 1202
Hyde, Charles Cheney, 1674
Hyde, Henry M., 1648
Hyman, Harold M., 795
Hyman, Sidney, 535, 592

Ickes, Harold L., 844, 960, 996
International Opium Commission, 1188
Iriye, Kira, 361, 1372
Israel, Fred L., 44, 1609; coau, 427, 1962
Israel, Jerry, 1394
Isely, Bliss, 2151
Izant, Grace (Goulder), 262

Jackson, Carlton, 664, 757
Jackson, Robert H., 1972, 2051
Jacob, C.E., 698
Jacob, Kathryn Allamong, coau, 1591
Jaffray, Elizabeth, 2159
James, Edward T., coau 2219
Jeffries, Ona Griffin, 2160, 2220

Jennings, David H., 1897, 1920
Jensen, Amy La Follette, 2161
Jernigan, Jay E., 1844
Jessup, Philip C., 1286, 1577
Johnson, Alvin S., 1038
Johnson, Arthur M., 905
Johnson, Carolyn W., 1518
Johnson, Charles, 1620
Johnson, Claudius I., 1498
Johnson, David E., 1797
Johnson, Donald B., coau, 463, 536, 627, 1777
Johnson, Haynes, 758
Johnson, Hiram, 1539
Johnson, James Weldon, 1126
Johnson, Nelson Trusler, 2314
Johnson, Tom Loftus, 845
Johnston, Charles, 906
Johnsnton, Richard, coau 1287
Jones, Charles A., 645
Jones, Cranston, 2333
Jones, Eliot, 881
Josephson, Harold, 1884
Josephson, Matthew, 241
Judson, F.N., 1107
Juergens, George, 538

Kahn, M.A., 1091, 1092
Kahn, Stephen, coau 1567, 1721
Kallenbach, Joseph E., 539, 665
Kane, Joseph Nathan, 207, 2278
Kanes, J.N. 540
Kahn, Stephen, coau 1567
Kanter, Arnold, 796
Kanter, Sanford, coau 2181
Kaplan, Milton, coau 2366
Kay, Richard S., 1947
Kayser, Pat, 263
Keefe, Arthur John, 2091
Kehl, James, 2162
Keller, Ulrich, 1402
Kellerman, Barbara, 541

Kellogg, Charles Flint, 1127
Kelly, Frank, 1770
Kemmerer, Edwin W., 932, 1179
Kendall, Sergeant, 2375
Kenkel, Joseph F., 1213
Kennan, George F., 1395
Kennan, Kossuth K., 1045
Kennedy, Jean L., 1845
Kennett, Teresa, 2359
Kennon, Donald R., 1516
Kenski, Henry C., 776
Kent, William, 64
Keso, Edward E., 1571
Kessel, John H., 628, 745
Kessler, Frank, 666
King, Willard Leroy, 1650
Kirk, Elise K., 2163
Kirk, H. Porter, coau 635
Kirkpatrick, Ivy Eugene, 846
Kirwan, Albert D., coau 1117
Kitchin, Claude C., 1541
Kittler, Glenn D., 717
Klapthor, Margaret Brown, 2221
Klein, Fannie J., 1948
Klein, Mary, 667
Klinkhamer, Marie C., 1699
Knox, Philander C., 65, 96, 1274, 1459, 1625
Koenig, Louis W., 542, 543, 668, 746
Kohlsaat, Herman Henry, 451
Konefsky, Samuel Joseph, 1668, 2043
Kosberg, Roberta L., 1898, 1921
Kosonski, Douglas, coau 2124
Kraditor, Aileen, 1924
Kraines, O., 1069
Krock, Arthur, 2279
Krooss, Herman E., 933; coau 1054
Krukones, Michael, G., 1798
Kurland, P.B., 1093

Kutler, Stanley I., 1973, 2008, 2092-94

LaFeber, Walter, 1329
LaFollette, Belle Case, coau 1544, 1712, 2242
LaFollette, Fola, coau 1544, 1712, 2242
LaFollette, Robert M., 66, 1543, 1546, 1713, 2243
Lafontaine, Charles V.S.A., 728
Laird, Archibald, 736
Lamar, Clarinda Pendleton, 1679
Lamb, Charles R., coau 1836
Lambeth, Harry J., 2095
Landis, James M., coau 1964
Lane, Anne W., coau 97
Lane, Jack C., 1601, 1602
Lane, William Coolidge, coau 2360
Langley, Lester D., 1644
Larkin, John Day, 1214
Larson, David R., 2344
Laski, Harold Joseph, 544, 669
Laughlin, J. Laurence, 934
Lawson, Don, 2179
Lawson, Steven F., 2096
Lea, James S., 699
League to Enforce Peace, 1899
Lease, Martin Harry, Jr., 670
Lee, Cuthbert, 2362
Lee, John R., 700
Leish, Kenneth W., 220, 2164
Lentz, Andrea D., coau 2345
Leonard, Lewis Alexander, 273
Leopold, Richard, 1578, 2245
Lerner, Max, 1669, 2044
Leroy, J.A. 452
Lester, Salamon, coau 530
Letwin, William 882
Leupp, Francis E., 866, 1738, 1739
Levine, Lawrence W., 1937
Lewin, Nathan, 1662

Lewinson, Paul, 11238
Lief, Alfred, 1564, 1714
Link, Arthur S., 1163, 1164, 1715, 1716, 1772
Lippmann, Walter, 847
Liss, Sheldon, 399
Little, Herbert, 2097
Livermore, Seward W., 817, 1322, 1336
Livezey, William E., coau 1411
Lodge, Henry Cabot, 67, 98, 1551, 1552, 1554, 1900
Logan, Logna B., 2222
Logan, Rayford Whittingham, 1109; coau 1129
Longacre, Richard P., 671
Longworth, Alice Roosevelt, 1559
Longworth, Nicholas, 1556
Loots, Barbara Kunz, 2165, 2223
Lorant, Stefan, 2363-65
Loss, Richard, 593
Lott, Davis Newton, 718
Lovell, S.D., 1846
Low, A. Maurice, 1800-1
Lowdnes, Charles L. B., 2007
Lowell, A. Lawrence, 1901
Lowitt, Richard, 1565-66, 1718
Lowry, E.G., 1630, 2146
Lubalin, E., coau 597
Luce, Stephen Bleeker, 818
Luke, James, 2280
Lyle, Eugene P., 299
Lynch, Frederick, 2281, 2326

MacAdam, Hastings, 1741
McAdoo, William Gibbs, 1938
McBee, Silas, 453
McCall, Samuel Walter, 1215
McCardle, Richard E. 998
McCarran, Patrick A., 777
McConnell, Burt, coau 2224
McConnell, Brant, 545
McConnell, Jane, coau 2224
McCoy, Donald R., 1847, 1848
McCullough, David, 400, 1403
McCully, Richard T., 935
Maciarmid, John, 729
McDonough, John J., coau 94
McDougall, William, 1130
McGinney, Brian, 401
McGraw, Thomas K., 1651
McGuffy, Richard T., 1046
McHale, Francis, 242, 2244
McKee, Marguerite Miller, 1203
McKenna, Marian C., 1499
Mackenzie, George C., 759
McLaughlin, James Angell, 883
McMaines, Howard F., 454
MacMurray, John V.A. 1354
MacVeagh, Franklin, 69, 1468, 1802
Mack, Gerstle, 1404
Mackay, H.B., 280
Maddox, Robert James, 1500, 1902
Magill, Frank Northen, 208
Mangold, George B., 943
Mann, Arthur, 848
Mann, James R., 70
Manners, William, 243, 1773, 1803
Manning, Helen Taft, 2193, 2201, 2202
Mansfield, Harvey C., Sr., 546
Marable, Manning, 1131
Maranell, G.M., 594
Marburg, Theodore, coau 42, 68, 1914
Marchand, C. Roland, 1903
Marcus, Maeva, 2009
Marcy, Carl Milton, 1070
Margulies, Herbert F., 1904
Marks, Frederick W. III, 363
Marks, Rudolph, 2143
Martin, Albro, 1197
Martin, Asa Earl, 1865
Martin, Edgar, 2335

Martin, Fenton S., coau 491
Martin, Lawrence, 1344
Mason, Alpheus Thomas, 245, 961, 1444, 1974-76, 2032, 2062, 2098-99
Matthews, Dorothy M., coau 687, 805
Mauer, Donald J. 611
May, Ernest R., 798
Meacham, J.L., 1406
Meadows, Martin, 1538
Means, Marianne, 2225
Meier, August, 1132, 1133, 1165; coau 1120
Menendez, Albert J. 2149
Merrill, Marion, coau 547
Merrill, Samuel, coau 547
Merritt, Ella A., coau 945
Merseky, Roy, coau 2000
Merz, Charles, 1939
Meyer, George von Lengerke, 71, 936, 1174, 1181, 1471, 1472
Meyer, Herman H.B., 1265; coau 937
Mikell, William E., 701
Milhollen, Hirst Dillon, coau 2366
Miller, Arthur A., 1079
Miller, Arthur Selwyn, 672, 1977
Miller, August, coau 1140
Miller, Elizabeth W., 1111
Miller, Kelley, 1135, 1166
Miller, William M., 787
Miller, Zayne L., 286, 287, 300
Millett, Allan R., 799
Milligan, Nancy Miller, 1167
Milton, George Fort, 673, 760
Minger, Ralph Eldin, 314, 315, 364, 365, 366
Mischler, Wendell W., 28
Mohraz, Jane E., coau 1835
Montgomery-Massinberg, Hugh, 274
Moody, Eric N., 1805

Moody, William Henry, 72
Moore, Barbara, 730
Moore, John Bassett, 1422
Moore's Who Is Who in Ohio, 2346
Moos, Malcolm, 629, 630
Moran, Thomas F., 2284
Morgan, Howard Wayne, 455, 456, 457, 1849
Morgan, James, 209
Morgan, John Heath, coau 1309
Morganston, Charles E., 647, 761, 1617
Morison, Elting E., 1479; coau 100, 322
Morland, Robert L, 1850
Morris, Edmund, 316
Morris, James M., 1204
Morris, Jeffrey B., 2100
Mott, Thomas Bentley, 1622
Moum, Kathleen D., 1851
Mowry George E., 317, 458, 595, 849, 1719, 1720, 1743, 1774, 1806
Mugridge, Donald H. 492
Mullen, William F., 675
Munro, Dana G., 367, 1333, 1397, 1645
Murphy, Arthur B., 2285
Murphy, Bruce Allen, 1654, 1978, 2033
Murphy, G.M.P., 368
Murphy, Paul L. 1979
Murphy, Walter F., 1980, 2010, 2101; coau 1981
Murray, Robert H. 369; coau 2286
Myers, Elisabeth P., 246, 2247
Myers, Gustavus, 1982
Myrdal, Gunnar, 1136

Nagel, Charles, 73, 778, 779, 1476
Nagel, Stuart S., 2102
Nathan, Richard P., 762

National Bureau of Economic Research, 1047
Neals, Thomas H., 612
Nearing, Scott, coau, 1334, 1463
Needham, David Charles, 1137
Needham, Henry Beach, 1752
Nelson, Daniel A., 2066
Nelson, John K., 1905
Ness, Gary, 318
Neu, Charles E., 370, 371, 372
Neuberger, Richard L., 1567, 1721
Nurnberger, Ralph D., 1435, 1906
Neumann, William L., 1373
Neustadt, Richard E., 676
Nevins, Allan, 548
Newlands, Francis J., 74, 99, 1560, 1561
Nikolaieff, George A., 677
Ninkovitch, Frank, 1398
Noble, David W., 853
Norris, George, 75
Norris, George W., 850, 867, 1275, 1288, 1563, 1568
Noyes, Alexander D., 1048
Nye, Russell B., 851, 1722

Odegard, Peter H., 459, 1940
Ogden, Gerald R., 963
Ogg, Frederic, 1049
Oh, John C. H., 780
Ohio Historical Society, 102
Osborn, George C., 1171
Osgood, Robert E., 1315
Osofsky, Gilbert, 1170
Oulahan, R. V. 460
Overacker, Louise, 633
Ovington, Mary White, 1139
Owen, Robert Latham, 938, 1569, 1572
Owsley, Clifford C., 719

Pach, Alfred, 2367
Pachter, Marc, 2368
Page, Arthur W., 1101
Page, Thomas Walker, 1216
Page, Walter H., 1002
Painter, Estella, 1838
Paolucci, Henry, 1316
Paper, Lewis J., 2104
Parks, E. Taylor, 1360
Parks, Lillian Rogers, 2166, 2167
Parr, Marilyn K., coau 94
Parris, Judith, coau 617
Patterson, Bradley H, 747
Patterson, Caleb Perry, 551, 596
Patterson, Raymond Albert, 247, 319, 2248
Paullin, Charles Oscar, 825
Peabody, R.L., coau 597
Peffer, E. Louise, 963
Peltason, Jack Walter, coau 1022
Penick, Elmo R., 1445
Penick, James, Jr. 964, 1445
Percy, Michael B., coau 1287
Perkins, Bradford, 405, 1345, 1370
Perkins, Dexter, 1317, 2052
Perkins, George, 76
Perling, Joseph Jerry, 2180, 2197
Perry, Enos J., 264
Peterson, Harold, R., 1337
Peterson, Svend, 634
Phillips, David Graham, 852, 1631
Pier, Arthur S., 1776. 1852
Pinchot, Amos, 77
Pinchot, Gifford, 965, 1003
Pinci, A. V., 1807
Pinkett, Harold T., 966
Pious, Richard M., 552, 598
Plesure, M., 2147
Plishke, Elmer, 1306
Ploski, Harry A., coau 1640

Plumlee, John P., coau, 1030
Poindexter, Miles P., 78, 1276, 1289, 1573
Poland, Eleanor, 1284
Polsby, Nelson W., 553
Porter, Dorothy B., 1112
Porter, Kirk H., coau 463, 627, 1777
Potter, P.B., 702, 826
Post, Charles Johnson, 1246
Post, Robert C., 2369
Potts, E. Daniel, 720
Powell, Anna I., 1389
Powell, John Harvey, 1217
Powell, Lewis F., Jr., 2107
Pratt, Julius W., 1318
Prindville, Kathleen, 2226
Pringle, Henry F., 1813; *Theodore Roosevelt*, 249, 461, 2288; and *William Howard Taft*, 248, 265, 308, 321, 460, 463, 1141, 1277, 1723, 1778, 1893, 1326, 1437, 1983, 2168, 2250
Puerto Rico, Governor, 1413
Pugach, Noel H., 1632
Purdy, Virginia, 2370
Pusey, Merle J., 2053, 2105, 2106
Putney, Bryant, 599

Quarles, Benjamin, coau, 1119
Quinn, Sandra L., coau 2181
Quint, Howard H., 1853

Raat, William D., 1378
Radosh, Ronald, 2198
Ragan, Allen E., 250, 1984, 2251
Rakestraw, Lawrence, 1009
Ramsey, John W., 1031
Ranson, Edward, 1596
Raper, Charles Lee, 1175
Rappaport, Armin, 802
Ratner, Sidney, 1050
Ravis, W. J., 2136

Reed, Thomas B., 1250
Reedy, George E., 555
Regier, Cornelius C., 854
Rehnquist, William H., 2107
Reid, John Gilbert, 373
Reid, John Philllip, coau 1949
Reinfeld, Don, 2371
Reischauer, Edwin O., 1374
Reit, Seymour, 2169
Rennie, Thomas, 2148
Renninger, W. Daub, 1205
Reynolds, Bradley M., 1363
Rhodes, James Ford, 464, 1218
Richardson, Dorsey, 2045
Richardson, Elmo R., 967, 1446, 1815
Ripley, William Z., 1198
Rippy, J. Fred, 1361, 1379
Robbins, Edwin Clyde, 1266
Robbins, Roy M., 968
Roberts, Charles, 679
Robinson, Edgard E., 1816
Rockoff, Hugh, 1032
Rodabaugh, Karl, 949
Rodell, Fred, 1985
Roosevelt, Theodore, 79, 100, 251, 322, 466, 912, 913, 1724, 1818-22,
Root, Elihu, 1576, 1907
Rorvig, Paul, 1823
Rose, Richard, 705
Roseboom, Eugene H., 467, 635; coau 636
Rosebush, James S., 2227
Rosenthal, Robert H., 1753
Rosewater, Victor, 637, 1780
Ross, Edward A., 855
Ross, Ishbel, 275, 288, 294, 301, 1986, 2186, 2199, 2204
Ross, Thomas Richard, 969
Rossiter, Clinton, 556, 706
Rowe, Joseph Milton, 374

Rowland, Buford, 130
Rubin, Eva R., 1987
Rublee, George, 914
Rudwick, Elliott M., 1142, 1143; coau 1134
Russell, Francis, 557, 638
Rutledte, Anna Wells, 2378

Sadler, Christine, 2182
Salvatore, Nick, 468, 1856
Sander, Aldred D., 856
Sanders, A.H., 1252
Sands, W.F., 1335, 1464
Sayer, Wallace S., 950
Sayre, John R., coau 1590
Schaffter, Dorothy, coau, 680, 805
Schick, Allen, 707
Schieber, Clara Eve, 2366
Schimmel, Barbara B., 2057
Schlachter, Gail, 485
Schlesinger, Arthur M., Jr., 428, 639, 2292; coau 427
Schlesinger, Arthur M., 600, 2293
Schlup, Leonard, 1587
Schmidt, Benno C., Jr., coau 1957
Scholes, Marie V., coau 1327, 1465
Scholes, Walter V., 1466; coau 1327, 1465
Schriftgiesser, Karl, 1857
Schubert, Glendon A., Jr., 1086, 1087
Schultz, Louis Peter, 558, 2290-91
Schulzinger, Robert D., 1319
Scigliano, Robert G., 1088, 1089, 1988
Scott, Andrew MacKay, coau, 1925
Scott, Anne Firor, coau 1925
Scott, Emmet J., coau 1144
Scott, James Brown, 1919; coau 1907
Seager, Henry Roberts, coau 884
Seldman, J.S., 1051

Selden, C.A., 2170
Seligman, Edwin R. A., 1052, 1065
Seuling, Barbara, 2171
Severn, Bill, 252, 2252
Shannon, David A., 1858, 1859
Shapiro, Martin, 1989
Sharfman, Isiah Lee, 885
Shaw, Albert, 470, 2108
Shelley, Fred, 31
Sherman, James Schoolcraft, 80, 1579
Shibley, G.H., 471
Shriver, Phillip, R., 43, 1623
Shufeldt, Robert Wilson, 1146
Sikes, G.C., 1456
Simmons, Furnifold M., 81
Simons, Henry, 1053
Sims, William Sowden, 82, 1614
Sinclair, Andrew, 1860, 1941
Skefos, Catherine Hetos, 2109
Skolnik, Richard, 1687
Slade, W.A., coau 937
Slayden, Ellen M., 2228
Small, Miriam Rossiter, 2046
Small, Norman Jerome, 681
Smalley, Harrison, 1200
Smith, Bessie White, 266, 282
Smith, Don, 2128
Smith, F.F., 1189
Smith, Herbert A., 1990
Smith, Herbert Knox, 83
Smith, Marie D., 2172
Smith, Robert F., 1364
Smith, Roy C., 828
Smith, S.C., 648
Smock, Raymond H., coau 1125
Snowbarger, W.E., 376
Sobel, Robert, 493
Socolofsky, Homer E., 1511
Solvick, Stanley D., 323, 857, 870, 1253, 1254, 1256
Southern, David, 1147

Spector, Ronald, 1605, 1611
Speiser, Ephraim A., 1383
Spencer, Samuel R., Jr. 1148
Sponholtz, Lloyd Luther, 1782
Spooner, John C., 1582
Spracher, William C., 601
Sprout, Harold, coau 806, 1908
Sprout, Margaret, coau, 806, 1908
Stagner, Stephen, 2111
Stahl, Rose, 1015
Stanwood, Edward, 560, 1219, 1290
Steamer, Robert J., 1991
Steffens, Lincoln, 472, 858
Stein, Meyer L., 561
Stephens, George A., 918
Stephenson, D. Grier, Jr., 1950
Stephenson, Nathaniel, 1494
Stevens, F.W., 362
Stevens, Richard G., 1656
Stevenson, Francis Seymour, 1384
Stevenson, Frederick Boyd, 1825, 1826
Stewart, David Michael, 1992
Stewart, Kate, 32
Stickley, G., 473
Stimson, Henry L., 1478; coau 1480
Stockbridge, Frank Parker, 1827
Stoddard, Henry Luther, 253, 640, 1501, 1509, 1519, 1525, 1527, 1530, 1550, 1675, 2296
Stowe, Lyman Beecher, coau 1144
Straight, Willard, 85
Strange, C. D., 1828
Strum, Philippa, 641, 1993, 1994, 2034
Studenski, Paul, coau 1054
Sullivan, Mark, 859
Sulzner, George, coau 498
Sumberg, Alfred D., 474, 475
Sumner, Helen L., coau, 945
Sutton, Ottie K., 608
Swartz, W.G., 1291

Sweetman, Jack, 807
Swindler, William F., 1095, 2113
Szekely, Kalman, 613

Taft, Alfonso (father), 276
Taft, Charles Phelps (son), 87, 254, 2187
Taft, Helen Herron (Mrs. W. H. Taft), 256, 291, 731
Taft, Helen (daughter). See Manning, Helen Taft.
Taft, Horace Dutton (brother), 255, 2315
Taft, Robert Alphonso (son), 88, 2325
Taft, William H.: 1-25, 34-41, 106-9, 111-202, 267, 282, 289, 290, 302, 337, 378-95, 478, 479, 871, 887, 888, 1149, 1176, 1224-28, 1356, 1439-41, 1831, 1834, 1866-79, 1883, 1909, 1911-14, 1926, 1942, 2012-22, 2114-23, 2316; and messages to Congress, 191-96; and coau 1447, 2126
Tansill, Charles G., 1346
Tarbell, Ida Minerva, 1220
Tarr, Joel Arthur, 1025
Taussig, Frank William, 1278, 1292
Taylor, Tim, 210, 562
Tebbell, John, coau, 563
Tedesco, Paul H., 1221
Teger, Stuart H., coau 2124
Terrell, M.C., 396
Thacher, Thomas, 890, 924
Thernstrom, Stephan A., 1915
Thomas, A.E., 2138
Thompson, Carol, 602
Thompson, Charles Willis, 257, 2297, 2298
Timberlake, James H., 1943
Timbers, Edwin, 1096

Tindall, George B., 1150
Tinneman, Ethel Mary, 1636
Tittle, W., 2139
Tiveton, D. Jerome, 1293
Tobey, J.A. 946
Tompkins, D.A., 1260
Tompkins, Dorothy L.C., 737, 738
Torrey, George B., 2376
Tourtello, Arthur Benson, 564
Touster, Saul, 2047
Towle, K.A., 708
Tracy, R.G., 808
Trask, David F., coau 1307
Trask, Roger R., coau 1307
Tucker, David M., 1682
Tucker, Louis Leonard, 268
Tucker, Robert Whitney, 2188, 2200, 2205
Tugwell, Rexford G., 480, 565, 566
Tulis, Jeffrey, coau, 659
Turner, Edward Raymond, 1387
Turner, George Kibbe, 782, 872, coau 1833

Umbreit, Kenneth Bernard, 1995
Underwood, Oscar, 1854, 1585
U.S. Bureau of the Budget, 1034
U.S. Bureau of Labor Statistics, 944
U.S. Congress. Conference Committee, 61st Cong., 1st Sess., 1222
U.S. Congress. House, Committee on Judiciary, 763
U.S. Congress. House, Committee on the Philippines, 339
U.S. Congress. House, Committee on Ways and Means, 1223
U.S. Congress. House, Committee to Investigate the Concentration of Control of Money and Credits, 940
U.S. Congress. Senate Library, 678
U.S. Department of Agriculture, 101

U.S. Department of State, 1190, 1280, 1390
U.S. Library of Congress, 211, 647, 801
U.S. Library of Congress, Division of Bibliography, 1268
U.S. Information Service, 1267
U.S. National Monetary Commission, 939
U.S. National Park Service, 2338
U.S. Tariff Commission, 1208
U.S. President [Taft], 970, 1281, 1294-97
Urofsky, Melvin I., 925

Vagts, Alfred, 1367
Van Alstyne, Richard W., 1332
Van Dusen, Michael H., coau, 696
Van Hise, Charles R., 892
Van Riper, Paul P., 952
Varg, Paul A., 1357, 1358, 1399
Verrill, Alpheus H., 1414
Vevier, Charles C., 1647
Vestal, Alice M., coau 2339
Vexler, Robert I., 1491, 1581
Villard, Oswald Garrison, 2299, 2300
Vinyard, Dale, 567
Vivian, James F., 568
Viviani, James F., 1862

Wadsworth, James Wolcott, 2317
Wainwright, Richard, 830
Walker, Albert Henry, 893, 894, 895, 1055, 1056, 1283
Walker, E.R., 1691
Walker, Jack L., coau 536
Walker, Kenneth R., 2301, 2302
Walker, Samuel J., coau 353, 1305
Walls, Louise H., coau 97
Walter, Daniel C., 105
Walters, Everett, 1531

Waltman, Jerold L., 1057
Walton, Haynes, Jr., coau 646
Wann, Andrew J., 764
Warner, Hoyt, L., 860
Warren, Francis E., 1586
Warren, Sidney, 569, 642, 682
Washburn, Mabel T.R., 277
Wasby, Stephen L., 1996
Washington, Booker T., 89
Watson, James E., 2303
Watts, James F., Jr., 1683, 1700, 2037, 2054
Watts, Sarah Miles, coau 563
Wayne, Stephen J., coau 521, 522
Webb, Edwin Y., 90
Weekly Law Bulletin and Ohio Law Journal, 292
Weir, H.C., 734
Welles, Sumner, 1418
Welliver, Judson, 1759
Wellman, Walter, 340, 481
Wells, David A., 1066
Wells, Maggie, coau 742
Wert, S.T., 1017
West, H.L., 733
Whitaker, Arthur P., 1338, 1407
White, Anthony G., 753
White, Eugene Nelson, 1058
White, G. Edward, 1997
White, Jack, 1157
White, John, 1059, 1151
White, S.E., 1018
White, William Allen, 1726, 1727, 1861, 2304, 2305
Whiteman, Marjorie M., 1426
Whitney, David C., 520, 2306, 2372
Wickersham, George, 91, 1191
Wickersham George W., 896, 926-28, 1481-84
Widenor, William C., 1555
Wiebe, Robert H., 861, 862, 873, 929

Wiegand, Wayne A., 831, 1475
Wigdor, Alexandra K., 1952
Wilcox, M., 783
Wildavsky, Aaron, 577
Wilensky, Norman M., 1593, 1783
Wiley, Harvey Washington, 1192
Wilkins, Roy, 2318
Willard, Martha, 33
Williams, Benjamin H., 1229
Williams, Daniel Roderick, 341
Williams, George Fred, 483
Williams, James, coau, 1140
Willis, H. Parker, 941, 1489
Wilson, Francis Maris Huntington, 92, 1633, 1634
Wilson, Fred Taylor, 2373
Wilson, James, 1486, 1498
Wilson, Janet, coau 2219
Wilson, V., 572
Wilson, William L., 1039
Wilson Woodrow, 573, 1262, 1263
Winkler, John K., 484
Winston, Michael R., coau 1115
Winter, Ella, coau 863
Wise, Sidney, 574
Withers, John Lovell, 683
Witt, Elder, 1998
Witte, John F. 1060
Wold, Karl, 2144
Wolf, Simon, 2308
Wood, Leonard, 93, 1599
Woodward, C. Vann, 1152, 1153
Woodward, William, 722
World Book Encyclopedia, 212
Wormuth, Francis D., 1916
Wright, Hamilton, 1193
Wright, Herbert F., 1467
Wright, T.P., Jr. 397
Wynar, Lubomyr, 6514

Zabriske, Edward H., 1417
Zangrando, Robert L., 1154

Zanjani, Sally Springmeyer, 1762
Zeitler, Glen, coau 1837
Zink, Howard, 304

Zorn, Anders, 2377
Zorn, Walter Louis, 278

Index to Subjects

Ainsworth, Fred Clayton, 1595, 1596
Aldrich, Nelson W., 46, 1492-94, 1741
Anderson, Chandler P., 47

Bacon, Robert, 1618, 1619
Ballinger, Richard A., 48, 956-1019, 1442-46
Bernstorff, Johann von, 1635-37
Beveridge, Albert J., 1495-96
Borah, William A., 49, 1498-1501, 1902
Brandeis, Louis D., 50, 1650-52
Bristow, Joseph L., 51, 1503
Bryan, William Jennings, 425-29, 447-50, 470, 1767
Burton, Theodore E., 1504
Butler, Nicholas Murray, 52
Butler, Pierce, 2035
Butt, Archibald Willingham, 1597-98

Cannon, Joseph Gurney, 53, 1506-9, 1734, 1752, 1756
Capper, Arthur, 1511
Carnegie, Andrew, 54
China, 1647, 1649
Clapp, Moses, 55, 1513
Clark, Champ, 1516, 1827
Clark, John H., 2036
Contemporary newspapers, 102-5
Coolidge, Calvin, 1847, 1848, 1861
Cox, George Barnsdale, 283, 300
Crane, Charles R., 1620
Crane, Winthrop Murray, 1518-19
Cummins, Albert B., 56, 869

Dawson, Thomas C., 1621
Day, William R., 2037

Debs, Eugene V., 455, 456, 468, 1709, 1768, 1856
Dewey, George, 1605-6
Dickinson, Jacob McGavok, 51, 1449-52
Dollar Diplomacy, 1645, 1647-49
Dolliver, Jonathan, 58, 969, 1524-25, 1725, 1733
Du Bois, W.E.B., 1118, 1131, 1142-43

Elkins, Stephen Benton, 1526-27

Fisher, Walter L., 972, 995, 1014, 1454-56
Fiske, Bradley A., 1607-8
Foraker, Joseph Benson, 60, 284, 408, 1530-1
Frankfurter, Felix, 1654-56
Frick, Henry Clay, 886

Gary, Elbert H., 889
Gilbert, Cass, 2336-37
Gompers, Samuel, 475, 1102
Gore, Thomas P., 1534
Great Britain, 411-15

Hale, Eugene, 1536-38
Harding, Warren G., 1860, 1885, 1897, 1917-18, 1920-21
Harlan, John M., 1662
Harrison, Benjamin, 61
Hearst, William Randolph, 484
Herrick, Myron T., 1622-23
Hitchcock, Frank, 1458
Holmes, Oliver Wendell, 1665-69, 2038-47
Hughes, Charles Evans, 1049-52

Israel, Fred, coau

Johnson, Hiram, 63, 1540

Kent, William, 64
Kitchin, Claude C., 1542
Knox, Philander C., 65, 1460-67, 1626-31

LaFollette, Robert M., 66, 472, 1547-49, 1712, 1785, 1824
Lamar, Joseph Rucker, 1678-79
Lane, Franklin K., 97
League to Enforce Peace, 1887, 1899, 1901
Lodge, Henry Cabot, 67, 98, 1553-55, 1900
Longworth, Nicholas, 1557-59
Luce, Stephen Bleeker, 1610-3
Lurton, Horace Harmon, 1682-83
McKenna, Joseph, 2054
McReynolds, James C., 2055-57
MacVeagh, Franklin, 69, 1469
Mann, James R., 70
Manning, Mrs. Helen Taft (daughter), 2203-5
Marburg, Theodore, 68
Meyer, George von Lengerke, 71, 1473-75
Moody, William Henry, 72

Nagel, Charles, 73, 1477
National Association for the Advancement of Colored People, 1127, 1154, 1165
National Labor Board, World War I, 1881
Newlands, Francis, J., 74, 99, 1,561-63
Nicaragua, 1639, 1644, 1645, 1648
Nonpartisan League, 1836, 1850-1, 1862

Norris, George W., 75, 1564-67, 1714-18

Owen, Robert Latham, 1570-1

Peckham, Rufus Wheeler, 1686-87
Perkins, George, 76
Pinchot, Amos, 77
Pinchot, Gifford, 967, 989, 998-1000, 1002, 1004-6
Pitney, Mahlon, 1690-1
Poindexter, Miles, P. 78
Progressivism, general, 832-73
Prohibition, 1927-43

Rice, Sir Cecil Spring, 1638
Reinsch, Paul S., 1632
Roosevelt, Theodore, 1704, 1710, 1716-17, 1719-20, 1748, 1750-51, 1764, 1766, 1773-74, 1776, 1780-1, 1786, 1793, 1796-1797, 1799, 1803-6, 1810, 1812-14, 1816-17, 1822-23, 1825
Root, Elihu, 1577-78

Sanford, Edward T., 2058
Sherman, James Schoolcraft, 80, 1580-81
Sims, William S., 82
Smith, Herbert Knox, 83
Spooner, John C., 84, 1583
Steffens, Lincoln, 863
Stimson, Henry L., 86, 1479-80
Stone, Harlan Fiske, 2059-62
Straight, Willard, 85
Supreme Court, the, 1944-2023
Supreme Court building, 2336
Sutherland, George, 2063

Taft, William Howard, 103-58, 264-66, 272, 284, 298-303, 307-8,

Index to Subjects 267

310, 313, 314, 317, 318, 320,
321-24, 335, 340, 341, 343,
346-57, 1116, 1135, 1836,
1857, 1858, 1865, 2082-85,
2095-97, 2100-1, 2105, 2111,
2125-40, 2230-54, 232-31

chronology of, pp. 1-16

and mansucript and archival sources of: Nos. 1-28; and published papers of, 29-44; and unpublished personal and administrative papers of presidental associates, 46-94; and published personal and administrative papers of presidential associates, 95-101; and published writings of, 106-201; and unpublished writings of, 202

and early life and career: Ohio environment of, 259-68; ancestry of, 269-78; early career of, 283-94

and pre-presidential career: Solicitor General and Federal Court Judge, 1890-1900, 295-98; in the Philippines, 1900-1904, 309-41; Secretary of War, 1904-1908, 342-77, 396-406

and elections, presidential: 604-46; of 1908, 409-84; of 1912, 1763-1833

elections of 1910: 1701-62

and biographies of: 203-58

inauguration of as president: 709-34

cabinet of: 735-42

as administrator: 753-83

as commander in chief: 784-831

presidential power: 485-602, 647-708; and presidential studies, 495-603

as president, 1909-1913: administration personnel, 1442-1634; Black Americans, 1108-1112; anti-trust crusade, 874-929; banking and currency reform, 930-41; Childrens' Bureau, 942-46; civil service, 947-52; conservation, 953-1019; direct election of senators, 1020-25; federal budget, 1026-34; federal corporation tax, 1035-39; foreign affairs, 1301-1626; government reorganization, 1067-72; immigration, 1079-88; the judicial system, 1089-96; labor, 1097-1107; messages to Congress, 190-201; Panama Canal, 330-32, 407-10; the Philippines, 327-30, 339, 341; parcel post, 1173-77; postal savings banks, 1178-82; public health,1183-93; railroad regulation, 1194-1200; shipping, 1201-6; Supreme Court justices, 1639-90; tariff reform, 1207-63; tariff reciprocity with Canada, 1264-97; women's suffrage, 1298-1300; world peace, 1427-41

post-presidential career: 1834-62; professor of law, 1863-76; on

World War I, 1877-80; member of National War Labor Board, 1881-82; on world peace, 1883-1921; on women, 1922-26; on prohibition, 1927-43

Chief Justice of the Supreme Court: 1944-2023, 2078, 2124; personnel of Taft's court, 2024-66; most important decisions of Taft's court, 2067-77

personal life: 2125-40; health, 2141-48; homes of, 2332-33; religion, 2149-52; marriage, 2153-77; children, 2178-2205; contributions to history, 2255-2308; oral histories, 2309-18

in memoriam: 2334-38; portraits of, 203-4; iconography, 352-93

Taft, Mrs. William Howard (wife), 2206-29
Taft, Alphonso (father), 273

Taft, Charles Phelps (son), 2184-88
Taft, Robert A. (son), 2189-2200

Underwood, Oscar Wilder, 1584-85

Van Devanter, Willis, 1692-95, 2066-68
Vilalobar, Marquis de, 1639
Villard, Osward Garrison, 1915

Warren Francis E., 1587
Washington, Booker T., 89, 1123-25, 1132, 1144, 1158
Watson, James E., 1588-89
White, Edward Douglass, 1696-1700
White, William Allen, 1727, 1844, 1845
Wichersham, George W., 91,
Wilson, Francis M.H., 92
Wilson, James, 1486-89
Wilson, Woodrow, 1702, 1706, 1715-16, 1765, 1767, 1770, 1772, 1781, 1794, 1886, 1917
Women's suffrage, 1922-26
Wood, Leonard, 93, 1601-3

Appendix
Serials Consulted

Agricultural History
Alabama Review
American Bar Association Journal
Americana
American Archivist
American Bar Association Reports
American Forests
American Heritage
American History Illustrated
American Historical Review
American Journal of International Law
American Journal of Legal History
American Journal of Political Science
American Journal of Sociology
American Magazine
American Mercury
American Neptune
American Quarterly
American Scholar
American Studies International
Annals of the American Academy of Political and Social Science
Annals of Wyoming
Antiques
Arena, The
Arizona and the West
Arizona State University Law Journal
Army and Navy Journal
Atlantic Monthly

Canadian Journal of Political Science
Capitol Studies
Catholic History Review
Century Magazine, The
Chautauqua

Church and State
Cincinnati Historical Society Bulletin
Collier's Magazine
Commoner, The
Congressional Record
Cornhill Magazine
Cosmopolitan Magazine
Craftsman Magazine
Crisis, The
Current History
Current Literature
Current Opinion

Diseases of the Nervous System

Editorial Research Reports
Explorations in Economic History
Everybody's Magazine

Filson Club History Quarterly
Foreign Affairs
Fortnightly Review
Fortune
Forum

George Washington Law Review
Georgia Historical Quarterly
Good Housekeeping Magazine

Hampton's Magazine
Harper's Weekly
Harvard Library Bulletin
Hispanic American Historical Review
Historian, The
Historical and Philosophical Society of Ohio Bulletin

History of Childhood Quarterly
History Teacher

Indiana Magazine of History
Independent, The
Inter-American Economic Affairs
International Record of
   Medicine

Jewish Social Studies
Journal of American Culture
Journal of American History
Journal of Church and State
Journal of Contemporary History
Journal of Economics and Business
Journal of Economic History
Journal of Forest History
Journal of Modern History
Journal of Negro History
Journal of Philosophy
Journal of Political Economy
Journal of Politics
Journal of Southern History

Kentucky Law Journal

LaFollette's Weekly Magazine
Life Magazine
Literary Digest, The
Living Age

McClure's Magazine
Maryland Historian
Maryland Historical Review
Massachusetts Historical Society
   Proceedings
Michigan Law Journal
Michigan Law Review
Mid-America
Midwestern Journal of Political
   Science
Military Affairs

Mississippi Valley Historical Review
Missouri Historical Review

Nation, The
National Geographic Magazine
Naval War College Review
   (NWCR)
Nebraska History
Negro History Bulletin
Nevada History Society Quarterly
New England Quarterly
New Republic, The
New York Historical Society
   Quarterly
New York History
New York Times Magazine
Nineteenth Century
North American Review
New Breeder's Gazette
North Carolina Historical
   Review
North Dakota Quarterly
Northwest Ohio Quarterly

Ohio Archaelogical and Historical
   Society Publications
Ohio Cues
Ohio Historical Quarterly
Ohio History
Ohio Law Bulletin and Reporter
Ohio State Law Journal
Outlook, The

Pacific Historical Review
Pearson's Magazine
Phylon
Policy
Political Science Quarterly
Presidential Studies Quarterly
Proceedings of the Academy of
   Political Science
Prologue

Public Opinion
Public Opinion Quarterly
Putnam's Magazine
Quarterly Journal of the Library of
  Congress
Queen City Heritage

Rendezvous
Review of Politics
Royal Historical Society
  Transactions
Russian Review

Saturday Evening Post
Saturday Review of Literature
Scientific American
Scribner's Magazine
Smithsonian Magazine of History
Society for Historians of American
  Foreign Relations Newsletter
South Atlantic Quarterly
Southwestern Social Science
  Quarterly
Stanford Law Review
Supreme Court Historical Society
  Yearbook
Supreme Court Review

Tennessee Historical Quarterly

U.S. Department of State, Papers
  Relating to the Foreign Relations
  of the United States (FRUS)
U.S. Naval Institute Proceedings
  (USNIP)
University of Pennsylvania Law
  Review

Vanderbilt Law Review

Washington Monthly
Weekly Law Bulletin and Ohio Law
  Journal
Western History
Western Political Quarterly
Wilson Quarterly
Wisconsin Magazine of History
Woman's Home Companion
World Today, The
World's Work, The

Yale Law Journal
Yale Review